VERSITY OF
VINGHAM

THE DOCTOR'S GUIDE
TO CRITICAL APPRAISAL

FOURTH EDITION

D1493002

Pas**tes**⁺

THE DOCTOR'S GUIDE TO CRITICAL APPRAISAL

FOURTH EDITION

Dr Narinder Kaur Gosall

BSc (Hons) PhD

Lead Tutor, The Critical Appraisal Company

Director, Superego Cafe Limited

Dr Gurpal Singh Gosall

MA MB BChir MRCPsych

Consultant General Adult Psychiatrist

and Foundation Program Lead,

Lancashire Care NHS Foundation Trust

Director, Superego Cafe Limited

© 2015 Pastest Ltd

Egerton Court
Parkgate Estate
Knutsford
Cheshire WA16 8DX

Telephone: 01565 752000

All rights reserved. No part of this publication may be reproduced, stored in a retrieval system, or transmitted, in any form or by any means, electronic, mechanical, photocopying, recording or otherwise without the prior permission of the copyright owner.

First edition 2006, Second edition 2009, Third edition 2012, Fourth edition 2015, Reprinted 2016

ISBN: 978 1 905635 979
A catalogue record for this book is available from the British Library.

The information contained within this book was obtained by the authors from reliable sources. However, while every effort has been made to ensure its accuracy, no responsibility for loss, damage or injury occasioned to any person acting or refraining from action as a result of information contained herein can be accepted by the publisher or the authors.

This book contains excerpts from clinical papers. The content and formatting of these excerpts may have been altered for teaching purposes. All excerpts are taken from Open Access articles distributed under the terms of the Creative Commons Attribution License (2.0–4.0), which permits unrestricted use, distribution, and reproduction in any medium, provided the original work is properly cited. No endorsement or criticism of the researchers is implied by the inclusion of the excerpts in this book

All characters appearing in the scenarios are fictitious. Any resemblance to real persons, living or dead, is purely coincidental. All the clinical scenarios are for teaching purposes only and must not be used to inform clinical practice.

Pastest Online Revision, Books and Courses

Pastest provides online revision, books and courses to help medical students and doctors maximise their personal performance in critical exams and tests. Our in-depth understanding is based on over 40 years' experience and the feedback of recent exam candidates.

Resources are available for:

Medical school applicants and undergraduates, MRCP, MRCS, MRCPCH, DCH, GPST, MRCGP, FRCA, Dentistry, Interview Skills, and USMLE Step 1.

For further details contact:

Tel: 01565 752000   Fax: 01565 650264

www.pastest.com   enquiries@pastest.com

Text prepared by Carnegie Book Production, Lancaster
Printed and bound in the UK by Bell & Bain Ltd, Glasgow

CONTENTS

SECTION I – CRITICAL APPRAISAL IN PRACTICE

Dedicated to our son, Dilip, whose boundless energy
and enthusiasm for life is contagious.

ABOUT THE AUTHORS

Dr Narinder Kaur Gosall BSc (Hons) PhD

Lead Tutor, The Critical Appraisal Company
Director, Superego Cafe Limited

Narinder Gosall studied in Liverpool and gained a PhD in neuropathology after investigating the role of the phrenic nerve in sudden infant death syndrome and intrauterine growth retardation. After working as a university lecturer she joined the pharmaceutical industry. She worked in a variety of roles, including as a Medical Liaison Executive and as a Clinical Effectiveness Consultant for Pfizer Limited. She has extensive experience in teaching critical appraisal skills to healthcare professionals and is an international speaker on the subject. She is the Lead Tutor at The Critical Appraisal Company and the editor of the online course at **www.criticalappraisal.com**.

Dr Gurpal Singh Gosall MA MB BChir MRCPsych

Consultant General Adult Psychiatrist and Foundation Program Lead, Lancashire Care NHS Foundation Trust
Director, Superego Cafe Limited

Gurpal Gosall studied medicine at the University of Cambridge and Guy's and St Thomas's Hospitals, London. He worked as a Senior House Officer in Psychiatry in Leeds before taking up a post as Specialist Registrar in the North West. He now works as a Consultant General Adult Psychiatrist, looking after patients in the Psychiatric Intensive Care Units at the Royal Blackburn Hospital and Burnley General Hospital. He has a long-standing interest in teaching, design and programming. He founded Superego Cafe, a medical education company which runs courses and websites for psychiatrists. **www.superegocafe.com**.

INTRODUCTION TO THE FOURTH EDITION

The pressure on healthcare services has never been greater. Many clinicians face the challenge of treating increasing numbers of patients more rapidly with a wider choice of interventions but with fewer resources. Effective interventions must be prioritised. Waste must be minimised.

While healthcare managers focus on financial spreadsheets and optimising service models, clinicians are tasked with improving clinical outcomes. Many turn to research papers to discover innovative ways of practising. Therein lies the danger – there is strong evidence and there is weak evidence.

Critical appraisal skills are now as much a part of the clinician's armoury as the ability to diagnose conditions and prescribe treatments. Critical appraisal skills allow clinicians to prioritise evidence that can improve outcomes. Such is the importance of acquiring these skills that critical appraisal is now routinely tested in medical, dental and nursing exams.

We wrote the first edition of this book 9 years ago to explain critical appraisal to the busy clinician. Our aim has always been for the book to be the one-stop solution for all clinicians. Based on our teaching experience, we took a unique back-to-basics approach that provided a logical and comprehensive review of the subject. This new edition expands on the award-winning third edition with a modified structure, new and updated chapters, new figures and scenarios, and more help with difficult topics. We've also included excerpts from real clinical papers to illustrate key concepts.

By reading this book you will appraise clinical papers with more confidence. We hope that you will learn to apply evidence to your practice that will make a real positive difference to your patients. In the end, boom or bust, that's all that really matters.

NKG, GSG
2015

ACKNOWLEDGEMENTS

We would like to express our thanks to Cathy Dickens (Senior Commissioning Editor), Rachel Clarke (Typesetter, Carnegie Publishing Ltd) and the PasTest team for their help and support with this book. Thanks also to Elizabeth Kerr, formerly of PasTest, who worked on the first edition.

We thank our teachers and colleagues for generously sharing their knowledge and for providing guidance. We are also indebted to all the doctors, dentists, nurses, psychologists, pharmacists, researchers and other healthcare professionals who have attended our critical appraisal courses and provided us with comments and helpful suggestions about our teaching materials.

We would like to express our gratitude to our families, who inspired us and gave us unconditional support during the writing of this book.

January 2015

EVIDENCE-BASED MEDICINE

INTRODUCING CRITICAL APPRAISAL

Scenario 1

Mr Lemming visited the car dealership. The salesman showed him to the new car. 'This is the latest and greatest,' explained the salesman. 'Faster, quieter and more efficient. The engine is revolutionary, the leather seats are suppler and the satellite navigation is outstanding.' Mr Lemming nodded in agreement as he flicked through the brochure. 'If you purchase this car,' said the salesman, 'you'll be the talk of the neighbourhood, sir.' Mr Lemming was convinced. Without a single question and without requesting a test drive, he immediately purchased the car and looked forward to his regular commute!

Scenario 2

Dr Brown read the latest issue of the journal. A randomised controlled trial on a new treatment caught his eye. The results showed the new treatment was better than a placebo tablet. It helped patients to improve faster and with fewer side-effects. The authors of the article recommended the new treatment as the first-line intervention. Without a further thought, Dr Brown was convinced that his patients would benefit. He expected to achieve better outcomes than his colleagues. He would be the talk of the department! The next day Dr Brown began prescribing the new medication to his patients.

Every year, thousands of clinical papers are published in the medical press. The vast range of topics reflects the sheer complexity of the human body, with studies all fighting for our attention. Separating the wheat from the chaff is a daunting task for doctors, many of whom have to rely on others for expert guidance.

In 1972, the publication of Archie Cochrane's *Effectiveness and Efficiency: Random Reflections on Health Services*[1] made doctors realise how unaware they were of the effects of healthcare. Archie Cochrane, a British epidemiologist, went on to set up the Cochrane Collaboration in 1992. It is now an international organisation, committed to producing and disseminating systematic reviews of healthcare interventions. Bodies such as the Cochrane Collaboration have made the lives of doctors much easier, but the skill of evaluating evidence should be in the arsenal of every doctor.

---

1   Cochrane AL. *Effectiveness and Efficiency: Random Reflections on Health Services.* London: Royal Society of Medicine Press, 1999.

Evidence-based medicine

Evidence-based medicine is the phrase used to describe the process of making clinical decisions about a patient's clinical state taking into account the best available research evidence, our clinical expertise and patient preferences[1]. As such, evidence-based medicine has had a tremendous impact on improving healthcare outcomes since its widespread adoption in the early 1990s.

The most widely quoted definition of evidence-based medicine is that it is *'the conscientious, explicit and judicious use of current best evidence in making decisions about the care of the individual patient'*[2]. The practice of evidence-based medicine consists of five steps, shown in Table 1.

EVIDENCE-BASED MEDICINE – THE FIVE STEPS		
1	Question	Formulate a precise, structured clinical question about an aspect of patient management
2	Evidence	Search for the best evidence with which to answer the question
3	Critical appraisal	Evaluate the evidence, critically appraising the evidence for its validity, impact and applicability
4	Application	Apply the results to clinical practice, integrating the critical appraisal with clinical expertise and with patients' circumstances and views
5	Monitor	Monitor the process, evaluating the effectiveness and efficacy of the whole process, and identifying ways of improving both for the future

Table 1 Evidence-based medicine – the five steps

Evidenced-based medicine begins with the formulation of a clinical question, such as *'What is the best treatment for carpal tunnel syndrome?'* This is followed by a search of the medical literature, looking for answers to the question. The evidence gathered is appraised and the recommendations from the best studies are applied to patients. The final step, which is often overlooked, is to monitor any changes and repeat the process. This may involve audits and surveys.

Although evidence-based medicine has led to a more consistent and uniform approach to clinical practice, it does not mean that clinicians practise identically.

1   Haynes RB, Devereaux PJ, Guyatt GH. Physicians' and patients' choices in evidence based practice. *BMJ* 2002; 324: 1350.
2   Sackett DL, Richardson WS, Rosenberg W, Haynes RB. *Evidence-based Medicine: How to Practise and Teach Evidence-based Medicine.* London: Churchill Livingstone, 1997.

Clinicians vary in their level of expertise, so not all the recommendations from clinical research can be followed. For example, the evidence might suggest that an intramuscular injection is the best treatment for a condition but the clinician might not have been trained to safely administer that treatment. In addition, patients differ in the interventions they find acceptable – some patients prefer not to have injections, for example, and interventions should be tailored to the needs of individual patients. Finally, a lack of resources can also restrict the choices available, particularly for new and expensive interventions.

Critical appraisal

In the process of evidence-based medicine, why do we need a step of critical appraisal? Why not take all results at face value and apply all the findings to clinical practice? The first reason is that there might be conflicting conclusions drawn from different studies. Secondly, real-life medicine rarely follows the restrictive environments in which clinical trials take place. To apply, implement and monitor evidence, we need to ensure that the evidence we are looking at can be translated into our own clinical environment.

Critical appraisal is just one step in the process of evidence-based medicine. It allows doctors to assess the research they have found in their search and to decide which research evidence could have a clinically significant impact on their patients. Critical appraisal allows doctors to exclude research that is too poorly designed to inform medical practice. By itself, critical appraisal does not lead to improved outcomes. It is only when the conclusions drawn from critically appraised studies are applied to everyday practice and monitored that the outcomes for patients improve.

As with most subjects in medicine, it is not possible to learn about critical appraisal without coming across jargon. Wherever we start, we will come across words and phrases we do not understand. In this book we try to explain critical appraisal in a logical and easy-to-remember way. Anything unfamiliar will be explained in due course.

Internal validity and external validity

Critical appraisal assesses the validity of the research and statistical techniques employed in studies and generates clinically useful information from them. It seeks to answer two major questions:

- Does the research have **internal validity** – to what extent does the study measure what it sets out to measure? We want to know how good the research methods used by the researchers are to answer the clinical question.

- Does the research have **external validity** – to what extent can the results from the study be generalised to a wider population? Studies are usually done in experimental and artificial settings – we want to know whether we will get the same results in real life settings.

If we change our practice based on a study with poor internal validity, we may have unrealistic expectations about our outcomes and be disappointed. We may also end up harming our patients by not offering alternative choices or by exposing them to new dangers.

Studies with good internal validity can have poor external validity, particularly if the conditions used in the study are far removed from everyday life. The challenge then is to find studies with good internal validity but with experimental conditions that mimic real clinical environments, so that the results can be applied to normal practice. As we shall see, as researchers implement methods to improve the internal validity, the external validity often suffers.

Efficacy and effectiveness

Two words that are useful to define now are 'efficacy' and 'effectiveness'. These words are sometimes used interchangeably but they have different meanings and consequences in the context of evidence-based medicine.

Efficacy describes the impact of interventions under optimal (trial) conditions.

Effectiveness is a different but related concept, describing whether the interventions have the intended or expected effect under ordinary (clinical) circumstances.

Efficacy shows that internal validity is present. Effectiveness shows that external validity (generalisability) is present.

The contrast between efficacy and effectiveness studies was first highlighted in 1967 by Schwartz and Lellouch[1]. Efficacy studies usually have the aim of seeking regulatory approval for licensing. The interventions in such studies tend to be strictly controlled and compared with placebo interventions. The people taking part in such studies tend to be a selective 'eligible' population. In contrast, effectiveness studies tend to be undertaken for formulary approval. Dosing regimens are usually more flexible and are compared with interventions already being used. Almost anyone is eligible to enter such trials.

It is not always easy and straightforward to translate the results from clinical

---

1   Schwartz D, Lellouch J. Explanatory and pragmatic attitudes in therapeutical trials. *Journal of Chronic Diseases* 1967; 20: 637–48.

trials (efficacy data) to uncontrolled clinical settings (effectiveness data). The results achieved in everyday practice do not always mirror an intervention's published efficacy data and there are many reasons for this. The efficacy of an intervention is nearly always more impressive than its effectiveness.

Scenario 1 revisited

Mr Lemming's drive to work in his new car was a disappointing experience. The journey had taken the same duration as the previous week. He hadn't noticed an appreciable difference in acceleration. The fuel consumption appeared to be the same. The leather seats may have been a bit more comfortable but then again, Mr Lemming remembered, he had no complaints about the seats in his old car. Later that evening he conveyed his disappointment to his wife. She shook her head in dismay and said, 'Darling, you always fall for the glossy brochure.'

Scenario 2 revisited

Dr Brown was called to the office of the Medical Director. An analysis of prescribing costs in his department showed his costs were much higher than his colleagues. 'For the last month you've been prescribing an expensive new treatment,' explained the Medical Director, 'but you're not getting better outcomes.' He was unwilling to concede to Dr Brown's request for more time. 'You've treated 50 patients so far with the new treatment,' he said, 'yet no more patients are being cured.' Dr Brown mentioned the journal article he had read but the Medical Director remained unimpressed. 'I read it too but I didn't alter my prescribing practice,' he said, shaking his head in dismay. 'It was obvious the efficacy data published in the trial was not going to translate into effectiveness data. It appears, Dr Brown, that my critical appraisal skills are better than yours.'

FORMULATING A QUESTION

The first step in adopting an evidence-based medicine approach is to formulate a precise, structured clinical question about an aspect of patient management.

P.I.C.O.

The question should be directly relevant to the problem at hand[1]. Broad questions such as, 'How do I treat diabetes mellitus?' and 'What causes bowel cancer?' are easy to understand but return too many results on searching the medical literature. The acronym 'P.I.C.O.', explained in Table 2, can frame the question so that it directs the search to relevant and precise answers[1].

P	Patient or problem	Describe your patient and their problem
I	Intervention	Describe the main intervention, exposure, test or prognostic factor under consideration
C	Comparison	In the case of treatment, describe a comparative intervention (although a comparison is not always needed)
O	Outcome	Describe what you hope to achieve, measure or affect

Table 2 Introducing P.I.C.O.

For example, a doctor assesses a new patient presenting with depressive symptoms. The doctor decides to prescribe antidepressant medication. The patient is worried about side-effects and asks the doctor if there are any other treatment options. The doctor has heard that cognitive behavioural therapy is also used to treat depression. The doctor carries out a search of the medical literature using the P.I.C.O. search strategy shown in Table 3.

1   Richardson WS, Wilson MC, Nishikawa J, Hayward RS. The well-built clinical question: a key to evidence-based decisions. *ACP J Club* 1995; 123(3): A12–13.

P	Patient or problem	In a man with depression...
I	Intervention	...is cognitive behavioural therapy...
C	Comparison	...compared to fluoxetine...
O	Outcome	...better at improving depressive symptoms?

Table 3 An example of the P.I.C.O. framework

SEARCH STRATEGIES

By adopting a sensible search technique you can dramatically improve the outcome of a search. You might begin by formulating a P.I.C.O. research question. This will enable you to perform a more structured search for the relevant information and will indicate where the information needs lie. Keywords, similar words or synonyms should then be identified, to search terms on the database.

When you start the search you want to ensure that the search is not too narrow – that is, that you get as many papers as possible to look at. This is done by **exploding your search**. This means that you can search for a keyword plus all the associated narrower terms simultaneously. As a result, all articles that have been indexed as narrow terms and that are listed below the broader term are included. If too many results are returned, you can refine the search and get more specific results – **focusing your search**. Filters can be used to increase the effectiveness of the search. Subheadings can be used alongside index terms to narrow the search. Indexers can assign keywords to an article. These words can also be weighted by labelling them as major headings. These are then used to represent the main concepts of an article. This can help focus the search even more.

Search engines are not normally case-sensitive – 'Diabetes' and 'diabetes' will return the same results. To search for a phrase, enclose it in **quotation marks** – 'treatment of diabetes mellitus' will only return items with that phrase, for example.

Boolean operators are used to combine together keywords and phrases in your search strategy:

- **AND** is used to link together different subjects. This is used when you are focusing your search and will retrieve fewer references. For example, 'diabetes' AND 'insulin inhalers' will return items containing both terms.

- **OR** is used to broaden your search. You would use OR to combine like subjects or synonyms. For example, 'diabetes' OR 'hyperglycaemia' will return items containing either term.

- **NOT** is used to exclude material from a search. For example, 'diabetes' NOT 'insipidus' will return items containing the first term and not the second.

Parentheses (nesting): This can be used to clarify relationships between search terms. For example, *'(diabetes or hyperglycaemia)' AND 'inhalers'* will return items containing either of the first two terms and the third.

Truncation: A **truncation** symbol at the end of a word returns any possible endings to that word. For example, *'cardio*'* will return 'cardiology', 'cardiovascular' and 'cardiothoracic'. There are a variety of truncation symbols in use, including a question mark (?), an asterisk (*) and a plus sign (+).

Wild cards: A **wild card** symbol within a word will return the possible characters that can be substituted. For example, *'wom#n'* will return 'woman' and 'women'. Common wild-card symbols include the hash (#) and the question mark (?).

Stemming: Most search engines will 'stem' search words. Stemming removes suffixes such as '-s', '-ing' and '-ed'. These variations are returned automatically when stem words are searched.

Thesaurus: This is used in some databases, such as MEDLINE, to help perform more effective searching. It is a controlled vocabulary and is used to index information from different journals. This is done by grouping related concepts under a single preferred term. As a result, all indexers use the same standard terms to describe a subject area, regardless of the term the author has chosen to use. It contains keywords, definitions of those keywords and cross-references between keywords. In healthcare, the National Library of Medicine uses a thesaurus called **Medical Subject Headings (MeSH)**. MeSH contains more than 27 000 terms[1]. Each of these keywords represents a single concept appearing in the medical literature. For most MeSH terms, there will be broader, narrower and related terms to consider for selection. MeSH can also be used by the indexers in putting together entries for MEDLINE databases.

Synonyms: Search engines might expand searches by using a thesaurus to match search words to other words with the same meaning.

Plus (+) symbol: Use a **plus (+)** symbol before a term that must appear in the search results. For example, *'+glucophage diabetes'* will return items that include the Glucophage brand name and diabetes rather than the generic name metformin.

Stopwords: Commonly found words, such as *'and'*, *'this'* and *'also'*, are not indexed. These stop words are words that, if indexed, could potentially

1   U.S. National Library of Medicine. Medical Subject Headings (MeSH). 2014. Available: http://www.nlm.nih.gov/pubs/factsheets/mesh.html. Accessed 1 September 2014.

return every document in the database if the word was used in a search statement[1].

Sources of information

There is no single definitive source of medical information. A comprehensive search strategy will use a number of different sources to ensure that all relevant material is retrieved.

1   U.S. National Library of Medicine. Stopwords. 2014. Available: http://www.nlm.nih.gov/bsd/disted/pubmedtutorial/020_170.html. Accessed 10 October 2014.

Not all journals are equal. Some journals are more prestigious than others. There can be many reasons for such prestige, including a long history in publishing, affiliation with an important medical organisation or a reputation for publishing important research. It is important to know which journal an article was published in – but remember, even the best journals sometimes publish poor articles and good papers can appear in the less prestigious journals.

Peer-reviewed journals

A **peer-reviewed** journal is a publication that requires each submitted article to be independently examined by a panel of experts, who are non-editorial staff of the journal. To be considered for publication, articles need to be approved by the majority of peers. The process is usually anonymous, with the authors not knowing the identities of the peer reviewers. In double-blind peer review, neither the author nor the reviewers know the others' identities. Anonymity aids the feedback process.

The peer-review process forces authors to meet certain standards laid down by researchers and experts in that field. Peer review makes it more likely that mistakes or flaws in research are detected before publication. As a result of this quality assurance, peer-reviewed journals are held in greater esteem than non-peer-reviewed journals.

There are disadvantages to the peer-review process, however. Firstly, it adds a delay between the submission of an article and its publication. Secondly, the peer reviewers might guess the identity of the author(s), particularly in small, specialised fields, impairing the objectivity of their assessments. Thirdly, revolutionary or unpopular conclusions can face opposition within the peer-review process, leading to preservation of the status quo.

Finally, it is worth remembering that peer review does not guarantee that errors will not appear in the finished article or that fraudulent research will not be published. There have also been instances where the peer review process itself has been shown to be defective. For example, a spoof paper concocted by *Science* in 2013 revealed little or no scrutiny at many open-access journals[1]. Acceptance of the obviously flawed paper was the norm, not the exception. In 2014 two publishers announced they were removing more than 120 papers

1   Bohannon J. Who's afraid of peer review? *Science* 2013; 342(6154): 60–65.

from their subscription services after a researcher discovered that the works were computer-generated nonsense[1].

Journal impact factor

A high number of citations implies that a journal is found to be useful to others, suggesting that the research published in that journal is valuable. However, simply ranking a journal's importance by the number of times articles within that journal are cited by others would favour large journals over small journals and frequently issued journals over less frequently issued journals.

A **journal impact factor** provides a means of evaluating or comparing the performance of a journal relative to that of others in the same field. It ranks a journal's importance by measuring the frequency with which the average article in a journal has been cited in a particular year. Impact factors are calculated annually by Thomson Reuters (formerly known as the Institute for Scientific Information) and published in the *Journal Citation Report* (JCR).

The impact factor of a journal is calculated as the number of citations in the current year to articles published in the two previous years, divided by the total number of articles published in the two previous years[2]. In 2014 *The New England Journal of Medicine* had an impact factor of 54.42[3] (the highest among general medical journals) and *The BMJ* had an impact factor of 16.3[4].

It is important to remember, in critical appraisal, that the journal impact factor cannot be used to assess the importance of any one article, as the impact factor is a property of the journal and is not specific to that article. Also, journal citation counts in JCR do not distinguish between letters, reviews or original research.

The **Immediacy Index** is another way from Thomson Reuters of evaluating journals. The Immediacy Index is the average number of times an article is cited in the year it is published[5]. It is calculated by dividing the number of citations

1   Van Noorden R. Publishers withdraw more than 120 gibberish papers. 2014. Available: http://www.nature.com/news/publishers-withdraw-more-than-120-gibberish-papers-1.14763. Accessed 1 September 2014.

2   Journal Citation Report (JCR). Philadelphia, USA. Thomson Institute for Scientific Information, 2005. JCR provides quantitative tools for ranking, evaluating, categorising and comparing journals.

3   NEJM. *Media Center Fact Sheet.* 2014. Available: http://www.nejm.org/page/media-center/fact-sheet. Accessed 1 September 2014.

4   The BMJ. *About The BMJ.* 2014. Available: http://www.bmj.com/about-bmj. Accessed 1 September 2014.

5   Thomson Reuters. *Immediacy Index.* 2012. Available: http://admin-apps.webofknowledge.com/JCR/help/h_immedindex.htm. Accessed 1 September 2014.

to articles published in a given year by the number of articles published in that year. This is useful for comparing journals specialising in cutting-edge research.

A journal can improve its impact factor by improving accessibility to its articles and publicising them more widely. In recent years there have been significant improvements in web-based access to journals and now some journals publish research articles online before they appear in print. Many journals issue press releases highlighting research findings and send frequent email alerts to subscribers. A rise in the percentage of review articles with citations to the journal itself can also boost a journal's impact factor. Review journals often occupy the first-ranked journal position in the JCR subject category listings.

As impact factors provide a quantitative measure of the quality of a journal it is perhaps not surprising that there have been scandals where impact factors have been manipulated. Some journal editors have engaged in coercive self-citation, pressurising researchers to add citations from the editor's journal, even when the manuscript was not lacking in attribution[1].

Ingelfinger rule

The Ingelfinger rule, named after Franz Ingelfinger, a former editor of *The New England Journal of Medicine,* stipulates that neither an original research article nor any of its pictures or tables may be published in more than one outlet[2]. This rule was originally implemented to protect the newsworthiness of the journal. It is now a widely adopted principle within the scientific community and serves to ensure research is subjected to peer review and published in the scientific literature before it is touted to the public or the profession.

1   Wilhite AW, Fong EA. Coercive citation in academic publishing. *Science* 2012; 335(6068): 542–43.
2   Relman AS. *The Ingelfinger Rule.* 1981. Available: http://www.nejm.org/doi/full/10.1056/NEJM198110013051408. Accessed 1 September 2014.

ORGANISATION OF THE ARTICLE

The majority of published articles follow a similar structure.

Title: This should be concise and informative, but sometimes an attention-grabbing title is used to attract readers to an otherwise dull paper. The title can influence the number of people who read the article, which can in turn lead to increased citations.

Author(s): This should allow you to see if the authors have the appropriate academic and professional qualifications and experience. The institutions where the authors work might also be listed and can increase the credibility of the project if they have a good reputation for research in this field. Be wary of 'guest' or 'gift' authors who did not contribute to the article. These authors might have been added to make the list of authors appear more impressive or to enhance the authors' curricula vitae, often on a reciprocal basis. Conversely, a 'ghost' author is someone who contributed to a piece of work, but who is left uncredited despite qualifying for authorship. The International Committee of Medical Journal Editors (ICMJE) recommends that authorship be based on the following four criteria[1]:

1. Substantial contributions to the conception or design of the work; or the acquisition, analysis, or interpretation of data for the work.

2. Drafting the work or revising it critically for important intellectual content.

3. Final approval of the version to be published.

4. Agreement to be accountable for all aspects of the work in ensuring that questions related to the accuracy or integrity of any part of the work are appropriately investigated and resolved.

All those designated as authors should meet all four criteria for authorship, and all who meet the four criteria should be identified as authors. Those who do not meet all four criteria should be acknowledged[1].

Abstract: This summarises the research paper, briefly describing the reasons for doing the research, the methods used, the overall findings and the conclusions made. Reading the abstract is a quick way of getting to know the

---

1   Recommendations for the Conduct, Reporting, Editing, and Publication of Scholarly Work in Medical Journals in http://www.icmje.org/recommendations/browse/roles-and-responsibilities/defining-the-role-of-authors-and-contributors.html. December 2013. Accessed 10 October 2014.

article, but the brevity of the information provided in an abstract means that it is unlikely to reveal the strengths and weaknesses of the research. If the abstract is of interest to you, you must go on to read the rest of the article. Never rely on an abstract alone to inform your clinical practice!

Introduction: This explains what the research is about and why the study was carried out. A good introduction will include references to previous work related to the subject matter and describe the importance and limitations of what is already known.

Method: This section gives detailed information about how the study was actually carried out. Specific information is given on the study design, the population of interest, how the sample of the population was selected, the interventions offered and which outcomes were measured and how they were measured.

Results: This section shows what happened to the individuals studied. It might include raw data and might explain the statistical tests used to analyse the data. The results can be laid out in tables, diagrams and graphs.

Conclusion / discussion: This section discusses the results in the context of what is already known about the subject area and the clinical relevance of what has been found. It might include a discussion on the limitations of the research and suggestions on further research.

Conflicts of interests: Articles should be published on their scientific merit in order to maintain public trust in the scientific process[1]. A conflict of interest exists when professional judgment concerning a primary interest (such as how many subjects improve in a study) may be influenced by a secondary interest (such as financial gain)[1]. Perceptions of conflict of interest are as important as actual conflicts of interest[1]. Conflicts of interest can be held by anyone involved in the research project, from the formulation of a research proposal through to its publication, including authors, their employers, a sponsoring organisation, journal editors and peer reviewers. Conflicts of interest can be financial (eg research grants, honoraria for speaking at meetings), professional (eg being a member of an organisational body) or personal (eg a relationship with the journal's editor). Ideally, authors should disclose conflicts of interest when they submit their research work. **A conflict of interest does not necessarily mean that the results of a study are void.**

---

1   Recommendations for the Conduct, Reporting, Editing, and Publication of Scholarly Work in Medical Journals in http://www.icmje.org/recommendations/browse/roles-and-responsibilities/defining-the-role-of-authors-and-contributors.html. December 2013. Accessed 10 October 2014.

Ileal-lymphoid-nodular hyperplasia, non-specific colitis, and pervasive developmental disorder in children
Wakefield AJ, Murch SH, Anthony A, et al. *Lancet* 1998; 351: 637–41.

This study raised the possibility of a link between the measles, mumps and rubella vaccine (MMR) given to children in their second year of life and inflammatory bowel disease and autism. This was widely reported by the media. The MMR scare reduced vaccination rates to 80% nationally, leading to a loss of herd immunity and measles outbreaks in the UK. Later it was revealed that the lead author was being funded through solicitors seeking evidence to use against vaccine manufacturers and he also had a patent for a single measles vaccine at the time of the study. Ten of the study's 13 authors later signed a formal retraction[1]. The editor of the Lancet said the research study would never have been published if he had known of a serious conflict of interest.

[1] Murch SH, Anthony A, Casson DH, et al. Retraction of an interpretation. *Lancet* 2004; 363: 750.

SECTION B

AIMS AND OBJECTIVES

A common misconception is that the study design is the most important determinant of the merits of a clinical paper. As soon as the words 'randomised controlled trial' appear, many clinicians assume that the study is of great value and that the results can be applied to their own clinical practice. If this approach were true, then there would be no need for any other type of study.

Research projects are done to answer questions. The critical appraisal of a paper must therefore begin by understanding the **aims and objectives** at the heart of the paper.

The clinical question is normally stated in the title of the paper. The first few paragraphs of the paper should explain the reasons why the clinical question needs to be answered. There might be references to, and a discussion of, previous research. It is quite legitimate to repeat research if the researchers are proposing to use better methods or to confirm earlier results, particularly if those results were controversial or suggested big changes should be made to customary practice.

The primary hypothesis

As the researchers are conducting a scientific experiment, the clinical question is formalised into a position statement that will be proven true or false in the experiment – this is the **primary hypothesis**. It is also known as the **a priori hypothesis** – ie the hypothesis is generated prior to data collection. The hypothesis is usually the same as or closely related to the clinical question. Table 4 shows an example of a clinical question and primary hypothesis.

CLINICAL QUESTION	EXPERIMENT	PRIMARY HYPOTHESIS	STUDY DESIGN
What is the best analgesic medication for back pain?	Let's compare paracetamol and ibuprofen in back pain	Paracetamol gives better back pain control than ibuprofen	A randomised controlled trial comparing the efficacy of paracetamol versus ibuprofen in the treatment of back pain

Table 4 Designing a research project

Note that not all studies are designed to test a hypothesis. Some studies, such as case reports or qualitative studies, can be used to generate hypotheses.

TO SUMMARISE, A GOOD STUDY WILL ....

Give a summary about what is already known about the topic area.

Explain why more research is needed.

Explain how the new research differs from research already published.

Clearly state the clinical question and/or primary hypothesis.

A study should, ideally, be designed and powered to answer one well-defined primary hypothesis.

However, researchers may want to do more than one analysis in a study. For example, as well as finding out which one of two treatments is best, they may also want to determine if there was any differences between just the elderly patients or if there were differences in the incidence of a side effect. These additional comparisons are called **subgroup analyses**.

The danger with doing many subgroup analyses and highlighting only the positive differences is that the researchers may be accused of **data dredging**.

Data dredging

Data dredging occurs when researchers collect excessive amounts of data on the groups in the study and/or do multiple comparisons of the groups looking for any differences in outcomes. The more analyses that are done, the more likely it is a difference between the groups will be found.

Statistical significance and the alpha level are discussed later in this book (see page 178). You may wish to return to this chapter later to fully understand the problem caused by data dredging. Briefly, if one outcome is being compared, a statistically significant result can arise purely by chance and mislead the researchers into thinking something is happening when it isn't. If two outcomes are being compared, each result can be statistically significant purely by chance, so, if the probabilities of this happening are combined, a significant result will arise by chance more often than if only one outcome is being compared.

Performing many subgroup analyses has the effect of greatly increasing the chance that at least one of these comparisons will be statistically significant, even if there is no real difference (a type 1 error). As a result, conclusions can be misleading. Deciding on subgroups after the results are available can also lead to bias.

Multiple hypothesis testing on the same set of results should therefore be avoided. Subgroup analyses should be restricted to a minimum and, if possible, subgroup analyses should be pre-specified in the aims and objectives whenever possible. Any additional analyses suggested by the data should be acknowledged as exploratory for generating hypotheses and not for testing them. The Bonferroni correction (see page 186) may be employed to adjust the results for multiple testing.

Researchers often overlook the issue that the methods they use to answer one clinical question may be suboptimal to answer other questions. The pressure to get published means that researchers may be tempted to engage in data dredging to find positive results.

Subgroups and ethics

In a 2010 Supplementary guidance the General Medical Council states, 'Restricting research subjects to subgroups of the population that may be defined, for example, by age, gender, ethnicity or sexual orientation, for legitimate methodological reasons does not constitute discrimination.'[1]

TO SUMMARISE, A GOOD STUDY WILL ....
Specify any subgroup analyses as part of the aims and objectives.
Minimise the number of subgroup analyses.
Not collect excessive data.
Not introduce additional subgroup analyses later in the paper.
Not intend to switch focus to the subgroup analyses instead of the primary hypothesis.
Not intend to publish subgroup analyses as separate papers.

1   General Medical Council. Good Practice in Research and Consent To Research (Supplementary Guidance). London: GMC, 2010.

Scenario 3

Dr Edwards designed a case–control study to investigate the relationship between alcohol consumption and lung cancer. She recruited 700 people into her study, both healthy controls and people with lung cancer. She questioned each person on their alcohol history. To her surprise, she found a significant relationship, showing that alcohol consumption increased the risk of lung cancer, such that the finding was unlikely to have happened by chance alone. She submitted her article to The BMJ.

Most clinical questions are about whether a relationship exists between an **exposure** and an **outcome**.

The exposure could be to a risk factor or to a treatment:

- Does using sunbeds increase the risk of skin cancer? Here the exposure is a risk factor (sunbed use) and the outcome is skin cancer.

- Do cholesterol lowering drugs reduce the risk of heart disease? Here the exposure is a treatment (cholesterol lowering drugs) and the outcome is heart disease.

The researchers hope to find evidence that a relationship exists. Sometimes the clinical question appears simple but in real life the situation is more complex, so that even if researchers do find evidence that a relationship exists, it might not be the complete answer.

For example, suppose researchers want to know if living in a city is associated with an increased risk of heart disease. In an experiment the researchers compare people living in a city with people living in the countryside. The results show that city people are more likely to have the outcome. However, even though the relationship is proven, there may be other reasons why the relationship exists. The findings may be explained by the existence of a third factor, a confounder.

A **confounder** has a triangular relationship with both the exposure and the outcome, but, most importantly, it is not on the causal pathway (Figure 1). It makes it appear as if there is a direct relationship between the exposure and the outcome or it might even mask an association that would otherwise have been present.

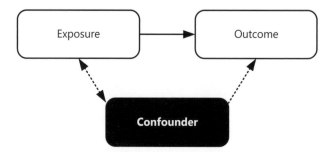

Figure 1 The relationship between the exposure, confounder and outcome

In the above example, it may be that the city people are more likely to be stressed because of their employment than people who live and farm in rural areas. Stress is a confounding factor. Stress is associated with living in the city and stress is independently associated with heart disease. If it is missed as an important factor, stress will mislead the researchers into simply concluding that having a city address is linked to an increased risk of heart disease. That would cause panic in the majority of the population!

To be a confounding factor, the variable must be associated with:

- the exposure, but must not be the consequence of the exposure
- the outcome, independently of the exposure (ie not an intermediary).

In the example in Figure 2, living in the city appears to be associated with heart disease. Stress is a confounding factor. It is associated with city living and it is a risk factor for heart disease, even in people who do not live in the city.

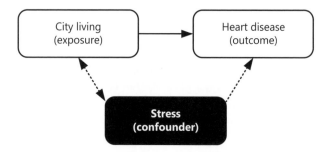

Figure 2 Stress is a confounding factor

The reverse is not true. City living does not confound the relationship between stress and heart disease, even though it is associated with stress. Having a city address is not a risk factor for heart disease independently of stress (Figure 3).

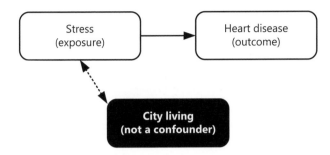

Figure 3 City living is not a confounding factor

When confounders are mentioned, we are usually referring to positive confounding. A **positive confounder** results in an association between two variables that are not associated:

- Example: The association between city living and heart disease is positively confounded by stress. People who live in a city might be stressed. Stress is a risk factor for heart disease, even for those people who do not live in the city.

Negative confounding also exists. A **negative confounder** masks an association that is really present:

- Example: The association between poor diet and coronary heart disease can be negatively confounded by exercise. People who exercise regularly might compensate for the effects of a poor diet, making it appear that poor diet is not as strongly associated with coronary heart disease.

Confounding can cause overestimation or underestimation of the true association and can even change the direction of the observed effect. An example is the confounding by age of an inverse association between level of exercise and heart attacks (younger people take more rigorous exercise), causing overestimation.

Identification of confounders
When researchers are designing their study, they should consider the possibility of confounding based on their knowledge and intuition. A list of possible confounding factors is usually given in the methods section. The researchers will normally collect data on how many subjects have one or more confounding factors.

Dealing with confounders

Once identified, there are a number of techniques that can be used to deal with confounding. Measures can be taken to

- eliminate confounding factors altogether (exclusion criteria – page 57)
- nullify their effects by spreading them equally between the different groups of the study (matching – page 68, randomisation – page 72)
- account for their effects on the results using statistical techniques (eg regression – page 202).

Scenario 3 revisited

Dr Edwards received a letter from the editor of The BMJ. The editor wrote, 'Although a most interesting conclusion, the results of the study are less impressive when confounding variables are considered. Unfortunately, smoking as a confounder has been overlooked. I'm afraid that we cannot consider publishing your study results. I wish you better luck in the future.'

TO SUMMARISE, A GOOD STUDY WILL ....
Accept the possibility that confounding may be an issue.
List confounding factors and explain their impact on any relationship under investigation.
Describe how confounding factors were controlled at the design and analysis stage.

Bias means mistake. Mistakes can happen at any time during the study. Mistakes don't happen because of bad luck – mistakes happen because of poor research techniques. The consequence is that the results generated are wrong. Wrong results may lead to wrong conclusions. Wrong conclusions applied to clinical practice may cause harm to patients.

The difference between bias and confounding

Bias leads to the wrong results

If a study suffers with a bias, **the results data are incorrect** due to the bias. The conclusion is correct judged solely on the collected data but had there been no bias, different results would have been generated.

- Example: In a study, a group of patients are aware they are receiving a new treatment. Another group of patients are aware they are receiving an old treatment. The new treatment group report fewer symptoms in the study. The researchers conclude that based on the data the new treatment is better than the old treatment. However, had patients not had expectations of how well they were expected to do in their respective groups, the results may have been different.

Confounding leads to the wrong conclusion

If a study suffers with a confounding problem, the results data are correct but **the conclusion is wrong**. The interpretation of the results is wrong because the researchers don't appreciate the entire situation.

- Example: Researchers mistakenly conclude that having a city address is linked with an increased risk of heart disease because there were more heart disease cases in city people compared to a group of people living in rural areas. However, the researchers are unaware of stress as a confounding factor, which is the underlying reason for the results data.

Confounding differs from bias in that confounding is not caused by a mistake made by the researchers. Confounding arises from a real-life relationship that already exists between the exposures and outcomes under consideration.

Types of bias

Bias can happen at any time in the study and there are many types of bias. We'll be highlighting sources of bias in the following chapters and explaining methods used to reduce the risk of bias. Two types of bias which are commonly seen in studies are selection bias and observation bias.

Selection bias occurs when there is a problem with the way subjects are recruited and allocated to groups.

Observation bias occurs when there is a problem with the way data are gathered in the study, such that the results have been unduly influenced by the expectations of researchers and subjects.

TO SUMMARISE, A GOOD STUDY WILL ....

Strive to use methods to minimise the risk of bias.

Acknowledge the presence of bias when it occurs and discuss how the results may have been influenced.

Suggest how future researchers should modify their methods to reduce the risk of bias if possible.

SECTION C

STUDY DESIGNS

The clinical question determines which study designs are appropriate.

- One clinical question can be answered by more than one study design.
- One study design cannot answer all clinical questions.

The type of clinical question determines the types of studies that will be appropriate.

Study designs fall into three main categories:

1. **Observational descriptive studies** – the researcher reports what has been observed in one person or in a group of people.
2. **Observational analytical studies** – the researcher reports the similarities and differences observed between two or more groups of people.
3. **Experimental studies** – the researcher intervenes in some way with one group of people and reports any differences in the outcome between this experimental group and a control group where no intervention or a different intervention was offered.

Examples of different study designs will be described in the next four chapters. The advantages and disadvantages of the different designs might include references to terms that we have not yet covered.

It is also possible to classify studies by their clinical question. Such studies, such as prognostic (or survival) studies and diagnostic studies, are described in section G.

Terms used to describe studies

Longitudinal: Deals with a group of subjects at more than one point in time. Subjects are usually seen regularly and assessed over days, weeks, months or years.

Cross-sectional: Deals with a group of subjects at a single point in time (ie a snapshot in time). Subjects are usually seen once and assessed.

Parallel: The groups receive different interventions and the experiment can proceed in the groups independently of each other and/or at the same time.

Prospective: Deals with the present and the future (ie looks forward). Data are collected as they are generated.

Retrospective: Deals with the present and the past (ie looks backwards). Pre-existing data are collected.

Ecological: A population or community is studied, giving information at a population level rather than at an individual level.

Explanatory: The study takes place in an ideal setting, such as a medical research centre, to determine if an intervention can work and how it might work. Often a new drug is compared to a placebo with subjects who are as homogeneous as possible. These studies produce efficacy data[1].

Pragmatic: The study takes place in an ordinary setting, such as an outpatient clinic or hospital ward, to determine if an intervention works in real-life conditions. These studies produce effectiveness data[1]. The results are more reflective of everyday practice, as long as the patients selected are representative of the patients who will receive the treatment. Often a new treatment is compared with a standard treatment rather than with a placebo. Pragmatic trials tend to be difficult to control and difficult to blind, and there are difficulties with excessive drop-outs.

An intervention that is shown to be efficacious in an explanatory study may not always be effective in a pragmatic study.

---

1   Roland M, Torgerson DJ. Understanding controlled trials: What are pragmatic trials? *BMJ* 1998; 316: 285.

OBSERVATIONAL DESCRIPTIVE STUDIES

In observational descriptive studies the researcher describes what has been observed in a sample. Nothing is done by the researcher to the people in the sample. There is no control group for comparison. These studies are useful for generating ideas for research projects.

Case report

The experience of a single person is described in a case report.

Case reports are easy to write, but they tend to be anecdotal and cannot usually be repeated. They are prone to chance association and bias. Their value lies in the fact that they can be used to generate a hypothesis.

A famous case report was about Phineas Gage, a railroad worker in Vermont, USA. In 1848 he suffered an accident during a blast explosion in which an iron rod was driven through his head, destroying his left frontal lobe[1]. In the following years his behaviour and personality changed. His symptoms included irritability, inappropriate profanity and poor judgement. The case report gave rise to the idea that specific parts of the brain had defined functions. The full story can be read on Wikipedia at http://en.wikipedia.org/wiki/Phineas_Gage.

[1] Phineas Gage http://en.wikipedia.org/wiki/Phineas_Gage. Accessed 10 October 2014.

The Yellow Card Scheme, run by the MHRA and the Commission on Human Medicines, is used to collect case reports from both health professionals and the general public on suspected adverse drug reactions. Yellow Card reports are evaluated to find previously unidentified potential hazards and other new information on the side-effects of medicines. Further information is available on the scheme's website at https://yellowcard.mhra.gov.uk.

Case series

A group of people are studied in a case series. Case series are useful for studying rare diseases.

A famous case series was published as a letter in the Lancet in 1961[1], in which WG McBride wrote, 'Sir, Congenital abnormalities are present in approximately 1.5% of babies. In recent months I have observed that the incidence of multiple severe abnormalities in babies delivered of women who were given the drug thalidomide during pregnancy, as an antiemetic or as a sedative, to be almost 20%. Have any of your readers seen similar abnormalities in babies delivered of women who have taken this drug during pregnancy?' The link with congenital abnormalities led to the withdrawal of thalidomide from the market.

[1] McBride WG. Thalidomide and congenital abnormalities. Lancet 1961; 2: 1358.

There are hardly any journals devoted to publishing case reports and case series alone. These studies are more likely to be found in poster presentations in conferences and as letters or rapid responses in journals. Case reports and case series are low down in the hierarchy of evidence as they may be simply reporting events that have occurred by chance. However, they are useful for identifying new diseases, symptoms and signs, aetiological factors, associations, treatment approaches and prognostic factors.

There is no need to do a 'critical appraisal' of a case report or a case series, as the studies are purely narrative. One should never dismiss a case report or a case series without asking the question, 'Could there be any truth in the findings?'

Scenario 4

Dr Richards, a General Practitioner, smiled as she read the final draft of her research paper. Her survey of 50 patients with fungal nail infections demonstrated that more than half of them had used a public swimming pool in the month before their infection developed. She posted a copy of the paper to her Public Health Consultant, proposing she submit the article to the Journal of Public Health.

In observational analytical studies the researcher reports the similarities and differences observed between subjects in two or more groups. These studies are useful for investigating the relationships between risk factors and outcomes. The two types, cohort and case–control studies, differ in their initial focus.

- Cohort studies focus initially on recruiting subjects with a risk factor. At the start of the study there are two groups of subjects – one with a risk factor and one without.

- Case–control studies focus initially on recruiting subjects with an outcome. At the start of the study there are two groups of subjects – one with an outcome and one without.

Cohort study

Cohort means group. In a cohort study a group of subjects exposed to a risk factor are matched to a group of subjects not exposed to a risk factor. At the beginning of the study no subject has the outcome. Both groups are followed up to see how the likelihood of an outcome differs between the groups (Figure 4). The researcher hopes to show that subjects exposed to a risk factor are more likely to have the outcome compared with the control group.

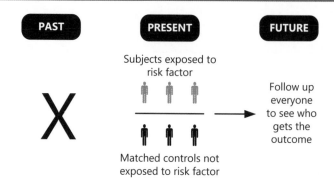

Figure 4 Cohort study design

Cohort studies are used to investigate the consequences of exposure to risk factors, so they are able to answer questions about aetiology and prognosis. They can give a direct estimation of disease incidence rates. They can also assess temporal relationships (the sequence of events that lead to a person developing an outcome) and multiple outcomes.

It can take a long time from exposure to the development of the outcome. Cohort studies are therefore expensive to set up and maintain. Bias becomes a problem if subjects drop out of the study over time, as the characteristics of the subjects at the end of the study may be dissimilar to those at the start.

The mortality of doctors in relation to their smoking habits; a preliminary report
Doll R, Bradford Hill A. *British Medical Journal* 1954; 1: 1451–55.

A cohort study which examined the relationship between smoking and lung cancer: 24 389 doctors were divided into two groups, depending on whether or not they were exposed to the risk factor (smoking). Twenty-nine months later, an examination of the cause of 789 deaths revealed a significant and steadily rising mortality from deaths due to lung cancer as the amount of tobacco smoked increased.

Cohort studies are also known as 'prospective' or 'follow-up' studies.

Sometimes a study is described as a **retrospective cohort study**. This sounds paradoxical but a retrospective cohort design simply means that the researchers identified a cohort study already in progress and added another outcome of interest. This saves the researcher time and money by not having to set up another cohort from scratch. Importantly, at the start of the retrospective cohort study, subjects were divided into two groups depending on the presence or absence of a risk factor; no-one had the outcome.

An **inception cohort** is a term used to describe a group of subjects who are recruited at an early stage in the disease process but before the outcome is established.

Case–control study

Subjects who have the outcome (the cases) are matched with subjects who don't have the outcome (the controls). All the subjects are asked about whether they have been exposed to one or more risk factors in the past (Figure 5). The researchers hope to show that the cases are more likely to have been exposed to the risk factor(s) compared with the controls.

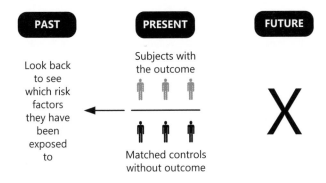

Figure 5 Case-control study design

Case–control studies are also known as 'case comparison' or 'retrospective' studies. They are used to investigate the causes of outcomes. Case–control studies are often carried out when new diseases appear so we can better understand why some people are becoming unwell. They are particularly useful in situations where there is a long time period between exposure and outcome, as there is no waiting involved.

Case–control studies are usually quick and cheap to do because few subjects are required, but it can be difficult to recruit a matching control group. The major difficulty with case–control studies is the need to rely on recall and records to determine the risk factors to which the subjects have been exposed. The temporal relationship between exposure and outcome can be difficult to establish as subjects tend to forget about the sequence of events such as symptom appearance.

Smoking and carcinoma of the lung: preliminary report
Doll R, Bradford Hill A. *British Medical Journal* 1950; 2: 739–48.

A case–control study in which patients who had suspected lung, liver or bowel cancers were asked about past exposure to risk factors, including smoking. Those with lung cancer were confirmed as smokers, and those who were given the all-clear were non-smokers.

Studying rare risk factors or outcomes

If the relationship between a risk factor and disease is being investigated and the risk factor is rare, the best way to guarantee a sufficient number of people with the risk factor is by using a cohort design. It would be unwise to choose a case–control design. Case–control studies start by recruiting subjects with and subjects without an outcome. Many people would need to be recruited in order to find the few that have been exposed to the rare risk factor.

If it is the outcome that is rare, the best way to guarantee a sufficient number of people with the outcome is by using a case–control design. It would not be a good idea to choose a cohort design. Cohort studies start by recruiting subjects with and subjects without a risk factor. A large number of people would need to be followed up to detect the few who have the rare outcome.

Case–cohort and nested case–control studies

A **nested case–control study** is done in a population taking part in a cohort study. Once sufficient numbers of outcomes have been reached in the cohort population, the case–control study can be used to investigate exposures not previously taken into consideration at baseline. The cases in the study are matched to controls in the same cohort. A nested case–control study helps to reduce costs.

In a **case–cohort study** cases are recruited just as in a traditional case–control study. The difference is that the control group is recruited from everyone in the initial cohort (the population at risk at the start of the risk period), regardless of their future disease status. The control group is a sample of the full cohort.

Association or causation?

Observational analytical studies are often used to show the association between exposure to a risk factor and an outcome. Association does not necessarily imply causation, however. Deciding if a causative relationship exists is made easier by using Sir Austin Bradford Hill's nine considerations for assessing the question, 'When does association imply causation?'[1]:

- **Strength:** Is the association strong enough and large enough that we can rule out other factors?

- **Consistency:** Have the results been replicated by different researchers, in different places or circumstances and at different times?

- **Specificity:** Is the exposure associated with a very specific disease?

- **Temporality:** Did the exposure precede the disease?

- **Biological gradient:** Are increasing levels of exposure associated with an increased risk of disease?

- **Plausibility:** Is there a scientific mechanism that can explain the causative relationship?

- **Coherence:** Is the association consistent with the natural history of the disease?

- **Experimental evidence:** Is there evidence from other randomised experiments?

- **Analogy:** Is any association analogous to any previously proved causal association?

For establishing whether a causal relationship exists between a microorganism and a disease, for example, Koch's postulates, named after the German physician, are useful, although their use is limited because there are exceptions to the rules[2].

- The bacteria must be present in all cases of the disease.

- The bacteria must be isolated from the host with the disease and grown in pure culture.

- The disease must be reproduced when a pure culture of the bacteria is inoculated into a healthy host.

- The bacteria must be recoverable from the experimentally infected host.

Rothman and Greenland introduced the concepts of **sufficient cause** and **component cause** to illustrate that discussing causation is rarely a

1   Bradford Hill A. The environment and disease: association or causation? *Proceedings of the Royal Society of Medicine* 1965; 58: 295–300.
2   Koch's postulates. http://en.wikipedia.org/wiki/Koch's_postulates. Accessed 10 October 2014.

straightforward matter[1]. A cause of a specific disease event was defined as an event, condition or characteristic that preceded the disease event and without which the disease event either would not have occurred at all or would not have occurred until some later time.

A 'sufficient cause', which means a complete causal mechanism, can be defined as a set of minimal conditions and events that inevitably produces disease.

It might be that no specific event, condition or characteristic is sufficient by itself to produce disease. A 'component cause' might play a role as a causal mechanism but by itself might not be a sufficient cause. The component cause must act with others to produce a causal mechanism. Component causes nearly always include some genetic and environmental factors.

Rothman's pies are used to illustrate these concepts. The pie chart is shown divided into individual component slices. The pie as a whole is the sufficient causal complex and is the combination of several component causes (the slices of the pie).

Cross-sectional study

In a cross-sectional study, the prevalence of the exposure and the outcome in a population at one point in time is determined. Researchers do not follow-up the subjects, so there is no information on the temporal sequence of events. Although cross-sectional studies may be able to establish association, they cannot determine any cause and effect relationship between the exposure and the outcome, which limits their usefulness.

Scenario 4 revisited

Dr Richards' colleague was less enthusiastic about the findings. He wrote, 'Interesting though the results are, your chosen study design shows merely an association between swimming pools and fungal nail infections. I think you wanted to know whether a causative relationship exists. I'm afraid a cross-sectional survey cannot answer that question. Before you panic the general public, may I suggest you go back to the drawing board and, based on your question, choose a more appropriate study design?'

1   Rothman KJ, Greenland S. Causation and causal inference in epidemiology. *American Journal of Public Health* 2005; 95(Suppl 1): S144–50.

In experimental studies the researcher intervenes in some way to measure the impact of a treatment.

Uncontrolled trial

If all the subjects in the study are given the same treatment, the study is described as **uncontrolled** (Figure 6).

Group

Figure 6 Uncontrolled trial design

Controlled trial

In controlled trials subjects in the study are given one of two treatments (Figure 7). The treatment under investigation is given to the experimental group. A standard intervention, a placebo treatment or no treatment is given to the control group for comparison. The researchers report any differences in the outcome between the experimental group and the control group.

Experimental group

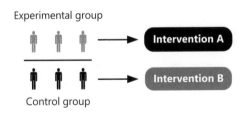

Control group

Figure 7 Controlled trial design

Usually the experimental and control groups are compared together in a research project. If historical controls are used, the experimental group is compared with old data in a control group.

Some trials have more than two groups.

Randomised controlled trial

This is the gold-standard design for studying treatment effects. Subjects do not choose which group they go into. Subjects are randomly allocated a treatment, which minimises selection bias and might equally distribute confounding factors between the treatment arms, depending on the randomisation strategy. Randomised controlled trials are a reliable measure of efficacy and allow for meta-analyses, but they are difficult, time-consuming and expensive to set up. There can be ethical problems in giving different treatments to the groups.

Crossover trial

All the subjects receive one treatment and then switch to the other treatment halfway through the study (Figure 8). The researchers assess which treatment made the subjects feel better.

Figure 8 Crossover trial design

The washout period is used to minimise carry-over effects. Its duration has to be long enough so that the first intervention does not interfere with the second intervention because of a long half-life or discontinuation/withdrawal effects.

To prevent order effects, the design can be more elaborate, with the subjects split into groups to receive the interventions in different orders (Figure 9).

Figure 9 Crossover trial design

Crossover trials are often used to study rare diseases where the lack of subjects would make a conventional trial underpowered. In a crossover trial each subject is providing twice as much data compared to a more conventional study design.

The crossover design has another advantage. A researcher in a treatment study needs to ensure that the subjects in the two arms are similar, so that any difference in outcome can be attributed to the presence or absence of treatment. In a crossover study the subjects are their own controls, so matching is almost perfect. The word 'almost' is used here on purpose: usually in research studies the results in the experimental arm are compared with the results in the control arm at the same point in time (parallel arms); in a crossover design, the comparison takes place at different time points. This can be a problem if something changes that means dissimilar conditions exist at the two time points.

n-of-1 trial

In an 'n-of-1' trial a single subject is studied and receives repeated courses of the experimental drug and control treatment in a random or alternate order (Figure 10). The trial can be blind or open label. The subject reports on their progress regularly. This can establish effectiveness in that subject because it can reveal whether clinical improvement occurs only at the time of being in receipt of the experimental drug and can also help indicate the most helpful dose. The generalisability of the findings is minimal.

Figure 10 n-of-1 study design

Factorial study

Experimental trials need not limit themselves to evaluating one intervention at a time. Factorial randomised trials assess the impact of more than one intervention and can give researchers an insight into how different interventions interact with one another (Figure 11).

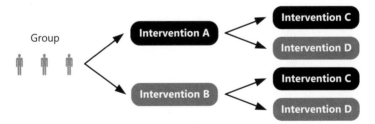

Figure 11 Factorial study design

For example, a researcher might wish to randomise subjects to receive an antidepressant versus placebo and then an antipsychotic versus placebo. The different treatment groups are shown in Table 5.

		ANTIDEPRESSANT	
		Yes	**Placebo A**
ANTIPSYCHOTIC	**Yes**	Group 1 Antidepressant + Antipsychotic	Group 2 Placebo A + Antipsychotic
	Placebo B	Group 3 Antidepressant + Placebo B	Group 4 Placebo A + Placebo B

Table 5 Factorial trial design

Audit

Aspects of service provision are assessed against a **gold standard**, which can be a regulatory standard, a national guideline, a local protocol or generally accepted best practice. Sometimes it is necessary to devise a gold standard in the absence of a published one.

Data on the service are collected and compared with the gold standard. A change is then implemented in the running of the service, hopefully to improve performance, and the audit cycle is completed by another collection of data (Figure 12).

To be labelled as an audit, the project must contain at least two cycles of data collection. The project can cycle indefinitely.

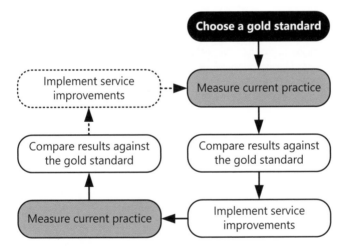

Figure 12 The audit cycle

Audits provide information on the effectiveness of services, but they are resource-hungry and take clinicians away from clinical work. Audits do not usually require ethical approval.

Surveys

In a survey a group of subjects is questioned. Surveys can identify patterns and help to plan service provision. A **census** is a special kind of survey in which data on every person and/or household in a population are collected.

Surveys cannot distinguish between cause and effect.

In a **qualitative survey** opinions are elicited from a group of subjects, with the emphasis on the subjective meaning and experience. Such studies can be used to study complex issues. The inquiry can be via interviews, focus groups or participant observation. However, it can be difficult to get information, record it and analyse the subjective data.

Economic analysis

This type of study assesses the cost and/or utilities of intervention. Such analyses help to prioritise services, but it is difficult to remain objective because assumptions have to be made.

Systematic review and meta-analysis

A systematic review attempts to access and review systematically all of the pertinent articles in the field. A meta-analysis combines the results of several studies and produces a quantitative assessment.

Bringing a drug to the market can take several years and cost hundreds of millions of pounds (Figure 13). The developmental process usually begins with the identification of a biological target that is linked with the aetiology of a disease. Compounds are formulated to act on this target. The chosen compound is then transformed and packaged in such a way that it can be administered to patients to give the maximum benefit and the minimum of side-effects. This transformation process involves a series of trials on animals and humans that are subject to the rigorous controls required by the regulatory authorities and local ethics committees.

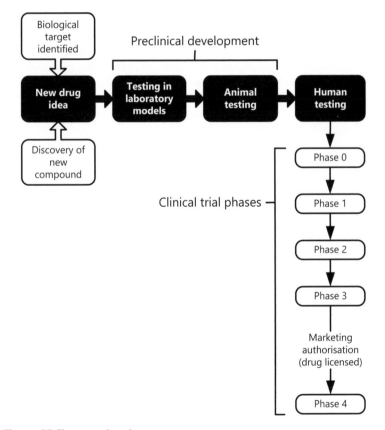

Figure 13 The research pathway

Clinical trial authorisations are needed for all new products in development. Applications for such authorisations in the UK are assessed by the medical, pharmaceutical and scientific staff at the Medicines and Healthcare products Regulatory Agency (MHRA), an agency of the Department of Health.

Clinical trial phases

Clinical trials of experimental drugs consist of five phases.

Phase 0 clinical trials

These studies are also known as human microdosing studies. A small number of people are given sub-therapeutic doses of the drug. The aim is to elicit information on pharmacodynamics and pharmacokinetics, particularly oral bioavailability and half-life of the drug[1].

Phase 1 clinical trials

These are the earliest trials in the life of a new drug or treatment. The researchers test a new drug or treatment in a small group of **healthy people** for the first time, to assess its safety, establish a dosage range and identify any side-effects. These trials aim to help in the evaluation and understanding of the behaviour of the molecule or compound. The healthy volunteers are normally compensated for the time they are giving up but are not given financial incentives to take part in research.

Phase 2 clinical trials

About seven out of every ten new treatments tested at phase 1 in healthy volunteers proceed to phase 2 trials and are tested on **people with the relevant illness**. At this stage, the study drug or treatment is given to a larger group of people to assess its effectiveness and safety profile.

Phase 3 clinical trials

At this stage, the study drug or treatment is given to large groups of **people in clinical settings** to make further assessments of its effectiveness, dose range and duration of treatment, and to monitor side-effects. These trials compare the new treatment with the best currently available treatment (the standard treatment).

Providing satisfactory results are gained from phase 3 studies, a drug will get a **marketing authorisation**, which sets out its agreed terms and conditions of use, such as indications and dosage. Even drugs with a high risk-to-benefit

---

1   Phases of clinical research. http://en.wikipedia.org/wiki/Phases_of_clinical_research. Accessed 10 October 2014.

ratio can be approved, for example if the drug enhances the quality of life of patients with terminal illnesses.

Phase 4 clinical trials

Phase 4 trials, also known as **post-marketing surveillance studies**, are carried out after a drug has been shown to work, has been granted a licence and has been marketed. Information is collected about the benefits and side-effects of the drug in different populations. Data on long-term usage are also collected. These studies involve monitoring the safety of medicines under their usual conditions of use, and they can also be carried out to identify any new safety concerns (**hypothesis generating**) and to confirm or refute these concerns (**hypothesis testing**).

SECTION D

SELECTING SUBJECTS

After stating the clinical question and the type of study design chosen, researchers will usually begin the methods section by describing the **recruitment** of subjects and their **allocation** into different groups.

Although this may appear to be a straightforward exercise, many researchers find recruiting subjects to be a frustrating experience because of the time it takes. Shortcuts are often taken to speed up recruitment and get an adequate sample size.

Controlled trials involve dividing subjects into two or more groups so that different interventions can be compared. The researchers need to ensure that the groups are as similar as possible in order that any comparisons done between them are fair.

Poor techniques for recruiting and allocating subjects may result in **selection bias**.

POPULATIONS AND SAMPLES

Researchers identify the **target population** they are interested in. It is rarely feasible to include everyone in the target population in the trial. Instead the researchers recruit a **sample population**, that is, they take a representative proportion of the target population. The sample population is defined by **inclusion criteria** and **exclusion criteria**. The researchers experiment on the sample population. The results from this sample are then generalised to the target population (Figure 14).

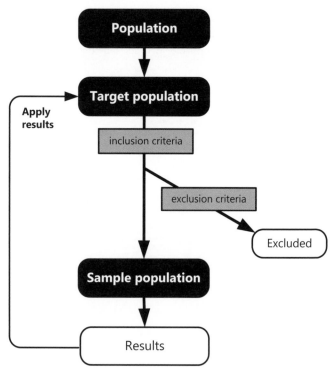

Figure 14 Describing people at different stages of a study

Inclusion criteria

Inclusion criteria are a list of criteria which must be met by a person in the target population to be included in the sample population.

Exclusion criteria

Exclusion criteria are a list of criteria which if met by a subject lead to that subject not being allowed into the sample population, even if the subject meets the inclusion criteria.

Exclusion criteria fall into three main categories.

The subject is too unwell to take part in the study

Trial protocols are highly specific about what will happen to subjects in different groups. In order to make comparisons fair, differences between the groups should be minimal. If a subject has a comorbid condition and takes part in a trial, that subject may not receive interventions and privileges that they will benefit from, even if they are unrelated to the aims and objectives of the study. For example, a patient who has just suffered a stroke may be deprived of medication and physiotherapy because they are not specified in the trial protocol. Such patients are also likely to drop out of the study when their unmet needs become too great.

There is also an ethical concern about putting patients at risk. The last thing a researcher wants is for a patient to die or deteriorate significantly in a trial. A further challenge is showing that severely ill patients were able to give informed consent to take part in the trial.

To avoid these complications, patients who are already too unwell are often excluded from sample populations.

The subject may become unwell during the study

For ethical reasons, exclusion criteria may exclude subjects who are well but may become unwell in the study should they take part. These subjects usually have allergies or intolerances to the drugs used in the study or they are taking medications that may interact with the study drugs.

The risk to the unborn child and breastfed baby may also be considered for exclusion by not allowing pregnant and breastfeeding women into the sample.

The subject has a confounding factor

Confounding factors can mislead researchers into making the wrong conclusion. One method of dealing with confounding factors is to exclude subjects with confounding factors from the sample population.

The exclusion criteria can include one or more confounding factors. This means that subjects with the confounding factors are not allowed into the sample. The end result is that confounding due to these factors is no longer an issue.

SEE EXCERPT 1

Excessive use of exclusion criteria

There are two main concerns with having too many exclusion criteria:

1. It will be harder to recruit a sample population, resulting in a smaller sample size, less confidence about the results and a greater risk of a type 2 error.

2. There will be diagnostic purity bias (a subtype of selection bias). The results may not be generalisable to the target population.

As a result, if it appears there will be excessive exclusion criteria, the researchers may limit the list by using other ways of dealing with confounding factors (eg matching, randomisation, statistics).

Sampling methods

There are five common techniques that are used to obtain a sample from a population:

1. **(Simple) random sampling:** Every person in the target population has an equal chance of being selected. The researchers usually have access to a database holding details of the target population. Random sampling is also known as **representative sampling** or **proportionate sampling** because all groups should be proportionately represented.

2. **Systematic sampling:** Every n^{th} member of the target population is selected once the first person has been chosen at random. This is also known as **quasi-random sampling**. It usually gives a representative sample of the population. **SEE EXCERPT 2**

3. **Stratified sampling:** People in the target population are put into subgroups or strata depending on one or more characteristics, such as ethnicity. A sample is drawn from each of the strata, usually randomly. This guarantees that people with certain characteristics are represented in the sample population. **SEE EXCERPT 3**

4. **Cluster sampling:** The target population is divided into similar and representative clusters. Some of these clusters are exhaustively sampled; other clusters are not used. **SEE EXCERPT 4**

5. **Convenience sampling:** Sampling is done as convenient, selecting people as they appear and often allowing the person to choose whether or not he or she is sampled. Convenience sampling is the easiest and potentially most dangerous. Good results can often be obtained, but just as often the data set can be seriously biased. Convenience sampling is used in qualitative studies.

EXCERPT 1

Adapted from: Lago-Deibe FI et al. The safety and efficacy of the tetanus vaccine intramuscularly versus subcutaneously in anticoagulated patients: a randomized clinical trial. *BMC Family Practice* 2014; 15: 147.

In patients treated with oral anticoagulants, subcutaneous injections of anti-tetanus vaccine are usually recommended to reduce the risk of bleeding. The objective of this study was to compare the safety and efficacy of intramuscular and subcutaneous injections of tetanus-diphtheria vaccine in patients treated with oral anticoagulants.

Inclusion criteria
- *Patients treated with oral anticoagulants, for whom administering of at least one dose of anti-tetanus vaccine was indicated.*

Exclusion criteria
- *Severe local reaction to previous doses with the whole circumference of the injected limb being affected.*
- *Peripheral neurological disorders due to previous doses.*
- *Severe anaphylactic reaction due to previous doses or any of the components.*
- *Poor haematological control (International Normalised Ratio [INR] > 4) in the last 2 months.*
- *Serious illness, terminal stages of diseases, immobilised, adversely affected by chronic pathology or immunosuppressive states.*
- *Pregnant or breast-feeding women.*

Commentary: Patients who are too unwell already, patients who may become unwell in the study and pregnant/breast-feeding women are excluded from the sample population.

EXCERPT 2

Adapted from: Al-Maskari F et al. Prevalence of risk factors for diabetic foot complications. *BMC Family Practice* 2007; 8: 59.

The aim of this study was to determine the prevalence and risk factors for foot complications among diabetic patients. The sample was to include diabetic patients of all ages and both genders, attending any diabetic centre or clinic.

In the absence of a diabetes registry or a computerised database for patients in the district, systematic random sampling within these units (centres/clinics) was used to select patients to be approached for participation in the study. Thus, every third diabetic patient visiting any of the participating centres and clinics was approached.

Commentary: An example of systematic sampling. Every third patient was approached.

EXCERPT 3

Adapted from: Bellis MA et al. National household survey of adverse childhood experiences and their relationship with resilience to health-harming behaviours in England. *BMC Medicine* 2014; 12: 72.

Researchers carried out a national household survey of adults resident in England to investigate the relationship between adverse childhood experiences and resilience to health-harming behaviours.

Sampling used a random probability approach stratified first by region (n = 10, with inner and outer London treated as two regions) and then small area deprivation in order to provide a sample representative of the English population. Samples for each region were proportionate to their population.

Commentary: An example of stratified sampling. Researchers divided the country into regions. Within each region, the population was further stratified by the level of deprivation, each of which was sampled. Consequently the researchers were able to recruit subjects of different economic statuses from all the regions of the country.

EXCERPT 4

Adapted from: Manandhar K et al. Estimating the prevalence and burden of major disorders of the brain in Nepal: methodology of a nationwide population-based study. *The Journal of Headache and Pain* 2014; 15: 52.

The aim of the study was to assess the prevalence and burden attributable to major disorders of the brain in Nepal in order to inform health policy.

The population of interest were adults aged 18–65 years who were Nepali speaking and living in Nepal. We selected, employed and trained groups of interviewers to visit randomly selected households by cold-calling. Households were selected from 15 representative districts out of 75 in the country through cluster sampling. One participant was selected randomly from each household.

Commentary: An example of cluster sampling. The nation was divided into 75 clusters but only 15 clusters were sampled.

TO SUMMARISE, A GOOD STUDY WILL ....

Define the target population.

Describe the sampling method.

List the inclusion criteria and relate them to the aims of the study.

List and explain the exclusion criteria.

Illustrate how many people were included and excluded, often in the form of a flowchart or table.

Explain how the sample size was determined.

Comment on how well the sample population represents the target population.

SELECTION BIAS

Scenario 5
General Practitioner Dr Stevenson wanted to know whether smoking cannabis was dangerous. In her clinics she asked patients if they smoked cannabis and, if the answer was yes, whether they had any health concerns. The results were extremely disturbing. There was a strong association between cannabis smoking and poor health. She wrote to the editor of the Addiction Journal, urging him to rapidly publish her study in order to highlight the risks.

Scenario 6
Mr Pahal, Consultant Plastic Surgeon, was interested in how many patients would use a hospital website to access information about postoperative care. He placed an advertisement in The Times newspaper and recruited 90 people for his survey. He concluded that 80% of patients would definitely visit a hospital website for more information about the management of surgical wounds. He put forward a proposal to the Hospital Board for funding the development of such a website.

The sample population should be representative of the target population so that the results from the sample population can be generalised to the target population.

Selection bias occurs when the researchers recruit a sample population that is unrepresentative of the target population. The sample population differs in some significant way from the population that generated the sample population, such that any results and conclusions drawn from the sample population cannot be generalised to the population as a whole.

Selection bias can be further divided into **sampling bias**, which is introduced by the researchers, and **response bias**, which is introduced by the study population.

Examples of **sampling bias** include:

- **Berkson (admission rate) bias:** This arises when the sample population is taken from a hospital setting, but the hospital cases do not reflect the rate or severity of the condition in the community population. The relationship between exposure and disease is unrepresentative of the real situation. For example, if one looked at how many cigarette smokers developed lung cancer, the answer would be different if the research was done on a respiratory ward instead of in the community. **SEE EXCERPT 5**

- **Diagnostic purity bias:** This arises when comorbidity is excluded in the sample population, such that the sample population does not reflect the true complexity of cases in the population. For example, if there are excessive exclusion criteria, the subjects in the study are 'too pure' and tend to do well with interventions in the study. In reality, patients are more complex; comorbidities and lifestyle factors may adversely impact treatment success rates.

- **Neyman bias (incidence-prevalence bias, survival bias):** This occurs when the prevalence of a condition does not reflect its incidence. Usually this is due to a time gap between the onset of a condition and the actual selection of the study population, such that some individuals with the condition are not available for selection. This bias often affects studies on conditions which are rapidly progressive, such as pancreatic cancer, with some patients dying before they can take part in the study. The researchers end up only testing interventions on the patients with milder forms of illness yet suggesting their results can be applied to the whole clinical population.

- **Membership bias:** This arises when membership of a group is used to recruit subjects. The members of such a group might not be representative of the population. The usual problem is that people who join organisations, such as cancer charities, are more motivated to look after their health than the typical person in the target population. These members tend to adhere to trial protocols well, whereas in real life people don't care so much about maintaining their health and healthy lifestyle. **SEE EXCERPT 6**

- **Historical control bias:** This arises when subjects and controls are chosen across time, such that secular changes in definitions, exposures, diseases and treatments can mean that such subjects and controls cannot be compared with one another.

Response bias occurs when individuals volunteer for studies but they differ in some way from the population. The most common reason for such a difference is that the volunteers are more motivated to improve their health and therefore participate more readily and adhere to the trial conditions better. Typical methods of selecting subjects that might lead to a response bias include advertising for volunteers in newspapers, radio stations and television channels. **SEE EXCERPT 7**

Confusingly, the term 'response bias' can also be used to describe an observation bias (see page 98).

Avoiding selection bias with large sample sizes

One way that researchers can minimise or even eradicate the problem of selection bias is to have the whole target population data in the experiment. This may be feasible when researchers have access to comprehensive databases which provide all their data requirements. **SEE EXCERPT 8**

Allocation and selection bias

Selection bias can happen not only at the recruitment stage of a study but also when subjects are allocated to different arms. **The group of subjects in each arm should be representative of the target population.** If the subjects are not representative, a selection bias has occurred during the allocation process.

Researchers and subjects should not be allowed to decide which subjects go into specific groups. If we allow researchers and subjects to decide, selection bias is inevitable. In experimental studies, for example, researchers want the experimental group to be composed of subjects who will do well in the study and the control group to be composed of subjects who will do poorly in the study. The composition of each group is then not representative of the target population and selection bias has occurred.

Sampling and selection bias

Even if steps are taken to reduce the risk of selection bias, a **sampling error** can also happen by chance. Large sample sizes and probability sampling help to minimise sampling error.

EXCERPT 5

Adapted from: Wen J et al. Risk factors of earthquake inpatient death: a case control study. *Critical Care* 2009; 13: R24.

Researchers in China did an epidemiological study on the determinants of the mortality of patients hospitalised after an earthquake.

A selection bias (eg admission rate bias or Berkson bias) should be noted. One of the most important exclusions from hospital-series case-control studies are at-scene deaths. As most earthquake deaths do occur outside the hospital, it is a critical exclusion for trauma death numbers. Therefore, the causes of death for hospitalised patients may dramatically differ from at-scene deaths.

Commentary: In their discussion, the researchers note a potential Berkson bias if their results are applied to all earthquake victims. They explain that the findings from the victims admitted to hospital are not necessarily applicable to earthquake victims who died before getting to hospital.

EXCERPT 6

Adapted from: Ruston A et al. Diabetes in the workplace – diabetic's perceptions and experiences of managing their disease at work: a qualitative study. *BMC Public Health* 2013; 13: 386.

The aim of this study was to explore the perceptions and experiences of employees with type 1 and type 2 diabetes.

The inclusion criteria for the study were current or recent employment and mode of treatment. People with type 1 diabetes need to administer insulin either through daily injections or through an insulin pump and generally attend specialist centres, only some of which support the use of insulin pumps. To ensure inclusion of those using insulin pumps and multiple injections the study utilised a national database of people with type 1 diabetes. The database was compiled from users of an online support organisation which advocates access to insulin pumps and other diabetes technologies in the UK. People with type 2 diabetes were recruited via local diabetes clinics in two general practices in south east England.

Commentary: There is a selection problem in the form of a membership bias. The type 1 diabetic patients that were recruited were members of an online support organisation. They are more likely to have a positive outlook on life with diabetes but may not be representative of all type 1 diabetic patients. Ideally all patients should have been recruited from outpatient clinics.

EXCERPT 7

Adapted from: Russell G et al. Parents' views on care of their very premature babies in neonatal intensive care units: a qualitative study. *BMC Pediatrics* 2014; 14: 230.

Researchers explored parents' views and experiences of the care for their very premature baby on a neonatal intensive care unit.

A qualitative study of preterm birth where all eligible parents whose baby was born at one of three hospitals in the previous six months were invited to take part. Parents were eligible to take part if they had a baby born before 32 weeks gestation and spoke English well. Parents were recruited from three tertiary care centres in South East England by posters in the neonatal units or by letter of invitation. Letters were either posted or given to parents if they had been on the neonatal unit for longer than two weeks and met the eligibility criteria. Parents returned a card indicating their willingness to participate.

Commentary: In the discussion the researchers acknowledge the possibility of response bias. The results may not be applicable to all parents who give birth to a very premature baby. For example, there is a higher incidence of very preterm birth in certain ethnic groups and in women from very deprived areas. The current sample comprised largely white, educated and married parents. As parents responded to a letter of invitation only, it was not possible to collect information about parents who did not accept the invitation to take part.

EXCERPT 8

Adapted from: Lass J et al. Antibiotic prescription preferences in paediatric outpatient setting in Estonia and Sweden. *Springer Plus* 2013; 2: 124.

A study was done to compare the paediatric outpatient antibiotic use in two countries – Sweden and Estonia.

We conducted a descriptive drug utilisation study based on the Estonian Health Insurance Fund and Swedish Prescribed Drug Register database. Both are nationwide prescription databases, containing electronically submitted data of all prescription medicines dispensed by the pharmacies. We identified all prescriptions for systemic antibacterial drugs released for children aged less than 18 years between January 1 and December 2007, from both databases.

Commentary: The study avoided selection bias by comparing data on all prescriptions in the two countries. The data were held on national databases allowing relatively easy collection and retrieval.

Scenario 5 revisited

The editor of the Addiction Journal was scathing in his feedback. 'Unfortunately your study has a fundamental issue with selection bias. Your sample comprises your clinic patients, a group who already have health concerns. You should have sampled people in your whole community to see how many cannabis smokers suffered health problems. I suspect that would have taken a lot longer and your results would be much less impressive.'

Scenario 6 revisited

Mr Pahal's proposal was rejected by the Hospital Board. In their conclusions, they commented, 'A non-representative sample was used to generate the findings. The population that the hospital serves is dissimilar to that which reads The Times newspaper in a number of respects, including, but not limited to, lower literacy levels and less internet access. Mr Pahal should consider selecting a more representative sample for future proposals, to avoid selection bias.'

TO SUMMARISE, A GOOD STUDY WILL ....

Allow sufficient time and resources to recruit subjects without resorting to shortcuts.

Explain how the selection process minimised selection bias.

Acknowledge any mistakes or methodological compromises that were made.

Make suggestions on how any mistakes can be avoided in future research, if possible.

MATCHING

Scenario 7

Dr Field investigated the impact of ethnicity on educational achievement in secondary school pupils. She recruited 50 pupils aged 14 years old of Asian ethnicity from one school and a control group of 50 pupils aged 14 years old of white ethnicity from a neighbouring school. The gender ratio in each group was the same. Her study showed that the Asian pupils fared worse in exams taken 2 years later. She submitted her cohort study to the Journal of British Epidemiology, writing that she had shown that Asian pupils were less intelligent than their white counterparts. She expected her research would make the front pages of newspapers.

Ideally, in a study with more than one arm the subjects in each arm should be as similar as possible apart from exposure to the risk factor or intervention of interest.

In cohort and case–control studies, the researchers recruit the experimental group first before recruiting a control group. The experimental and control groups are usually **matched**, which means that for every subject in the experimental group there is a control subject who has similar values of the matching variables. It is usual for the researchers to recruit the control group from the same location as the experimental group in the expectation that the resulting groups will be similar.

Examples of matching variables include:

- **Demographic factors** – age, gender, ethnicity
- **Lifestyle factors** – smoking status, alcohol drinking status, drug misuse status
- **Disease factors** – diabetes, heart disease, bowel cancer
- **Treatment factors** – anti-hypertensives, cholesterol-lowering drugs

SEE EXCERPT 9

Matching and confounding factors

The issue of confounding can be dealt with using exclusion criteria in a study. However, if there are many confounding factors, it is not possible to deal with all of them using exclusion criteria without causing selection bias.

One other tactic is to allow subjects with confounding factors into the study but distribute them equally in the different groups. The confounding factors will then have equal influence in all the groups, nullifying their effect when it comes to looking for differences between the groups.

Matching can be used to distribute confounding factors evenly. Study participants are chosen to ensure that potential confounding variables are evenly distributed in the two groups being compared. This ensures that any confounding factor that has been identified in the experimental group can also be replicated in the control group.

SEE EXCERPT 10

Matching must be used with caution because, like restriction, it can limit the sample size and possible analysis strategies. It can be difficult to find matching controls, especially with large numbers of matching variables. In these situations, matching may be abandoned in favour of using statistical analyses later on to adjust for those variables which would have been matched had there been a sufficient number of controls. This is easier to do in large studies. In small studies, matching is preferred.

There might be a table in a clinical paper comparing the baseline characteristics of subjects in the different arms. A failure of matching is shown by a significant difference in one or more characteristics between the arms. Whether this difference impacts on the study's internal validity depends on whether the characteristic has an important influence.

EXCERPT 9

Adapted from: Okebe J et al. A comparative case control study of the determinants of clinical malaria in The Gambia. *Malaria Journal* 2014; 13: 306.

The study reassessed the importance of known risk factors and reviewed demographic and socio-economic determinants of malaria risk in the population.

Cases were children aged six months to 12 years with confirmed malaria attending the outpatient clinics of the study clinics. To select a route along which the search for a suitable control will follow, a trained field staff stood at the doorstep of the index case's house and spun a pen on the ground. The team then visited households in the direction of the long axis of the pen, visiting until a potential age-matched child was found. On finding such a child, additional criteria for recruitment; residence in the area in the previous six months, no history of malaria treatment in the preceding two weeks and a negative rapid antigen test for malaria were checked after obtaining a written consent from the child's mother or other responsible adult available.

Commentary: An example of matching primarily using demographic factors, with the assumption that children in the same locality will be good matches.

EXCERPT 10

Adapted from: Physical activity and renal cell carcinoma among black and white Americans: a case–control study. *BMC Cancer* 2014; 14: 707.

Renal cell carcinoma has a higher incidence in blacks than in whites. Physical activity may influence the risk of renal cell cancer, but the evidence is inconsistent. This case–control study investigated this relationship.

Blacks and whites between 20 and 79 years of age with an incident, histologically-confirmed diagnosis of renal cell carcinoma during the enrolment period were eligible to participate. Controls were selected from the general population and frequency matched to cases on sex, age (5-year intervals) and race.

Commentary: The researchers recruited the cases first. Controls were selected from the rest of the population and matched on three variables to keep the two groups as similar as needed.

Scenario 5 revisited

Dr Field's research was rejected by the journal. The editor dismissed the paper with a cursory reply. 'Apart from matching the pupils by age and gender, you forgot to match on other important characteristics. The baseline characteristics show that the second school which generated the control group, for example, serves a much wealthier population than the first school which is set in a deprived inner-city area. Unfortunately as you have not dealt with such disparities, publishing this research would be a terrible slur on Asian pupils.'

TO SUMMARISE, A GOOD STUDY WILL ....

Describe how matching was done and any difficulties encountered.

List and justify the matching criteria.

Minimise the matching criteria to avoid recruitment problems.

Provide a table comparing the baseline demographic and prognostic characteristics of the different groups, highlighting significant differences.

Scenario 8

Dr Gilbert wanted to investigate a new treatment to lower the risk of coronary artery disease. He invited 60 people to take part in his randomised controlled trial. Half the subjects would receive the new treatment and half would receive a placebo intervention. He looked at the people as they sat in the outpatient clinic's waiting room. He decided that those sitting on the left would be allocated to the treatment group and those sitting to the right would be allocated to the control group.

Randomisation ensures that all the people entering into a study have an equal chance of being allocated to any group within the study. Allocation of subjects to specific treatment groups in a random fashion ensures that each group is, on average, as similar as possible to the other group(s).

Note that random sampling is not the same as randomisation. Random sampling comes earlier in the study and is used to recruit a sample population from the target population. Randomisation aims to allocate the recruited subjects to one of the intervention groups.

Random number generation

Successful randomisation requires that group allocation cannot be predicted in advance. Some methods of allocation, such as alternate allocation to treatment group or methods based on patient characteristics, are not reliably random. These allocation sequences are predictable and not easily concealed, and can therefore reduce the guarantee that allocation has been random and that no potential participants have been excluded by pre-existing knowledge of the intervention.

Instead, researchers use a variety of techniques to generate a random sequence that can be used to decide allocation:

- computer random number generation – the most popular method
- random number tables – contain a series of numbers that occur equally often and which are arranged in a random fashion; numbers usually have two or more digits
- shuffled cards or envelopes – contain all the allocations but are picked out by the researcher or subject in a random order.

Randomisation methods

Randomisation methods can be divided into:

- Fixed randomisation: The randomisation methods are defined and allocation sequences are set up before the start of the trial. Examples include simple randomisation, block randomisation and stratified randomisation.

- Adaptive randomisation: The randomised groups are adjusted as the study progresses to account for imbalances in the numbers in the groups or in response to the outcome data. An example is minimisation.

Fixed randomisation

Simple randomisation

Each subject's allocation is decided at random as each subject is recruited into the study, independently of any other factors (Figure 15). Methods include flipping a coin (for studies with two groups), rolling a die (for studies with two or more groups), random number tables and computer-generated random numbers.

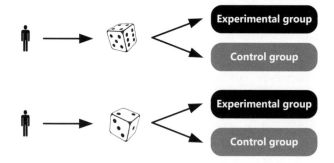

Figure 15 Simple randomisation – subjects are recruited and allocated individually to one of the groups by a random process

With simple randomisation, confounding factors, known and unknown, have an equal chance of entering either group, but at any one time the result can still be unequal group sizes and unequal distribution of confounding factors, particularly in small trials.

Block randomisation

Block randomisation is used to ensure that there are equal numbers of patients in each arm. When subjects are recruited into the sample population, they are not allocated immediately. Instead, subjects are placed into blocks (Figure 16). The block size varies between studies.

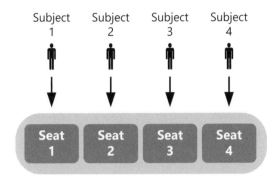

Figure 16 In block randomisation, subjects are first placed in a block

When the block is filled with subjects, the subjects are allocated in equal numbers into the different groups of the study (Figure 17). The process is repeated with as many blocks as required to reach the desired sample size.

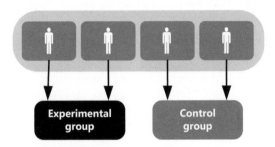

Figure 17 When a block is filled, the subjects are allocated in equal numbers into the groups

The order of the allocation when the block is filled can be randomly permuted to stop the researchers having an influence. For example, four allocations in a random order could be placed in the four seats in a block. Some clinical papers refer to this method as 'permuted block randomisation'.

SEE EXCERPT 11

Stratified randomisation

Block randomisation allocates subjects in equal numbers to the different groups. Sometimes researchers want to have factors equally distributed too. For example, the researchers may want equal numbers of patients with severe illness in each group, rather than risk getting an asymmetrical distribution of severity, which would make comparisons between the groups unfair. An extension of block randomisation, called stratified randomisation can help.

In stratified randomisation there are blocks for subgroups that need to be distributed equally. For example, let's suppose the researchers want equal numbers in two groups but also want to distribute severity of illness equally. They can use a block randomisation method that includes blocks for severity (Figure 18). When a subject is recruited, the severity of their illness is assessed and the subject is placed in the appropriate block. When blocks are filled, the subjects in the blocks are equally distributed into the groups. Not only will the groups have equal numbers but also equal numbers of patients with severe illness and mild illness.

SEE EXCERPT 12

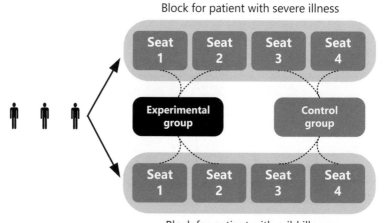

Block for patient with severe illness

Block for patient with mild illness

Figure 18 Stratified randomisation based on severity of illness

Stratified randomisation is often used to distribute known confounding factors equally into the groups. For example, if smoking cigarettes is a confounding factor and cannot be eliminated through exclusion criteria, the researchers could have a block for smokers to ensure they are equally distributed in the groups.

There can be different levels of stratification. For example, one could stratify on severity of illness and then on cigarette smoking status. In small studies it becomes impractical to stratify on more than one or two factors because some blocks will be at risk of not getting filled as there aren't enough subjects with the characteristics. Minimisation is an alternative method for achieving similarity between study arms.

Other forms of randomisation

Quasi-random allocation: A method of allocating subjects to different arms that is not truly random. For example, subjects could be allocated by date of birth, day of the week, medical record number, month of the year or the order in which they were included in the study (alternation). There is a greater risk of selection bias in quasi-randomised trials where allocation is not adequately concealed compared with randomised controlled trials with adequate allocation concealment. **SEE EXCERPT 13**

Cluster randomisation: Subjects are not randomised as individuals. Instead, a group of subjects, or a cluster, is randomised to the same arm together. In these studies the unit of analysis is the cluster, rather than the individual subjects in that arm. A summary statistic for the improvement in each cluster is often calculated and compared. Cluster randomisation is most commonly seen in public-health and primary-care research. For example, in a study on treatment options for back pain, all the patients in one primary care centre could be randomised to the physiotherapy intervention and all the patients at another centre could be randomised to the medication intervention. **SEE EXCERPT 14**

Cluster randomisation is not without problems. Firstly, clusters might be of different sizes yet be given equal weighting in the analysis. Secondly, as fewer data are generated by analysing clusters than would be generated by analysing individuals, the study loses power. Thirdly, individuals within a cluster tend to be more similar to each other than to members of other clusters, which can lead to an overestimation of the difference between the arms that has been caused by the intervention under investigation.

Factorial randomisation: Factorial randomised trials assess the impact of more than one intervention and can give researchers an insight into how different interventions interact with one another. **SEE EXCERPT 15**

Randomised consent method (Post-randomised consent design, Zelen's design): In this method subjects are consented *after* they have been randomised and allocated to a group[1]. This makes the consent process easier as subjects know which group there are in, improving recruitment, but there are new problems involving subjects and researchers knowing what the group allocations are in advance and high crossover rates.

---

1   Zelen's design. http://en.wikipedia.org/wiki/Zelen's_design. Accessed 10 October 2014.

Adaptive randomisation

In adaptive randomisation methods the probability of being allocated to a certain arm in the study is adjusted to maintain similarity between the arms. As an arm becomes imbalanced with subjects of a certain characteristic, the probability of future similar subjects also being allocated to the same arm reduces.

Minimisation is the most commonly used adaptive randomisation method. At the outset the researchers decide which factors they would like to be present in equal numbers in the different arms. The first subject recruited is allocated to an arm by a random method. Following subjects are allocated to the arm in such a way as to keep all the arms as similar as possible with regard to the predetermined factors. The allocation of each subject therefore depends on the characteristics of the subjects already enrolled. In small studies minimisation is more effective than randomisation in ensuring that the different arms are as similar as possible. Minimisation is also effective when multiple factors need to be distributed evenly. **SEE EXCERPT 16**

EXCERPT 11
Adapted from: Peters-Veluthamaningal C et al. Randomised controlled trial of local corticosteroid injections for carpal tunnel syndrome in general practice. *BMC Family Practice* 2010; 11: 54.
The study examined the effectiveness of carpal tunnel syndrome treatment by intracarpal corticosteroid injection.
For the randomisation procedure an electronic online randomization tool was used. Block randomisation was realised by creating 7 sets of blocks of 10 random numbers. Even numbers corresponded with active trial medication and uneven numbers with placebo to ensure equal numbers of allocation to active and placebo treatment.
Commentary: An example of block randomisation. The block size was 10 and 7 blocks were used, making a total sample size of 70 subjects. When each block was filled, 5 subjects went into the active group and 5 subjects went into the control group. The allocation was decided by a random number placed in each seat in the block; there were 5 even numbers and 5 odd numbers.

EXCERPT 12

Adapted from: Lin A T-L et al. Duloxetine versus placebo for the treatment of women with stress predominant urinary incontinence in Taiwan: a double-blind, randomized, placebo-controlled trial. *BMC Urology* 2008; 8: 2.

Researchers compared the efficacy of duloxetine with placebo in women with stress urinary incontinence. Success was defined as a 50% or greater reduction in incontinence episode frequency (IEF).

Randomisation was controlled by a computerised interactive voice response system at a central location for all study sites. Stratified randomisation using baseline IEF of < 14 or ≥14 episodes/week obtained from patient diaries was used to prevent potential imbalance in incontinence severity.

Commentary: An example of stratified randomisation. Block randomisation was used to ensure equal numbers of subjects in each arm. There were blocks for severe cases and blocks for mild cases, ensuring that severity was distributed equally in the two arms.

EXCERPT 13

Adapted from: Foo CL et al. Risk stratification and rapid geriatric screening in an emergency department – a quasi-randomised controlled trial. *BMC Geriatrics* 2014; 14: 98.

Researchers aimed to determine if triaging patients in the emergency department based on their risk improved outcomes.

Patients were randomised using the last digit of their national registration identity card number. Odd-numbered patients were allocated to the control group; even-numbered patients were allocated to the intervention group.

Commentary: The allocation procedure is an example of quasi-randomisation. In the discussion the researchers justified using this method because it minimised disruption in a busy emergency department. They acknowledge that their patient population was a convenience sample that matched the duty hours of the nurses. This may have led to selection bias.

EXCERPT 14

Adapted from: Bonnel C et al. Initiating change locally in bullying and aggression through the school environment (INCLUSIVE): study protocol for a cluster randomised controlled trial. *Trials* 2014; 15: 381.

In this study, the researchers measured the effectiveness of the INCLUSIVE intervention in reducing aggression and bullying in secondary schools. INCLUSIVE is a school-led intervention which combines changes to the school environment with the promotion of social and emotional skills and restorative practices.

Schools will be recruited from secondary schools in Greater London and the surrounding counties. Eligible schools will be allocated with a 1:1 ratio between intervention and control arms. The primary outcome will be an assessment of experience of violence and bullying measured using two scales at 36 months through student survey self-reports.

Commentary: Pupils were not randomised individually in this study. Instead, each school was randomised with all its pupils into either the intervention arm or the control arm. This is an example of cluster randomisation. One problem that might result is that pupils from a specific cluster have more features in common with each other than with pupils from other clusters.

EXCERPT 15

Adapted from: Parekh S et al. Improving diet, physical activity and other lifestyle behaviours using computer-tailored advice in general practice: a randomised controlled trial. *International Journal of Behavioral Nutrition and Physical Activity* 2012; 9: 108.

This study evaluated the effectiveness of an intervention on multiple lifestyle factors delivered through general practice.

Patients were randomised using a permuted block randomisation procedure. This 2 × 2 factorial design randomised participants into intervention or control group, and for early (3 month) or late (12 month) follow-up. For each GP the block length was varied between 4, 8 or 12 to accommodate four study groups. Thus they were randomised into four groups as follows: intervention with 3 + 12 months follow-up, intervention with 12 months follow-up only, control with 3 + 12 months follow-up or control with 12 months follow-up only.

Commentary: This is an example of factorial randomisation. Two different levels of intervention are being assessed. Firstly, patients are allocated to either the intervention or the control group. The patients in the intervention group received computer-tailored printed advice. Then the impact of two different follow-up strategies is also assessed in each group. To ensure equal numbers of patients in each combination, block randomisation is used with block sizes that are a multiple of four.

EXCERPT 16

Adapted from: Cuthbertson BH et al. A pragmatic multi-centre randomised controlled trial of fluid loading in high-risk surgical patients undergoing major elective surgery – the FOCCUS study. *Critical Care* 2011; 15: R296.

The aim of the study was to determine the effectiveness of pre-operative fluid loading in high-risk surgical patients undergoing major elective surgery.

Participants were randomised through an interactive voice response automated telephone randomisation service on the day before surgery. A minimisation algorithm was used, incorporating centre, age, sex and type of surgery.

Commentary: A minimisation procedure was used. Patients were allocated to groups depending on a number of defined characteristics that were to be kept as symmetrical as possible in the arms.

Scenario 8 revisited

A month later Dr Gilbert was busy working in his clinic when a receptionist asked him how his study was progressing. He thanked her for her interest and said it was going well. He explained how he divided the subjects into active and control groups. The receptionist looked bemused. Dr Gilbert asked her what the matter was. The receptionist answered, 'There's a television on the left side of the waiting room that is always showing the sports channel. The male patients tend to sit on the left side of the room and the women sit on the right! I was chuckling to myself when you described how you split people up! The left side group must have more men and more people interested in sport. I thought you said it was a randomised study?'

TO SUMMARISE, A GOOD STUDY WILL ....

Describe how random numbers were generated and by whom.

Describe the randomisation method that was employed.

Provide a table comparing the baseline demographic and prognostic characteristics of the different groups to show randomisation was effective.

Discuss how concealed allocation was achieved and monitored.

CONCEALED ALLOCATION

Scenario 9

Dr Robertson assessed an elderly woman with breathing difficulties and decided that she needed hospital treatment. He admitted the woman to a respiratory ward. The ward nurse asked if the patient was eligible for the study he was doing on the efficacy of a new nebuliser treatment. Dr Robertson replied that as the next subject to be recruited was to be allocated to the new treatment arm, he did not think he could risk it with this poorly patient, even though she met the inclusion criteria. He told the ward nurse that the patient would not be taking part in the trial.

Ideally when recruiting a subject, the researchers do not know which group the subject will be allocated to. The new subject will be placed randomly into one of the groups. Selection bias is avoided as all the groups will end up with the same variety of subjects.

However, it is worth remembering that researchers are under considerable pressure to get their research published. The ideal result in a treatment study is a significant difference in the outcomes of subjects in the treatment and placebo groups in favour of the new treatment. This difference can be exaggerated by unscrupulous researchers by recruiting the 'best' patients to the treatment group and the 'worst' patients to the placebo group.

This manipulation can arise even if randomisation is used to allocate patients to groups. This may appear implausible – how can researchers predict a random allocation sequence? The answer lies in the fact that the randomisation schedule is often published in advance and the researchers may have access to the schedule. If it is known that the next individual will be allocated to the new treatment group according to the randomisation schedule, an individual who is not expected to do well might be overlooked for recruitment into the study. Instead, the researcher might wait for someone who will do very well in the new treatment group. A selection bias will result as the subjects in each group are not representative of the target population.

Concealed allocation

Concealment means that the researchers cannot predict with any accuracy which group the next subject will be allocated to. Concealed allocation is a vital part of any randomisation strategy. Without a description of a concealment strategy, one must assume that randomisation has been compromised.

The worst-case scenario is a simple randomisation strategy in which the allocation sequence is available to the researchers and clearly and unambiguously lists the allocations.

There are a number of ways in which concealed allocation can be achieved. For example, with a centralised concealment scheme in a multicentre trial, the clinician checks for eligibility, gains consent, decides on whether to enrol patients and then contacts the randomisation service to obtain the treatment allocation. This contact can be made by telephone or electronically on the internet.

In situations in which remote randomisation might not be feasible, a set of tamper-evident envelopes that look identical may be provided to each site. The envelopes are opaque and sealed, and the sequence of opening the envelopes is monitored regularly. **SEE EXCERPT 17**

Another technique is to use coded containers in which treatments from numbered bottles that appear otherwise identical are administered sequentially. **SEE EXCERPT 18**

Within the envelopes and bottles is a random sequence of allocations.

As a result of concealed allocation, the researchers are unaware of the intervention in the group to which a subject will be allocated, should that individual agree to be in the study. This avoids both conscious and subconscious selection of patients into the study. Concealed allocation is a vital part of the randomisation process and protects against selection bias.

A good study will not have the same people recruiting and randomising subjects.

Concealed allocation and blinding

These two terms are often confused because they both involve keeping interventions secret. Concealed allocation is part of the randomisation and allocation procedures. It seeks to eliminate selection bias. Blinding happens after randomisation and aims to reduce observation bias (see page 100).

Importantly, concealed allocation can take place even in a study which is not blinded and vice-versa.

EXCERPT 17

Adapted from: Coleman S et al. A randomised controlled trial of a self-management education program for osteoarthritis of the knee delivered by health care professionals. *Arthritis Research & Therapy* 2012; 14: R21.

Researchers investigated whether a self-management programme for patients with osteoarthritis of the knee – the Osteoarthritis of the Knee Self-Management Programme (OAK) – implemented by healthcare professionals would lead to clinically meaningful improvements compared with a control group.

Participants were allocated to study groups using simple randomisation performed in batches of approximately 24 depending on recruitment success. Once a group of 24 volunteers were recruited, they were randomised to either the OAK or the control group. Twenty-four premade cards (12 interventions and 12 controls) in sealed opaque envelopes were placed in a box. An envelope was drawn from the box by an independent person to determine group allocation. Blinding of participants was not possible, owing to the nature of the intervention.

Commentary: The allocations were contained within the sealed opaque envelopes which were shuffled in a box. It was not possible for the researcher to predict what was in the envelope that the next recruited subject picked out of the box. Note that blinding was not possible in this study – blinding is different from concealed allocation.

EXCERPT 18

Adapted from: Kurt O et al. Treatment of head lice with dimeticone 4% lotion: comparison of two formulations in a randomised controlled trial in rural Turkey. *BMC Public Health* 2009; 9: 441.

This study on head lice compared the efficacy of dimeticone 4% lotion against lice and eggs with and without nerolidol 2% added.

Treatment allocation was in balanced blocks of 12 predetermined using a computer generated list. Allocation at the point of delivery was made from instruction sheets enclosed in opaque, sealed, sequentially numbered envelopes distributed to the investigators in batches of 12. As each participant was enrolled the investigator on site selected the next available numbered envelope from the allocation and the treatment was then applied from one of two series of numbered bottles.

Commentary: Randomisation was protected by a number of techniques. Subjects were placed in blocks of 12. Each subject in the block was given an opaque, sealed, sequentially numbered envelope leading them to a coded bottle. It was only on opening the bottle that the intervention would be revealed. It would not have been possible for the researchers to predict what intervention each subject would be receiving prior to recruiting them.

Scenario 9 revisited

Dr Robertson's study concluded that the new nebuliser treatment was of major benefit to patients with breathing difficulties and it would save lives if it was given as a first-line treatment. He presented his findings at the hospital's academic meeting and received a standing ovation. The ward nurse was in the audience. At the end of the presentation, when Dr Robertson invited questions and comments, she said, 'As you were aware of the treatments being given in each group and the allocation sequence, your selection of patients was biased and ended up widening the difference between the groups. Does selection bias not make your results invalid?'

TO SUMMARISE, A GOOD STUDY WILL ....

Include concealed allocation as part of the randomisation process.

Describe the people involved in recruiting and allocating subjects.

Discuss how concealed allocation was achieved and monitored.

PROPENSITY SCORING

Normally to study the effect of interventions, we use randomised controlled trials. In the experimental group, subjects get the new intervention. In the control group, subjects get the control treatment. Randomisation with concealed allocation ensures we get two groups which are broadly similar, so the comparison is fair.

However, in some situations it is not ethical to split people up into two groups. For example, we might want to compare how well smokers do with a certain intervention compared to non-smokers. It is not ethical to design groups in which one group of subjects will be made to smoke and the other group will not be smoking.

In these situations when a traditional randomised controlled trial is not possible, we turn to observational analytical studies. We get a group of people who are already smokers and compare them to a group of subjects who are not smokers.

In observational studies we normally use matching to try to get the two groups to be as similar as possible to make the comparison fair. With matching, we normally assume the two groups are broadly similar (they are usually sampled from the same target population) and we match on one or more variables.

In some situations the two groups may be very dissimilar, so that matching on a few variables is unsatisfactory. For example, there may be many factors which determine that a person smokes and these factors may not be present at all in non-smokers. In this situation propensity scoring can be used to try to make the comparison fair[1].

How does propensity scoring work? Propensity is a measure of how likely it is that a subject will be allocated to one group. In a randomised controlled trial using simple randomisation, for example, the propensity for each subject going into the experimental group is 0.5 (50%) and the propensity for each subject going into the control group is 0.5 (50%).

Let's go back to the example of smokers versus non-smokers. If there is a subject who drinks heavily, is hypertensive, lives in poverty and is unemployed, the

1   An Introduction to Propensity Score Methods for Reducing the Effects of Confounding in Observational Studies. *Multivariate Behav Res* May 2011; 46(3): 399–424. Available at http://www.ncbi.nlm.nih.gov/pmc/articles/PMC3144483/. Accessed 10 October 2014.

propensity for that subject to end up in the smoking group might be calculated as 0.75. We then look for someone who also has the same propensity score of 0.75 but is actually a non-smoker. We then have two subjects who can be compared fairly, as they have similar background variables. We repeat this over and over again with all the subjects, looking for propensity score matching in the two groups. Any subject who does not get a match is excluded from the trial.

The authors of a paper will normally explain what variables they used to calculate propensity scores and how they ensured they got matching propensity scores in the two groups.

SEE EXCERPT 19

EXCERPT 19

Adapted from: Yu P-J et al. Propensity-matched analysis of the effect of preoperative intraaortic balloon pump in coronary artery bypass grafting after recent acute myocardial infarction on postoperative outcomes. *Critical Care* 2014; 18: 531.

There is substantial variability in the preoperative use of intra-aortic balloon pumps (IABPs) in patients undergoing coronary artery bypass grafting post myocardial infarction. The objective of this study was to determine the effect of preoperative IABPs on postsurgical outcomes in this subset of patients.

Propensity score matching was used to match preoperative IABP patients to controls (non-preoperative IABP patients) on several potentially confounding variables. The probability of receiving a preoperative IABP (that is the propensity score) was calculated. Factors included in the model were: age, gender, body mass index, left ventricular ejection fraction (LVEF), preoperative creatinine, presence of comorbidities (cerebral vascular disease, diabetes mellitus, hypertension, smoking, hyperlipidemia, peripheral vascular disease, dialysis, congestive heart failure, chronic obstructive pulmonary disease), preoperative use of antiplatelet agents and/or anticoagulants including intravenous heparin, use of intravenous nitroglycerine, reoperation, time between myocardial infarction and CABG, coronary artery disease burden (number of vessels with > 70% stenosis, left main coronary artery disease > 50%), concurrent valvular disease, and preoperative hemodynamic instability. Each patient was matched to a single control, based on the propensity score.

Commentary: The researchers used propensity scoring to get matching subjects in the experimental and control arms. They have listed the factors that are used to calculate a propensity score for each subject that is in the experimental group.

TO SUMMARISE, A GOOD STUDY WILL ....

Explain the reasons why a randomised controlled trial design could not be used.

Describe the aims and objectives of the observational analytical study.

List the factors that are used to determine propensity scores.

Describe the statistical methods used to generate propensity scores.

Provide a table comparing the baseline demographic and prognostic characteristics of the different groups to show propensity scoring was effective.

Scenario 10

Dr Green smiled as the postman delivered the letter to her. The journal logo on the envelope told her she was about to read that her research had been accepted for publication. Her randomised controlled trial had shown a new angina treatment worked much better than the standard treatment. Her head-to-head trial was going to change medical practice worldwide. As she nervously opened the envelope, she wondered if in a year's time letters to her would be addressed to Professor Green. Her life would never be the same.

After recruitment and allocation into groups, the researchers may give information about the subjects. Details can include demographic characteristics, such as age and gender, as well as more fluid variables, such as smoking status. The baseline characteristics are usually given in the form of a table comparing the composition of the groups. **SEE EXCERPT 20**

The baseline characteristics give valuable information about the internal and external validity of the research.

- The sample population should be representative of the target population. Discrepancies may indicate a flawed recruitment campaign leading to selection bias.

- There should be broad symmetry across the groups. Any significant differences may point to a failure of matching or randomisation leading to selection bias.

- In some cases differences across the groups may reflect manipulation of allocation by researchers in order to get significant results.

- The closer the sample resembles your own clinical population, the more applicable the results will be to your patients.

EXCERPT 20

Adapted from: Yacoub R et al. Association between smoking and chronic kidney disease: a case control study. *BMC Public Health* 2010; 10: 731.

This study investigated the relationship between cigarette smoking and chronic kidney disease using a case–control design. Cases were patients who had chronic kidney disease. They were compared to controls who were normal people.

	Cases (n = 198)		Control (n = 371)		P value
	n	%*	n	%**	
Gender					0.57
Male	102	51.5	182	49	
Female	96	48.5	189	51	
Age (yr)					0.96
18–24	30	15.2	59	15.9	
25–34	28	14.1	48	12.9	
35–44	34	17.2	55	14.8	
45–54	44	22.2	92	24.7	
55–64	40	20.2	74	19.9	
≥65	22	11.1	43	11.5	
Medications					
Any HTN medication	91	45.9	149	40.1	0.18
ACEi	83	41.9	127	34.2	0.07
ARBs	15	7.6	26	7	0.81
Beta blockers	72	36.4	105	28.3	0.04
Analgesic	40	20.2	70	18.9	0.70
BMI					0.14
Underweight	7	3.5	26	7	
Normal weight	104	52.5	163	43.9	
Overweight	56	28.3	115	30.9	
Obesity	31	15.6	67	18	
HTN	58	29.3	92	24.8	0.25
Diabetes Mellitus	56	28.3	99	26.7	0.68

*Of cases (n = 198). **Of control (n = 371).

Commentary: The table shows the baseline characteristics of the two groups. Broad symmetry is expected if matching has been successful. A third column shows P values. The only statistically significant difference between the cases and controls is in the use of beta-blocker medication.

Scenario 10 revisited

Dr Green was flabbergasted. The journal had rejected her research! She scanned the letter but she wasn't really reading. She could not concentrate. All her hopes had been shattered. She would never live this humiliation down. She picked up the phone and called the editor. She angrily demanded an explanation; the research had demonstrated statistical significance. The editor was calm in his response. 'It's the baseline characteristics in table 1,' said the editor. 'There is a major difference in severity of illness across the two groups, isn't there? Patients in the experimental arm were much less ill than patients in the control arm – an obvious sign that randomisation was manipulated. I'm afraid we can't publish what is an unfair comparison between two drugs. Thanks for calling, doctor.'

TO SUMMARISE, A GOOD STUDY WILL ....

Give the baseline characteristics of the sample groups.

Highlight statistically significant differences between the groups at baseline.

Explain whether any differences between the groups are important.

OBSERVING SUBJECTS

After the allocation of subjects into groups, the researchers start their experiment. They expose subjects to different risk factors or interventions in each group. To assess the impact of the exposure, the researchers measure variables as the trial progresses and count how many subjects in each group achieve one or more outcomes at the end of the trial.

The effects of expectation may wreak havoc on the results. Researchers take a number of steps to protect their results from the influence of expectation, such as the use of blinding techniques and reliable measuring methods. If they succeed, the results will reflect the truth. If they fail, observation bias may rear its ugly head.

THE EFFECTS OF EXPECTATION

Scenario 11

Dr Singh, a rheumatologist, finished writing his first case report. He had seen a patient with arthritis. The patient had visited his GP and had, by the press of a wrong key on the computer, been mistakenly dispensed co-careldopa, a treatment for Parkinson's disease, instead of co-codamol, a painkiller. The patient had unwittingly taken the wrong treatment for a month and, far from experiencing no effect, his pain symptoms had dramatically improved. Dr Singh submitted his report to the Lancet, stating that this case had demonstrated for the first time the painkilling properties of anti-parkinsonism treatment and could lead to a new treatment approach.

Expectation can have a powerful effect on researchers and subjects. If a person expects a certain experience, there may be a conscious, subconscious or unconscious change in attitudes and behaviour to fulfil that expectation.

Researchers will be aware that a study that does find a difference between two groups is more likely to get published than a negative trial (publication bias). Although a clinical question should be approached with an open mind, researchers may expect subjects in the active group to do better than subjects in the control group. Motivations and expectations can be so powerful that they can alter the way the research is performed and the way the researchers collect data.

Subjects also may have expectations. They may, for example expect to get better faster if they are given a new drug. Conversely, if they are given an older treatment, they may expect to do less well. Subjects are human, and humans like to please. The subjects may want to please the researchers and this might lead them to give researchers the answers they think the researchers are hoping for rather than the true answer, which may disappoint the researchers.

So subjects can improve simply if they expect to get better with treatment. This effect is so powerful that subjects can improve even if they are unaware that they have been given a placebo or dummy treatment. A placebo does not have any therapeutic activity for the condition being treated.

Placebo effect

The placebo effect is the name given to the improvement seen in subjects when they are in receipt of a placebo treatment. The placebo effect is greater when a subject is given several pills instead of one pill, larger pills instead of smaller pills, and capsules instead of tablets.

One arm in an intervention trial is usually given the active treatment and the other arm is given a placebo treatment. The placebo is used to determine whether any difference in outcome is attributable to the active treatment or to the effect of expectation.

- If the improvement in the active arm is the same as that in the placebo arm, the improvement can be attributed to the placebo effect.
- If the improvement is greater in the active arm, the active treatment is having a beneficial effect over and above that due to the placebo effect.

Placebos

People do not volunteer for clinical trials hoping to be allocated to the placebo arm. However, trials need subjects in the placebo arm in order to measure the placebo effect.

Placebo treatments should be as similar as possible to the active treatment. They should look the same, feel the same, smell the same, taste the same and have the same mode of delivery. A placebo treatment should be sourced from the manufacturer of the active treatment in order to look as similar as possible and only differ in that it has no therapeutic activity. Subjects will then be less able to determine whether they are in the placebo arm and are more likely to continue in the trial. **SEE EXCERPT 21**

Some organisations argue that all new treatments should be compared in head-to-head trials with the current standard or best treatment, to see if the new treatment is significantly better. However, trials in which an active treatment is not compared with a placebo treatment cannot determine how much of any improvement is due to the placebo effect.

Sham treatment is a term used in non-pharmacological studies, where the intervention might be a device, a psychological treatment or a physical intervention.

Placebo effect by proxy

It is not just the subject who is taking the placebo who might benefit from the placebo effect. The people around the subject, including relatives, friends and healthcare professionals, also have a strong expectation of improvement, making themselves feel better that the subject is being treated and enhancing third-party reports of clinical outcomes, even if the subject does not actually improve[1].

Ethical considerations

It is not always ethical to use a placebo treatment. For example, in some conditions the patient's condition can deteriorate if given a placebo.

The World Medical Association's Declaration of Helsinki[2] states that the benefits, risks, burdens and effectiveness of a new intervention must be tested against those of the best current proven intervention, except in the following circumstances:

- where no current proven intervention exists – in this case the use of a placebo (or no treatment) is acceptable
- where for compelling and scientifically sound methodological reasons the use of placebo is necessary to determine the efficacy or safety of an intervention and the patients who receive placebo or no treatment will not be subject to any risk of serious or irreversible harm.

Nocebo response

Whereas the placebo effect refers to the improvement experienced by a subject taking a dummy treatment, the nocebo response refers to the opposite experience, where a negative effect of an intervention is experienced because of the subject's negative beliefs and expectations about the dummy treatment. It is not due to any biochemical effect. This explains why dummy treatments, including homeopathic remedies, can have side-effects.

The side-effect profile of a real treatment in a subject can be considered to be a combination of side-effects caused by the pharmacological action of the drug and side-effects due to the nocebo response.

1   Grelotti DJ et al. Placebo by proxy. BMJ 2011; 343: d4345.
2   World Medical Association. WMA Declaration of Helsinki – Ethical Principles for Medical Research Involving Human Subjects. 2013. Available: http://www.wma.net/en/30publications/10policies/b3/. Accessed 1 September 2014.

EXCERPT 21

Adapted from: Chan RYP et al. The effects of two Chinese herbal medicinal formulae vs. placebo controls for treatment of allergic rhinitis: a randomised controlled trial. *Trials* 2014; 15: 261.

This study evaluated the effects of two Chinese herbal formulae in treating allergic rhinitis over a 3-month follow-up, when compared to a placebo control group.

Two types of herbal medicine were prepared and bottled by the researcher and kept in the refrigerator of the clinic one day before use. The herbal and placebo medicines were in syrup form due to better taste and absorption and user-friendliness. A very small amount of fresh ginger was added to the placebo medication to establish a spicy taste and smell and be able to exert seasoning but no treatment effect in allergic rhinitis. With sugar and wheat powder added to the herbal medicines, the spicy taste and texture of the three kinds of syrups used for all of the three study groups were very similar. This similar form, colour and route of administration of the medication used among the three study groups was beneficial to provide a consistent and standardised format of medicinal treatment in this trial, as well as high levels of convenience and preference for people with chronic allergic rhinitis disease.

Commentary: The researchers prepared a placebo preparation that was of similar form, taste, texture and appearance to the herbal preparations.

Scenario 11 revisited

The editor of the Lancet wrote back to Dr Singh. He thanked Dr Singh for submitting his case report but noted that, 'The placebo effect of co-careldopa needs to be explored and will probably explain the beneficial effects seen. To really demonstrate the efficacy of co-careldopa for pain symptoms, I would suggest a placebo-controlled double-blind strategy is more appropriate. I'll be happy to publish these results if they can be replicated in a better study.'

TO SUMMARISE, A GOOD STUDY WILL ....

Explain the role of the placebo effect and nocebo response in any relationship under investigation.

Describe any placebo treatment used.

Describe how blinding was maintained when a placebo was used by describing its similarity to the active treatment.

Confirm that the study received ethical approval for using a placebo treatment.

OBSERVATION BIAS

Scenario 12

Consultant psychiatrist, Dr Thomas had a long-standing interest in the treatment of anxiety disorders. Her Clinical Director wanted her to set up a specialist clinic for patients with anxiety disorders, but needed to justify the expense to the Hospital Board. Dr Thomas sent a postal questionnaire to 500 patients of the Psychiatry Unit, asking them if they had ever been told they had a neurotic disorder. If the answer was 'yes', she asked them to describe the treatments offered and whether they would support the development of a specialist clinic.

Scenario 13

Nurse Smith wanted to illustrate the quality of care provided by her team to patients on a gastroenterology ward. She visited every patient on the day of their discharge home and took them through a questionnaire to rate the quality of the care they received during their hospital stay. She presented the near-perfect results to the matron and asked for a salary increase.

Observation bias, also known as 'information bias', occurs as a result of failure to measure or classify the exposure or outcomes correctly. The data collected are wrong in some way. The inaccuracy is usually caused by researchers and/ or subjects having knowledge of which group is which and having expectations about how each group should perform.

Observation bias can be due to the researchers or the subjects.

Examples of observation bias include:

- **Interviewer (ascertainment) bias:** This arises when the researcher is not blinded to the subject's group allocation in the study and this alters the researcher's approach to the subject and the recording of results. For example, if a researcher knows which group is which in a study, they may alter the way they question subjects in order to collect more favourable results from the experimental arm.

- **Response bias:** This arises in any study in which the subjects answer questions in the way they believe the researcher wants them to answer, rather than according to their true beliefs. Subjects who know they are in the experimental arm are more likely to give favourable responses than subjects in the control arm.

- **Hawthorne effect:** This arises when subjects alter their behaviour, usually positively, because they are aware they are being observed in a study.
- **Recall bias:** This arises when subjects selectively remember details from the past. This can be particularly problematic in case–control studies and in cross-sectional surveys.

Researchers need to take steps to reduce the risk of observation bias. Approaches include the use of blinding, reliable and valid measuring, and objective outcome measures.

Scenario 12 revisited

Dr Thomas's survey generated a surprising result, with only 1% of the sample having been diagnosed with a neurotic disorder. Her Clinical Director wrote to her, stating, 'Perhaps nowadays not many people are familiar with the term "neurotic". The use of the word "anxiety" might produce different results as it will eliminate observation bias. Please repeat the survey.'

Scenario 13 revisited

The matron was less than impressed. She commented, 'The results are good but what else did you expect if you asked patients about their views? They're hardly likely to give you negative comments. Perhaps I should ask an independent organisation to survey the patients at home? That will eliminate a response bias. I'm afraid a salary rise cannot be justified at this time. Now, back to work!'

BLINDING

Scenario 14

Dr Joseph analysed the results of a trial on the usefulness of psychological interventions in patients suffering chronic pain. In one arm of the study, the patients received 20 weekly sessions with a psychologist, exploring their perceptions of pain. In the control arm, the patients were invited to chat to a nurse about their daily routine. The psychologists dramatically reduced pain scores compared with the 'placebo' intervention. Dr Joseph wrote to his Hospital Board, suggesting that sessions with psychologists were a cost-effective intervention for his patients and could reduce the need for Pain Clinic appointments.

Scenario 15

Dr Webb was amazed by the results of her trial investigating a new mood-stabilising medication for patients with bipolar disorder. Compared with patients taking lithium, the patients taking the new treatment reported fewer symptoms and they were also pleased that they did not need regular blood tests to monitor drug levels. She submitted her results to the British Journal of Psychiatry and recommended that lithium should no longer be the gold-standard treatment for patients with bipolar disorder. She hoped that her results would be the topic of the journal's editorial.

The behaviour of researchers and subjects can be influenced by what they know or believe, resulting in an observation bias. If subjects in a trial are aware of whether they are receiving a placebo or an active intervention, the answers they give can be influenced by this knowledge. Similarly, the researchers might also be influenced by any awareness of which subjects are receiving the different interventions. The behaviour of study participants and researchers can lead to bias because the subjective answers and assessments might not actually mirror the truth. This bias often occurs at a subconscious level.

Blinding, sometimes called **masking**, overcomes this problem. A study is regarded as 'blind' when the subject and/or the researcher do not know what treatments are being administered. Blinding aims to eliminate observation bias.

Trial designs might involve:

- No blinding: This occurs in an **open-label trial**. Observation bias is problematic in such a trial design. **SEE EXCERPT 22**

- **Single blinding:** Either the researcher or the subject is blind to the allocation. **SEE EXCERPT 23**

- **Double blinding:** The researcher and the subject are not aware of the treatment being administered. The interventions should appear identical for each treatment group.

- **Triple blinding (blind assessment):** Knowledge of the treatment is concealed from the researcher, subject and the analyst processing the results (analysing data, examining a biopsy, using a rating scale, etc).

The blinding procedure should be clearly stated in the method section of the study.

Comparing dissimilar interventions

If the interventions are very different, it is obvious which group a patient is in. To blind the study, a **double-dummy technique** can be used, in which all the subjects appear to receive both interventions. However, in each arm one of two interventions is a placebo. **SEE EXCERPT 24**

Although desirable, blinding is not always possible. Open trials or single blind studies are often employed when investigating invasive or psychological interventions, for example.

Blinding can be compromised

A study might have used blinding but that does not mean that blinding cannot be compromised.

The groups in the trial should be treated equally as a result of blinding. Everything done to one group should be done to every group, including any monitoring requirements such as blood tests. If one group is treated differently, the blinding will be unravelled.

With natural curiosity, researchers and subjects will try to guess which arm is which. Different rates of side-effects, for example, can give the researchers and subjects clues that enable them to guess correctly which treatment a subject is receiving, which can lead to an observation bias and to subjects dropping out of the placebo arm.

Placebos may also be uncovered if they are without side-effects. This risk can be minimised by using a placebo that has been specially manufactured to cause temporary side-effects, in order to prevent the subject guessing that he or she is in the placebo arm.

EXCERPT 22

Adapted from: Chew KS et al. A randomized open-label trial on the use of budesonide/formoterol (Symbicort®) as an alternative reliever medication for mild to moderate asthmatic attacks. *International Journal of Emergency Medicine* April 2012; 5: 16.

Researchers compared Symbicort inhaler versus nebulised salbutamol in acute asthma.

In this study conducted from March until August 2011, we compared the effects of Symbicort® (at the strength of 160/4.5 mcg per inhalation) and nebulised salbutamol. Patients who consented to participate in this study were randomised to receive either two puffs of Symbicort® or nebulised salbutamol. Patients randomised to receive Symbicort® were given proper instruction on the inhalational technique using dummy turbuhaler devices.

Commentary: An example of an open-label study. An inhaler was compared to a nebuliser. Researchers and subjects were all aware of the interventions being administered. The nebuliser will be seen as the stronger treatment. This may affect the reporting of results.

EXCERPT 23

Adapted from: Shantz JAS et al. Sutures versus staples for wound closure in orthopaedic surgery: a pilot randomized controlled trial. *Patient Safety in Surgery* 2013; 7: 6.

Researchers compared sutures and staples in wound closure in terms of incidence of wound complications.

Patients allocated to the sutures intervention had their wounds closed using the suture material chosen by the primary surgeon. The primary surgeon also decided on the most appropriate technique of closure. Those allocated to the staples group were closed using a commercially-available stapler. Patients were blinded to treatment allocation by use of an adhesive bandage or plaster which remained in place until the first planned post-operative visit when the closure material was removed or the wound was checked, including the removal of steristrips in the case of absorbable subcuticular closure. Immediately prior to unblinding patients completed an outcome assessment survey including a questionnaire determining complication occurrence and a 100 mm VAS pain scale.

Commentary: An example of single blinding. The patients were unaware of whether they received sutures or staples. The surgeons were aware of the intervention given to each patient.

EXCERPT 24

Adapted from: Stricker K et al. A 6-week, multicentre, randomised, double-blind, double-dummy, active-controlled, clinical safety study of lumiracoxib and rofecoxib in osteoarthritis patients. *BMC Musculoskeletal Disorders* 2008; 9: 118.

Researchers compared lumiracoxib and rofecoxib in the treatment of osteoarthritis.

Patients were randomly allocated in the ratio of 1:1 to receive either lumiracoxib 400 mg od or rofecoxib 25 mg od. Lumiracoxib was provided as 2 × 200 mg tablets with matching placebos and rofecoxib as 25 mg capsules with matching placebos.

Commentary: The two interventions were different – one was 2 tablets and the other was a capsule. A double dummy technique was used to maintain the blind. Patients in both arms were given both treatments to take. In each arm, one of the interventions was a placebo.

Scenario 14 revisited
The Medical Director of the hospital wrote back to Dr Joseph, stating, 'It is hardly surprising that the psychotherapy patients got better. They were aware that they were getting the new intervention. While I accept that talking therapies are hard to blind, we must not rush into making costly decisions based on such trials.'

Scenario 15 revisited
Unfortunately the research article was rejected by the peer review process. The editor of the British Journal of Psychiatry wrote to Dr Webb, 'Unfortunately, blinding in your study was compromised because the patients taking lithium had regular blood tests. It was surely obvious who was taking lithium and who was taking the new mood-stabiliser drug. To maintain blinding and eliminate observation bias, everyone should have had the same blood tests. Sham results should have been reported for patients not taking lithium. I'm afraid that this major oversight means that I cannot publish your article.'

TO SUMMARISE, A GOOD STUDY WILL ....

Describe how blinding was implemented.

Discuss the use of placebos and sham interventions in helping to maintain blinding.

Discuss whether blinding could have been compromised.

ENDPOINTS

Scenario 16

There was an air of excitement in the regional audit meeting. The survival rates of patients discharged from coronary care units were about to be released. In the audience, Dr Taylor was looking forward to the report. Her switch to a new medication guaranteed her hospital would come top of the rankings for the first time. Before the switch she had read research which showed outcomes were better with the new treatment. As far as she knew, her hospital was the only one that had funded the new treatment and that was because of her recommendation! She allowed herself a gentle smile as she thought about spending her anticipated clinical excellence bonus payment on a holiday to the Caribbean.

Studies report results in terms of the endpoints that were measured. There are numerous endpoints that can be used in studies, eg mortality, disease progression, disability, improvement of symptoms and quality-of-life measures.

Ideally, changes in endpoints should help doctors to make better decisions for their patients and have some clinical significance.

There are three main types of outcome used in studies – clinical, surrogate and composite.

Clinical endpoint: A measurement of a direct clinical outcome, such as mortality, morbidity or survival. Clinical endpoints tend to be objective and easy to interpret.

Surrogate endpoint: A biomarker used as a substitute for a clinical endpoint. A surrogate endpoint is expected to predict clinical benefit (or harm or lack of benefit or harm) based on epidemiologic, therapeutic, pathophysiologic, or other scientific evidence[1]. The surrogate endpoint must fully capture the net effect of the intervention on the clinical endpoint. Although surrogate endpoints are believed to be predictive of important clinical outcomes, the relationship is not guaranteed. They are used because they allow effects to be measured sooner. **SEE EXCERPT 25**

---

1   Biomarkers and surrogate endpoints: preferred definitions and conceptual framework. *Clinical Pharmacology and Therapeutics* 2001; 69: 89–95.

For example, low-density lipoprotein (LDL) cholesterol level may be used as a surrogate marker for cardiovascular disease. Elevated LDL increases the risk of cardiovascular disease and reduced LDL decreases the risk. LDL is a useful surrogate despite the fact that beneficial changes may occur for the surrogate in most patients, but benefits in terms of clinical events occur only for a few[1].

Surrogate markers are also used in phase 1 and phase 2 clinical trials, ie during the early stages of drug development. They can also be used in phase 3 trials, but at this stage there needs to be careful consideration of how accurately the surrogate marker reflects the clinical outcome in question and whether it will be accurate and reliable. Sample sizes for studies using surrogate markers can be smaller and the trial does not have to be as long-lasting, because changes in the surrogate endpoints usually occur before the clinical event happens.

Composite endpoint: A combination of clinical events collectively make up the composite endpoint. If any one of these events occurs, the endpoint is reached[2]. Ideally, all events that make up the composite endpoint should be of similar importance to the patient and occur with similar frequency. **SEE EXCERPT 26**

Composite endpoints are useful to employ when individual clinical events occur infrequently. The problem of insufficient power in such a study is overcome by using a composite endpoint.

However, the danger with reading studies using composite endpoints is that the study may conclude that a beneficial effect was seen against all the clinical events when in fact one clinical event was responsible for achieving most of the composite endpoints[2].

Secondary endpoints are other characteristics that are measured in all study participants to help describe the effects of treatment.

Measuring endpoints – validity and reliability

As well as specifying which endpoints were used, a study should describe how these endpoints were measured or detected. Clinical endpoints tend to be objective and easily measured, eg whether the patient died, survived or was cured. Surrogate endpoints are more widely used but are more prone to subjective assessment and differences of opinion. Problems can arise if the measurements are not made consistently.

1   Moore RA. Endoscopic ulcers as a surrogate marker of NSAID-induced mucosal damage. *Arthritis Research & Therapy* 2013; 15(Suppl 3): S4.

2   Composite Endpoints and the CREST Trial. Available at http://www.evidenceinmedicine. org/2010/05/composite-endpoints-and-the-crest-trial.html. Accessed 10 October 2014.

Researchers use measuring techniques and instruments that have been shown to be valid and reliable. Validity refers to the extent to which a test measures what it is supposed to measure. Reliability refers to how consistent a test is on repeated measurements. Importantly, reliability does not imply validity.

The meaning of these two terms can be clarified by making an analogy with target practice (Figure 19): hitting the bull's-eye on the target is 'validity' or correctness; repeatedly hitting the same point is 'reliability' or consistency.

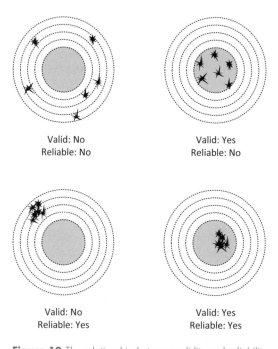

Valid: No
Reliable: No

Valid: Yes
Reliable: No

Valid: No
Reliable: Yes

Valid: Yes
Reliable: Yes

Figure 19 The relationship between validity and reliability

EXCERPT 25

Adapted from: Gardener H et al. Lipids and carotid plaque in the Northern Manhattan Study (NOMAS). *BMC Cardiovascular Disorders* 2009; 9: 55.

Lipids are associated with increased risk of stroke and cardiovascular disease, probably due to atherosclerosis. As part of a study to determine the incidence and risk factors of stroke, this cross-sectional analysis investigated the relationship between blood lipids and carotid plaque.

Low density lipoprotein has the strongest relation with carotid plaque ... Carotid plaque, particularly thick plaque and irregular plaque, has been shown to be a risk factor for vascular events, including stroke. Because lipids likely influence the risk of cardiovascular disease and stroke due to their effects on atherosclerotic plaque formation, carotid plaque may be used as a surrogate endpoint in epidemiologic and pharmacologic studies of lipid treatment.

Commentary: The authors discuss using carotid plaque as a surrogate endpoint in the study. Instead of waiting for cardiovascular disease and stroke, the use of the surrogate endpoint allows the trial to be shorter.

EXCERPT 26

Adapted from: MacHaalany J et al. Predictors and prognosis of early ischaemic mitral regurgitation in the era of primary percutaneous coronary revascularisation. *Cardiovascular Ultrasound* 2014; 12: 14.

In this study researchers sought to determine the predictors and prognosis of early ischemic mitral regurgitation after primary percutaneous coronary intervention (PCI) for ST-elevation myocardial infarction.

The rate of major adverse cardiac events was the composite of death, MI, stroke, re-hospitalisation for congestive heart failure, PCI or CABG and mitral repair or replacement.

Commentary: The outcome labelled as a major adverse cardiac event was a composite endpoint, comprising six different events.

Scenario 16 revisited

Dr Taylor was puzzled by the report. The mortality results for her hospital were no better than those of neighbouring hospitals. She scrutinised the data tables but could find no mistakes. The expensive new treatment had not improved her hospital's performance. Later that week she emailed the report's authors for their explanation. The reply was blunt and to the point: 'The research you refer to used surrogate outcomes. Instead of counting how many patients died following the new treatment, the researchers simply measured how many patients had more coronary artery occlusion. Although fewer patients had progressive disease with the new treatment, the relationship between coronary artery occlusion (a surrogate outcome) and death from myocardial infarction (a clinical outcome) is far from straightforward.'

TO SUMMARISE, A GOOD STUDY WILL ....

Clearly state the endpoint of interest.

Relate the endpoint to the clinical question.

Describe how the endpoint was detected and measured.

Acknowledge the shortcomings of using surrogate and composite endpoints.

Scenario 17

Dr Harrison looked at the next research proposal submitted for ethics approval. A junior doctor wished to compare the efficacy of a new thyroxine depot injection against that of thyroxine tablets in young men with hypothyroidism. She proposed a cohort study assessing the severity of symptoms by the television viewing time of each subject at home, as hypothyroid patients tended to be tired all the time. She hypothesised that thyroxine treatment would improve hypothyroid symptoms, marked by a reduction in the amount of television viewed.

Validity refers to the extent to which a test measures what it is supposed to measure. There are many subtypes of validity. The meaning of validity in this context is not to be confused with internal and external validity (see page 5).

Types of validity

Face validity

The extent to which the test, on superficial consideration, measures what it is supposed to measure. For example, a test measuring the exercise tolerance of patients and relating it to respiratory disease severity would have face validity. **SEE EXCERPT 28**

Content validity

The extent to which the test measures variables that are related to the parameter which should be measured by the test. For example, a questionnaire assessing angina severity would have content validity if the questions centred on the ability to do everyday tasks that made the heart work harder.

Criterion validity

This is used to demonstrate the accuracy of a measure or procedure by comparing it with another measure or procedure that has been demonstrated to be valid. Criterion validity can be concurrent or predictive.

- Concurrent validity: The extent to which the test correlates with a measure that has been previously validated. For example, a score on a rating scale for pain would have concurrent validity if it agreed with a previously validated rating scale.

- Predictive validity: The extent to which the test is able to predict something it should theoretically be able to predict. For example, a written examination would have predictive validity if it measured performance in secondary school and successfully predicted employment status in adulthood.

Construct validity

The extent to which the test measures a theoretical construct by a specific measuring device or procedure. For example, an IQ test would have construct validity if its results reflected the theoretical concept of intelligence. Constructive validity can be convergent or divergent.

- Convergent validity: The extent to which the test is similar to other tests that are measuring the same construct. For example, a digital thermometer would have convergent validity with a mercury-based thermometer if it returned similar results. **SEE EXCERPT 28**

- Divergent (discriminant) validity: The extent to which the test is not similar to other tests that are measuring different constructs. For example, a postgraduate assessment of critical appraisal skills of doctors would have discriminant validity if it returned results dissimilar to a multiple-choice question paper testing knowledge of diseases.

Incremental validity

The extent to which the test provides a significant improvement in addition to the use of another approach. A test has incremental validity if it helps more than if it were not used. For example, ultrasound scanning gives better estimates of fetal gestation age than clinical examination alone.

Scenario 17 revisited

Dr Harrison wrote back to the young researcher, stating that, 'Selecting patients and assessing them on the basis of their viewing habits seems inappropriate to me. Hypothyroid patients might do many things apart from increase their television viewing time (and I'm not even sure about that!), so it appears to me that a more valid assessment method is required.'

TO SUMMARISE, A GOOD STUDY WILL ....
Describe what was measured and how this related to the endpoints.

Scenario 18

Dr Nolan was supervising a class of first-year medical students. All the students were asked to take each other's blood pressure until they were comfortable using a sphygmomanometer. Dr Nolan noticed that, halfway through the session, some of the students looked bemused. He asked one student what the matter was. 'It's these sphygmomanometers,' said the student, 'They never give the same result twice!' After the session, Dr Nolan wrote to the Clinical Tutor, suggesting that an investment be made in better equipment.

Nearly all studies involve the measurement of one or more variables. Good research technique involves commenting on how good was the measuring in the study. Researchers may discuss measurement error and reliability.

Why is this important? In studies we want to know if subjects improve or deteriorate if they are exposed to a treatment or a risk factor. If the measuring in a study was in some way wrong, it may appear that subjects are improving or deteriorating when they are not. The wrong conclusion may be drawn and we may erroneously change our clinical practice.

Measurement error

Measurement error is the difference between the true value and the measured value, and refers to all sources of variability that cannot be explained by the independent variable[1]. It can be separated into systematic error and random error.

Systematic error

A systematic error is a consistent error made in a series of repetitive tests. For example, if an electronic weighing scale is poorly calibrated, it may give weight readings which are consistently lower than the true weights. No matter how many times the weight readings are repeated, the systematic error is the same. Systematic errors can be reduced by calibrating instruments, training researchers how to use the instruments and standardising procedures.

---

1   Bruton A, Conway JH, Holgate ST. Reliability: What is it, and how is it measured? *Physiotherapy* 2000; 86(2): 94–99.

A systematic error reduces **accuracy**, which is how close measurements are to the true values. Quantitatively, the systematic error is equal to the average value of the errors[1].

Random error

A random error is a variable error that occurs in a series of repetitive tests. For example, if an electronic scale is used to weigh an object repeatedly, a difference in weight readings points to a random error. If we average the weight readings over a series of tests, we can reduce the effect of the random errors.

A random error reduces **precision**, which is how much agreement there is between repeat measurements of the same quantity. Quantitatively, the random error is the deviation of the total error from its mean value[2].

Reliability

Reliability is the consistency of measurements. The measurements can be made by one rater at different times, or by more than one rater at one time or different times. Reliability is a measure of accuracy and precision, and therefore systematic error and random error. Reliability indicates how much variability in measurements is due to measurement error and how much is due to a true change.

Reliability can be quantified by a number of methods.

Test–retest reliability (intra-rater reliability)

Test–retest reliability assesses the level of agreement between assessments by one rater of the same sample at different times. The closer the agreement, the greater is the test–retest reliability of the instrument. **SEE EXCERPT 27 AND EXCERPT 28**

Quantitatively, the test–retest reliability is given by the correlation coefficient. The perfect value is 1.0 but correlation coefficient values above 0.7–0.8 are considered good[3]. In surveys, the test–retest reliability may be affected by a 'practice effect' – repeat testing may lead to higher scores if subjects in the sample 'learn' to answer the same questions[3].

1   Statistics.com. Systematic Error. 2014. Available: http://www.statistics.com/index.php?page=glossary&term_id=861. Accessed 1 September 2014.
2   Statistics.com. Random Error. 2014. Available: http://www.statistics.com/index.php?page=glossary&term_id=824. Accessed 1 September 2014.
3   Statistics.com. Test Retest Reliability. 2014. Available: http://www.statistics.com/index.php?page=glossary&term_id=867. Accessed 1 September 2014.

Parallel-forms reliability (alternate forms reliability)

Parallel-forms reliability assesses the level of agreement between assessments on the same sample using the test and, at a later time, an equivalent alternative form of the test. The closer the agreement, the greater is the parallel-forms reliability of the instrument.

The parallel-forms reliability can be quantified using a correlation coefficient.

The parallel-forms reliability tackles the problem inherent in test–retest reliability – that of the 'practice effect', although there may still be some change in responses between the tests. The main barrier to using parallel-forms reliability is to create an alternative version of the test that gives equivalent scores.

Internal consistency reliability

If a questionnaire instrument has several items which all address the same construct, then we usually expect each subject to get similar scores for those items. Internal consistency reliability assesses the reliability of an instrument by estimating how well items within the same instrument that reflect the same construct give the same results when used on a sample at one time.

Split-half reliability

In split-half reliability the instrument is divided into two parts, each containing symmetrical items testing similar constructs. The instrument is administered to a sample of subjects at one time. The closer the agreement between the two parts, the greater is the split-half reliability of the instrument. It solves the problem in parallel-forms reliability of creating an alternative version of the test.

Cronbach's alpha (α)

Within an instrument, there may be many ways of dividing up the instrument to measure split-half reliability. Cronbach's α is a measure of internal consistency and can be interpreted as the mean of all possible split-half coefficients[1]. By convention, if Cronbach's α is ≥0.7–0.8 there is acceptable agreement[2].
SEE EXCERPT 28

1   Trochim WMK. Types of reliability. 2006. Available: http://www.socialresearchmethods.net/kb/reltypes.php. Accessed 1 September 2014.
2   Lance CE, Butts MM, Michels LC. The sources of four commonly reported cutoff criteria – what did they really say? *Organizational Research Methods* 2006; 9(2): 202–20.

Inter-rater reliability (interobserver reliability)

Inter-rater reliability assesses the level of agreement between assessments made by two or more raters of the same sample at the same time using the same test. Inter-rater reliability is important when more than one researcher is involved with assessing subjects, such as in multicentre trials.

When the subjects' responses fall into categories, the inter-rater reliability is quantified by the **kappa statistic (κ)**[1], also known as Cohen's statistic or the chance-corrected proportional agreement statistic. The kappa statistic gives an indication as to whether any agreement is more than could be expected by chance. If the agreement is no more than expected by chance, then $\kappa = 0$. With perfect agreement, $\kappa = 1$. The unit of kappa implicitly assumes that all disagreements are equally serious. When the researcher can specify the relative seriousness of each kind of disagreement, **weighted kappa** may be used[1]. **SEE EXCERPT 29**

The **intraclass correlation coefficient** is a measure of reliability when tests are measuring quantitative variables. It describes the extent to which two continuous measures taken by different people or two measurements taken by the same person on different occasions are related. However, it gives no indication of absolute differences.

If the size of the difference between repeated measurements is of interest, the **Bland-Altman limits of agreement** can be used[2]. The difference between each pair of scores is plotted on the vertical axis versus their mean on the horizontal axis. Perfect agreement is shown by the points lying on the horizontal line through the zero value on the vertical axis. A poorer level of agreement is shown by points lying further away from the horizontal line. The presence of a systematic error is shown by the horizontal line not passing through zero. The mean and standard deviation of the differences between the pairs of scores can be calculated and then the 95% limits of agreement (as the mean difference plus or minus two standard deviations of the differences), and 95% confidence intervals for these limits of agreement. The 95% limits of agreement provide a range of error that may relate to clinical acceptability[3].

1   Fleiss JL, Cohen J. The equivalence of weighted kappa and the intraclass correlation coefficient as measures of reliability. *Educational and Psychological Measurement* 1973; 33(3): 613–19.

2   Bland JM, Altman DG. Statistical methods for assessing agreement between two methods of clinical measurement. *Lancet* 1986; 327(8476): 307–10.

3   Bruton A, Conway JH, Holgate ST. Reliability: What is it, and how is it measured? *Physiotherapy* 2000; 86(2): 94–99.

EXCERPT 27

Adapted from: Bjelland M et al. Development of family and dietary habits questionnaires: the assessment of family processes, dietary habits and adolescents' impulsiveness in Norwegian adolescents and their parents. *International Journal of Behavioral Nutrition and Physical Activity* 2014; 11: 130.

One aim of the project was to develop valid and reliable questionnaires to identify family processes and measure dietary behaviours in adolescents and their parents.

The test and retest were conducted 10–14 days apart ... For most of the items measuring intakes, meal frequency, work–family stress and communication the test–retest reliability was good (intraclass correlation coefficient > 0.61) to excellent (ICC > 0.81).

Commentary: The test–retest reliability of different aspects of the questionnaire is quantified by the researchers.

EXCERPT 28

Adapted from: Blum-Fowler C et al. Translation and validation of the German version of the Bournemouth questionnaire for low back pain. *Chiropractic & Manual Therapies* 2013; 21: 32.

The purpose of this study was to translate and validate the Bournemouth Questionnaire (BQ) for low back pain (LBP) into German. Face validity, test–retest reliability, construct validity and internal consistency of the translated questionnaire were checked.

The questionnaire was tested on 30 people. Each completed the questionnaire and was then asked the meaning of each questionnaire item as well as whether or not they had problems with the questionnaire format, layout, instructions or response scales ... A detailed report written by the interviewing person, including proposed changes of the pre-final version based on the results of the face validity test was then submitted to the expert committee.

Commentary: The researchers tested the German version of the questionnaire for face validity and adjusted the questions in the final version.

The questionnaire was tested for test–retest reliability. It was essential that no change or treatment occurred in between the two administrations. The two versions given before and after a 2 hour class ... Test–retest reliability was evaluated using the Intra-class Correlation Coefficient (ICC) ... The ICC values were above 0.91 and highly significant for all seven domains indicating acceptable agreement for all scales and the total score.

Commentary: The researchers assessed test–retest reliability by repeating the questionnaire two hours apart. The reliability was quantified by a correlation coefficient and was found to be acceptable.

108 low back pain patients from five different chiropractic practices were asked to fill in the new German version of the BQN, the German version of the Oswestry Disability Index (ODI) and the German version of the SF-36 Health Survey prior to the start of their chiropractic treatment. Four weeks later each patient had to complete the 3 questionnaires again. The ODI and SF-36 were selected for comparison to the BQ LBP questionnaire as they contain similar subscales ... External construct validity shows the extent to which the BQN's scores concord with the scores of other instruments measuring the same theoretical hypotheses of the concepts under consideration. This was done using the Pearson's correlation coefficient comparing the 7 scales and total score of the BQN with the ODI as well as the BQN with the SF-36 for answers given at baseline and at 4 weeks after the start of treatment ... All correlations, with one exception, were statistically significant.

Commentary: The researchers assessed construct validity by comparing the results of the questionnaire with two other valid measures.

The internal consistency of the BQN, which measures the degree to which items that make up the total score are all measuring the same underlying attribute, was assessed using Cronbach's α. ... Cronbach's α was 0.86 at baseline for the total pre-treatment scores and 0.94 for the total post-treatment scores indicating acceptable consistency.

Commentary: The internal consistency of the German questionnaire was quantified by Cronbach's α and found to be acceptable.

EXCERPT 29

Adapted from: Wright B et al. Examiner and simulated patient ratings of empathy in medical student final year clinical examination: are they useful? *BMC Medical Education* 2014; 14: 199.

The researchers assessed the rating of empathy in examinations by simulated patient (actors) in terms of inter-rater reliability compared with clinical assessors or correlation with overall examination results.

Inter-rater reliability was measured between clinical examiners and actor simulated patients in the OSCE, using the individual empathy scores for each station. Overall the reliability as measured by the intraclass correlation coefficient (ICC) is 0.645, indicating substantial agreement. The station 'Addressing concerns about a colleague's conduct' shows excellent reliability of 0.754 with the lowest reliability on the station 'Suicide risk assessment' 0.502. Other ICCs were 'Explaining a cancer diagnosis' 0.603 and 'Discharge planning concerns' 0.658.

Commentary: The researchers assessed the inter-rater reliability of empathy scores by clinical examiners and simulated patients, although the reliability varied between different stations.

Scenario 18 revisited

The Clinical Tutor wrote back to Dr Nolan, thanking him for his feedback. He went on, 'The issue of reliability is indeed an important one in blood pressure measurements. I don't think simply having a new set of sphygmomanometers will make much of a difference, however, because the reliability of the measure is never going to be perfect, no matter who uses the sphygmomanometer!'

TO SUMMARISE, A GOOD STUDY WILL ....

Provide evidence that measuring instruments are reliable, usually by referring to earlier studies.

Quantify reliability by reference to correlation coefficient values.

Describe how reliability was improved by training and standardisation.

BIAS REVISITED

Bias can occur at any time in a study. From recruiting and allocating to observing and measuring, if the researchers are not careful bias can be a problem. The end result is that the results generated will be wrong in some way and the wrong conclusion may then be drawn.

We have already discussed some types of bias. Some are easier to spot than others. For example, a table of baseline characteristics can indicate problems with selection bias. One clue to the existence of a problem is how much researchers write about the various bits of a study's methods. We expect lots of detail about how researchers sampled the target population, allocated subjects to the different groups, administered interventions and measured outcomes. A lack of detail, such as writing 'we randomised people into two groups' or 'we blinded people', should set alarm bells ringing. These processes are so labour intensive when done well that a brief description may be an attempt to rapidly move the reader on to other parts of the study.

Once the mistake has happened, there is little the researcher can do apart from admit the mistake and discuss its impact in the discussion section of the paper.

SECTION F

INTERPRETING RESULTS

The results section analyses what happened in the study. Collected data are summarised, compared and manipulated in order to arrive at a conclusion.

Broadly, the results section of many clinical papers can be broken down into four main parts.

1. **A description of the sample population results.** This involves summarising the results data in each group using mode, median and mean, rather than listing the results for every single subject. An accurate description requires observation bias to be minimised.

2. **An estimation of the true results in the target population.** The research was done on a sample population. Confidence intervals and standard errors are calculated to infer the target population results without having to experiment on the entire target population. Generalisation of the results to the target population requires selection bias to be minimised.

3. **A comparison of the sample results to see which group did better or worse.** This involves creating 2×2 tables and discussing risks, absolute risk reductions, relative risks, relative risk reductions, odds, odds ratios and numbers needed to treat.

4. **A calculation of whether the sample results are likely to be explained by chance or not.** This involves analysing data using statistical tests to generate probability values (P values) to accept or reject the null hypothesis, in the search for statistical significance.

Some results data are given in graphical format and some in the form of tables. It is always a good idea to quickly scan the results section for tables which may summarise the results data.

The chapters in this section follow the four steps outlined above, starting with a clarification of key terms.

BASIC STATISTICAL TERMS

Statistics is the mathematical science of collecting, organising, analysing, presenting and interpreting data.

Descriptive versus inferential statistics

Descriptive statistics
Used to organise or summarise data collected from a sample population. For example, there might be a table in the results section of a clinical paper which summarises the baseline characteristics of subjects in the different treatment arms.

Inferential statistics
Uses data collected from a sample population to make generalisations about the target population from which the sample population was drawn.

Variables, attributes and parameters

Variable
Any entity that can take on different values. Examples include sample size, gender, age and drug dosage. Variables can be **qualitative** or **quantitative** values.

Two further terms are used when describing relationships:

- An **independent variable** is manipulated in the study. It is also known as the 'experimental' variable.
- A **dependent variable** is affected by the change in the value of the independent variable. It is also known as the 'outcome' variable.

Attribute
A specific value of a variable. For example, gender has two attributes, male and female.

Parameter
Any numerical quantity that characterises a population. For example, the mean and the standard deviation are two parameters that characterise a normal distribution.

Accuracy versus precision

- **Accuracy:** How close the measurement is to its true value.
- **Precision:** How close repeat measurements are to each other.

Ideally, a measurement is accurate and precise but this isn't always the case. A result can often be very accurate but not precise or vice versa.

EPIDEMIOLOGY

Epidemiology is the scientific study of the distribution, causes and control of diseases in populations. Studies frequently provide epidemiological data to describe the disease or population of interest.

There are two main measures of disease frequency, **incidence** and **prevalence**.

Incidence
Incidence: The rate of occurrence of new cases over a period of time in a defined population (Figure 20). It is a measure of the risk of disease.

$$\text{incidence} = \frac{\text{number of new cases over a period of time}}{\text{population size}}$$

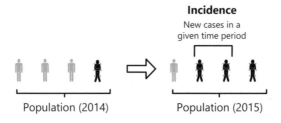

Incidence
New cases in a given time period

Population (2014)   Population (2015)

Figure 20 Incidence

The incidence can be given as a **crude rate**, which is the rate that applies to the whole population without any adjustment. **SEE EXCERPT 30**

A **specific rate** can be given, which only applies to a subgroup in the population.

- **Mortality rate:** This is a type of incidence rate that expresses the risk of death over a period of time in a population.

$$\text{mortality rate} = \frac{\text{number of deaths over a period of time}}{\text{population size}}$$

- **Standardised mortality rate:** The mortality rate is adjusted to compensate for a confounder, for example age. **SEE EXCERPT 31**

- **Standardised mortality ratio:** The ratio of the observed standardised mortality rate (from the study population) to the expected standardised mortality rate (from the standard population). The reference value is 100. Converting a mortality rate into a ratio makes it easier to compare different populations. The lower the ratio, the better.

- **Hospital standardised mortality ratio (HSMR):** A measure of overall mortality in hospitals, used in conjunction with other indicators to assess quality of care. The HSMR is adjusted for many factors, including sex, age, socioeconomic deprivation, diagnosis and method of patient admission to hospital. **SEE EXCERPT 32**

In 2009 a report by the Healthcare Commission detailed a catalogue of failings at Mid Staffordshire NHS Foundation Trust which were only uncovered when unusually high mortality rates at the hospital triggered alerts[1]. The HSMR for the hospital for 2005/06 was 127, meaning that 27% more patients died than might be expected. It was estimated that, between 2005 and 2008, 400 more people died at the hospital than would be expected. The Chairman of the Trust resigned, the Chief Executive was suspended and an independent inquiry was launched. The Mid Staffordshire NHS Foundation Trust Public Inquiry chaired by Robert Francis QC led to much soul-searching in a health service led astray by a target-driven culture.

[1] Investigation into Mid Staffordshire NHS Foundation Trust: Commission for Healthcare Audit and Inspection, March 2009, ISBN 978-1-84562-220-6.

- **Morbidity rate:** This is the rate of occurrence of new non-fatal cases of the disease in a defined population at risk over a given time period.

$$\text{morbidity rate} = \frac{\text{number of new non-fatal cases over a period of time}}{\text{size of population at risk}}$$

- **Standardised morbidity rate:** The morbidity rate is adjusted to compensate for a confounder.

- **Standardised morbidity ratio:** Ratio of the observed standardised morbidity rate (from the study population) to the expected standardised morbidity rate (from the standard population).

Prevalence

Point prevalence: The proportion of a defined population having the disease at a given point in time (Figure 21).

$$\text{point prevalence} = \frac{\text{number of people with the disease at a given time}}{\text{size of population at the same time}}$$

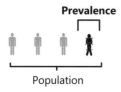

Prevalence

Population

Figure 21 Prevalence

Incidence and prevalence are related by the following equation

$$\frac{\text{prevalence at}}{\text{any time point}} = \text{incidence} \times \text{average duration of the disease}$$

Prevalence can be used with other factors rather than just disease. For example, the prevalence of risk factors can be calculated. **SEE EXCERPT 33**

Period prevalence: The proportion of a population that has the disease during a given time period (such as annual prevalence).

$$\text{period prevalence} = \frac{\text{number of people with the disease or developing the disease in a given time period}}{\text{size of population at the same time}}$$

Lifetime prevalence: This is the proportion of a population that either has or has had the disease at a given point in time.

EXCERPT 30

Adapted from: Linard ATS et al. Epidemiology of bee stings in Campina Grande, Paraíba state, Northeastern Brazil. *Journal of Venomous Animals and Toxins including Tropical Diseases* 2014; 20: 13.

This study investigated bee sting cases recorded between 2007 and 2012 in Campina Grande, Brazil.

A total of 459 bee sting cases were registered from January 2007 to December 2012 in the city of Campina Grande, with an average incidence rate of 28 cases per 100 000 inhabitants in 2007, 27 cases per 100 000 inhabitants in 2008, 24 cases per 100 000 inhabitants in 2009, 10 cases per 100 000 inhabitants in 2010, 13 cases per 100 000 inhabitants in 2011, and 14 cases per 100 000 inhabitants in 2012. Bee sting cases were registered in all months of the year, with higher incidence in the third trimester.

Commentary: An example of incidence data. The researchers give the number of new cases of bee stings in one year periods per 100 000 inhabitants.

EXCERPT 31

Adapted from: Roue T et al. The epidemiology of breast cancer in French Guiana 2003–2006. *Springer Plus* 2013; 2: 471.

A cancer registry collected data on breast cancer between 2003 and 2006 in French Guiana. The incidence and mortality of breast cancer were estimated by researchers.

Between 2003 and 2006, there were 147 new cases of breast cancer, which corresponded to a crude incidence rate of 36.7 per 100 000 women. The standardised incidence rate was 47.1 per 100 000 women. The crude mortality rate by breast cancer was 8.0 per 100 000 women. The standardised mortality rate was 11.0 deaths per 100 000 women.

Commentary: An example of crude and age-standardised incidence and mortality rates. The age-standardised mortality rate takes into account the age structure in the sample population. In this excerpt it is the numbers of deaths per 100 000 women that would occur if the sample population had the same age structure as the standard population and the sample population age-specific mortality rate applied.

EXCERPT 32

Adapted from: Heijink R et al. Measuring and explaining mortality in Dutch hospitals; The Hospital Standardized Mortality Rate between 2003 and 2005. *BMC Health Services Research* 2008; 8: 73.

Indicators of hospital quality, such as hospital standardised mortality ratios (HSMR), have been used increasingly to assess and improve hospital quality. The aim of this study was to describe and explain variation in new HSMRs for the Netherlands.

The total number of in-hospital deaths decreased between 2003 and 2005. In all years the hospital with the highest HSMR had an HSMR score about 1.5 times as high as the average score and about twice as high as the lowest score.

	2003	2004	2005
Total deaths	34391	32408	31808
HSMR Mean and all hospitals	100	90	83
HSMR Mean in 7 academic hospitals	117	103	94
Min–Max HSMR	74–151	62–140	57–120
HSMR between 2003 and 2005 (average 2003 = 100)			

Commentary: The table shows the HSMR data from 2003 to 2005. The Min–Max HSMR row shows there are considerable differences between hospitals. The researchers noted the comparatively higher HSMRs in academic hospitals and explained that this may result from (good quality) high-risk procedures, low quality of care or inadequate case-mix correction.

EXCERPT 33

Adapted from: Epidemiology of smoking among Malaysian adult males: prevalence and associated factors. *BMC Public Health* 2013; 13: 8.

Researchers described the prevalence of smoking in Malaysia with data gathered from national surveys.

A total of 7113 out of 15639 respondents interviewed were current smokers (46.4%). The prevalence of smoking declined with age; with 59.3% among 21–30 year olds, 56.8% among 31–40 year olds, 48.5% among 41–50 year olds, and 35.0% among those aged 61 and above. There were fewer smokers among those with higher education attainment (31.4%), monthly household income of at least RM3000 (39.2%), and among working professionals (32.3%). Smoking was higher among the Malays (55.9%) and people of other indigenous ethnic groups (53.8%) than the Chinese (36.0%) and Indians (35.0%).

Commentary: Examples of prevalence data.

Data can be classified as either qualitative or quantitative.

Qualitative data

Qualitative data are also known as **categorical** or **non-numerical** data. Examples of qualitative data:

- Gender: male, female
- Marital status: single, married, divorced, widowed
- Colour: red, yellow, blue, silver, green
- Outcome: cured, not cured

If there are only two possible attributes for a categorical variable, the term **binary data** can be used. The term **multicategory data** is used when there are more than two possible categories.

Quantitative data

Quantitative data are also known as **numerical** data and are classified as either discrete or continuous.

Discrete data have a finite number of possible values and tend to be made up of integers (or whole numbers). Counts are examples of discrete data:

- Number of pupils absent each day at school: 7, 3, 13, 14, 4
- Waiting time to see a doctor in days: 2, 1, 3, 2, 4, 2, 1

Continuous data have infinite possibilities. Continuous data values can include decimal places:

- Diameter of tumours: 1.23 cm, 1.78 cm, 2.25 cm
- Weight of patients: 67.234 kg, 89.935 kg, 101.563 kg

Measuring instruments and data collection

The measuring instrument used to measure data will determine the type of data collected:

- Fun weighing machine – results given as 'skinny', 'normal', 'fat', 'too fat' (qualitative data)
- Digital weighing scale – results given in kg to two decimal places (quantitative continuous data)

Converting quantitative data to qualitative data

Quantitative data can be converted into categorical data by using cut-off points (see Table 6). For example, biological measurements or results from rating scales are often converted into disease/no-disease categories or cured/not-cured categories. **SEE EXCERPT 34 AND EXCERPT 35**

This is because categorical data are easier to tabulate and analyse. However, the conversion means some data are discarded and it gets harder to detect a statistically significant difference. Also subjects at either side of the cut-off point end up with very different levels of risk.

BLOOD PRESSURE (QUANTITATIVE DATA)		BLOOD PRESSURE (CATEGORIES)
80/40 mmHg		Hypotensive
120/70 mmHg		Normotensive
145/85 mmHg		Normotensive
160/85 mmHg	⇨	Normotensive
150/100 mmHg		Hypertensive
165/105 mmHg		Hypertensive

Table 6 Converting quantitative data to categorical data

If we look forward to 2×2 tables, in each row we tabulate how many subjects got the outcome and how many did not by the end of the study. The 2×2 table is categorical data, with each subject in each group placed in one of two categories.

EXCERPT 34

Adapted from: Association and predictive value analysis for metabolic syndrome on systolic and diastolic heart failure in high-risk patients. *BMC Cardiovascular Disorders* 2014; 14: 124.

The aim of this study was to examine the relationship between metabolic syndrome and heart failure.

We enrolled 347 patients ... Systolic blood pressure and diastolic blood pressure values were the means of two physician-obtained measurements on the left arm of the seated participant. Hypertension was diagnosed if the blood pressure ≥140/90 mmHg and/or the patient was undergoing current antihypertensive therapy.

Commentary: The quantitative data on blood pressure were converted into qualitative data (hypertension or no hypertension) by defining a cut-off reading (140/90 mmHg) and/or by the use of antihypertensive therapy.

EXCERPT 35

Adapted from: Kajeepeta S et al. Sleep duration, vital exhaustion, and odds of spontaneous preterm birth: a case–control study. *BMC Pregnancy and Childbirth* 2014; 14: 337.

Researchers investigated the relationship between maternal sleep duration and vital exhaustion in the first six months of pregnancy and preterm birth.

Maternal report of vital exhaustion in early pregnancy was ascertained by asking women: 'During the first 6 months of your pregnancy, how often did you feel exhausted (except after exercise)?' Response choices were: (1) never; (2) once per month; (3) 2–3 times per month; (4) 4 times per month; (5) every week; and (6) every day. For multivariable analyses, we collapsed responses into a dichotomous variable with 'never' comprising the responses never, and 'ever' comprising all other responses.

Commentary: For the purposes of a statistical analysis, the researchers converted the responses for a question about feeling exhausted into two categories.

MEASURING DATA

A scale of measurement is used to assign a value to a variable. There are four types of measurement scales, listed below in order of increasing complexity. The measurement scale determines the types of statistics that can be used to analyse the data.

Nominal scales

A nominal scale is organised in categories which have no inherent order and which bear no mathematical relationship to each other (Figure 22). A nominal scale simply labels objects, eg:

- Gender: male, female
- Hair colour: blond, brunette, brown, black, ginger

Figure 22 A nominal scale has no order to the categories

Ordinal scales

An ordinal scale is organised in categories that have an inherent order or rank (Figure 23). The categories are not given a numerical value, so the interval between categories is not meaningful, eg:

- Social class: I, II, III, IV, V
- Severity of disease: mild, moderate, severe

Figure 23 An ordinal scale has an order to the categories

Interval scales

An interval scale is organised in a meaningful way, with the differences between points being equal across the scale. Interval data have no true starting point. The value zero on an interval scale has no special meaning; it is simply another point of measurement on the scale.

- The Celsius temperature scale is an example of an interval scale: 0°C does not mean there is no temperature, as minus temperatures are possible too. Also, although 80°C is as different from 40°C as 40°C is from 0°C, it does not mean that 80°C is twice the temperature of 40°C, as the scale does not start at 0°C (Figure 24).

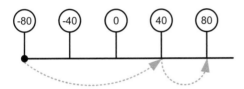

Figure 24 An interval scale does not start at a true zero

Ratio scales

A ratio scale is the same as an interval scale but there is a true zero. There is no number below zero.

- The Kelvin temperature scale is an example of a ratio scale:

0 K means there is no temperature as it signifies that all thermal motion has ceased. Also, 80 K is as different from 40 K as 40 K is from 0 K and 80 K is twice the temperature of 40 K (Figure 25).

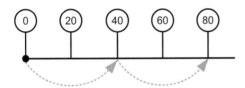

Figure 25 A ratio scale starts at a true zero

Using scales

Qualitative data tend to be measured on nominal or ordinal scales. Quantitative data tend to be measured on interval or ratio scales.

Nominal and ordinal data can be analysed with non-parametric statistics. Interval and ratio data can be analysed using parametric statistics.

Table 7 summarises the features of the different types of scales.

	NOMINAL	ORDINAL	INTERVAL	RATIO
Shows a difference	Yes	Yes	Yes	Yes
Shows direction of difference	—	Yes	Yes	Yes
Shows amount of difference	—	—	Yes	Yes
Has an absolute zero	—	—	—	Yes

Table 7 Measurement scales. Adapted from http://www.webster.edu/~woolflm/statwhatis.html

After data are collected, the information needs to be organised and summarised. Patterns or trends might emerge and this can help determine which statistical analyses should be performed on the data.

A **probability distribution** links all the possible values of a random variable in an experiment with the likelihood of the occurrence of each of these values.

- A coin is tossed once. The outcome can be head or tail. The probability of getting no heads is 0.5. The probability of getting one head is 0.5. This information displayed in a table would constitute a probability distribution.

Number of heads	Probability
0	0.5
1	0.5

- A coin is tossed twice. Each time the coin is tossed the outcome can be head or tail. The probability of getting no heads is 0.25. The probability of getting one head is 0.5. The probability of getting two heads is 0.25. This information displayed in a table would constitute a probability distribution.

Number of heads	Probability
0	0.25
1	0.5
2	0.25

Depending on whether a random variable is discrete or continuous, the probability distribution can be discrete or continuous.

The examples of tossing a coin are **discrete probability distributions**. It is only possible to get whole numbers of heads. For example, it is not possible to get 1.3 heads. As shown in the examples above, discrete probability distributions can be shown in tabular form. Each row of the table is concerned with one discrete value of the variable.

A continuous variable generates a **continuous probability distribution**. This type of distribution is best shown in a graphical format or expressed as an equation or formula.

There are three common probability distributions to consider:

- Binomial (discrete)
- Poisson (discrete)
- Normal (continuous)

Binomial distribution

In a **binomial experiment** there is a fixed number of runs in which a random variable can have two possible outcomes, the probabilities of which are the same in each run. Each run is independent. The outcome of each run does not affect the outcome of other runs.

The **binomial distribution** is the probability distribution of a binomial random variable. Tossing a coin five times and calculating the probabilities of getting from zero to five heads is an example of a binomial distribution.

The **Bernoulli distribution** is a special case of the binomial distribution in which an experiment on a variable with only two possible outcomes is run just once. Tossing a coin once and determining the likelihood of getting a head is an example of a Bernoulli distribution.

Poisson distribution

In a **Poisson experiment** there are repeated runs in which a random variable can have two possible outcomes. The mean number of outcomes that occur in a period of continuous space or time is known. The number of runs is not fixed.

The **Poisson distribution** can be used to determine the probability of getting an outcome in a Poisson experiment. For example, knowing that, on average, five babies are born every day on a maternity ward, one can calculate the likelihood that exactly six babies will be born tomorrow or the likelihood that fewer than three babies will be born tomorrow.

Normal distribution

The **normal probability distribution** is a **continuous** variable distribution. Many biological measures have an approximately normal distribution.

The normal distribution has many convenient mathematical properties. It has a characteristic bell-shaped distribution that is symmetrical about its mean value. This means that the mean is the same as the median and the mode. The normal distribution can be described completely by its mean and variance.

Central limit theorem

This is a theorem that states that no matter what the probability distribution of the original variables, the sum (or mean) of a large number of random variables is distributed approximately normally. This theorem allows the use of the normal distribution in creating confidence intervals and for hypothesis testing. It allows us to estimate the standard error (see page 151) from a single sample.

Reference ranges

These are a range of values or an interval which contains the values obtained from the majority of a sample of normal people. The normal distribution can be useful in calculating the reference ranges because of its unique properties.

Categorical data (mode, frequency)

Categorical data can be summarised using mode and frequency.

The **mode** (or **modal value**) is the most common value.

A **unimodal distribution** has a single peak – the mode (Figure 26).

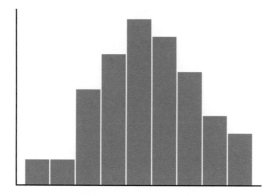

Figure 26 A unimodal distribution

A **bimodal distribution** has two modal values which signify local high points (Figure 27). This type of distribution can be seen if two sets of data are mixed.

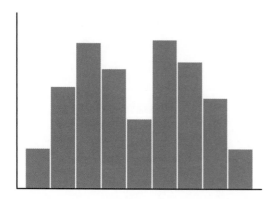

Figure 27 A bimodal distribution

A **multimodal distribution** has three or more local high points.

The **frequency** is the number of values in each category. For example, in Table 6 on page 130, the mode is 'normotensive' and the frequencies are:

- Hypotensive (1 observation)
- Normotensive (3 observations)
- Hypertensive (2 observations)

Presenting the frequencies as proportions is more useful than simply knowing the absolute frequency in each category. For example, 50% normotensive cases is more useful than knowing there were three normotensive observations. Ideally, the absolute numbers and proportions should be given together because the absolute frequencies are still needed for statistical analyses. **SEE EXCERPT 36**

EXCERPT 36

Adapted from: Citywide trauma experience in Mwanza, Tanzania: a need for urgent intervention. *Journal of Trauma Management & Outcomes* 2013; 7: 9.

This descriptive prospective study investigated trauma care in Tanzania.

During the period under study, a total of 5672 trauma patients were enrolled in the study. There were 3952 (69.7%) males and 1720 (30.3%) females with a male to female ratio of 2.3: 1. The age ranged from 2 months to 76 years with a median age of 28 years. The modal age group was 21–30 years accounting for 52.6% of cases.

Commentary: An example of the use of mode. The most common age category for trauma patients was 21–30 years of age with a frequency of 52.6%.

SUMMARISING NORMALLY DISTRIBUTED DATA

Normally distributed data (mean, standard deviation)

A **normal distribution**, also known as a **Gaussian distribution**, is a perfectly symmetrical, bell-shaped curve, as shown in Figure 28. The variable is on the x-axis. The frequency of different values of the variable is shown on the y-axis. Values in the middle of the x-axis occur frequently. Extreme values on the x-axis occur rarely.

Normal data can be summarised using mean and standard deviation.

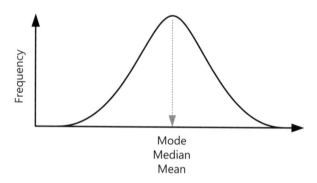

Figure 28 Normal distribution

Mean: The sum of all the values divided by the number of values.

$$\text{mean} = \frac{\text{sum of all the values}}{\text{the number of values}}$$

$$\bar{x} = \frac{\Sigma x}{n}$$

The mean uses all the data and is easy to calculate. However, it is not robust to outlying values and can be difficult to interpret.

The mean is also known as the **arithmetic mean**.

In a perfect normal distribution, the mean, median and mode are of equal value and lie in the centre of the distribution.

Weighted mean: In situations where some values of the variable are more important than other values, a weight can be attached to each value to reflect the relative importance of each value. If the weight is equal across all the values, the weighted mean is equal to the arithmetic mean.

Variance: The dispersion of values around the mean is indicated by the variance. This is equal to the average distance by which each individual observation differs from the mean value.

The variance is the sum of all the differences between all the values and the mean, squared and divided by the total number of observations minus 1 (the degrees of freedom):

$$\text{variance } (v) = \frac{\Sigma(x - \bar{x})^2}{n - 1}$$

Standard deviation (SD): A statistical measure that describes the degree of data spread about the mean – the amount the values will deviate from the mean. It is a measure of precision. It has the same units as the observations.

Standard deviation is calculated as the square root of the variance:

$$\text{standard deviation} = \sqrt{v} = \sqrt{\frac{\Sigma(x - \bar{x})^2}{n - 1}}$$

The extent of the bell shape in a normal distribution depends on the standard deviation. Key properties of the normal distribution are that we can calculate the proportion of the observations that will lie between any two values of the variable, as long as we know the mean and standard deviation.

If observations follow a normal distribution, the standard deviation is a useful measure of the spread of these observations (Figure 29).

- A range covered by 1 SD above the mean and 1 SD below the mean includes 68% of the observations (ie the area under the curve).
- A range of 2 SDs (actually 1.96) above and below the mean includes 95% of the observations.
- A range of 3 SDs (actually 2.58) above and below the mean includes 99.7% of the observations.

SEE EXCERPT 37

The larger the standard deviation, the greater the spread of observations around the mean.

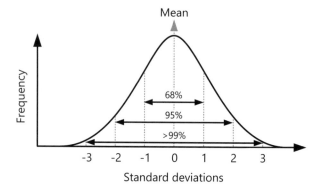

Figure 29 A normal distribution showing 1, 2 and 3 standard deviations

z score: Converts the value of an observation into the number of standard deviations that observation lies from the mean of the distribution. A z score is calculated by subtracting the mean from the observation and dividing the difference by the standard deviation. It is a dimensionless quantity. For example, a z score of 1.2 means the difference between the data point and mean value is +1.2 times the size of the standard deviation of the population. A negative z score indicates that the value of the data point is less than the mean. It is possible to calculate the probability of getting a value with a certain z score. **SEE EXCERPT 38**

Coefficient of variation: Used to compare studies using different units, which usually makes direct comparisons difficult. It is a measure of spread that is independent of the unit of measurement. The coefficient of variation is the ratio of the standard deviation and the mean and is expressed as a percentage.

$$\text{coefficient of variation} = \frac{\text{standard deviation}}{\text{mean}} \times 100$$

Standard normal distribution: A special case of the normal distribution in which the mean is zero, the variance (and standard deviation) is 1 and the area under the curve is equal to 1. Normal distributions can be converted to standard normal distributions. This transformation enables comparisons of distributions that have different means by showing them on the same scale.

Effect size: The effect size is used to compare the results of studies which used different outcome measures. It is calculated for each study by the following equation:

$$\text{effect size} = \frac{(\text{mean in experimental group} - \text{mean in control group})}{\text{standard deviation of the control group or both groups}}$$

It is also known as the **standardised mean difference**. The larger the value of the effect size, the greater the impact of the intervention.

Showing a distribution is normal

Certain statistical tests can only be used on data that are normally distributed. Different approaches can be used to show that a distribution is normal.

- Visual inspection: If the data are plotted on a graph, the data may visually appear to be a bell-shaped distribution.

- According to the central limit theorem, no matter what the probability distribution of the original variables, the sum (or mean) of a large number of random variables is distributed approximately normally. Therefore, the larger the sample size, the more likely it is that a normal distribution exits.

- Basic statistical tests: In a perfect normal distribution the mode, median and mean are the same value.

- Advanced statistical tests: Shapiro–Wilk test, Anderson–Darling test, Kolmogorov–Smirnov (K–S) test, Lilliefors corrected K–S test, Cramér–von Mises test, D'Agostino skewness test, Anscombe–Glynn kurtosis test, D'Agostino–Pearson omnibus test, and the Jarque–Bera test[1]. The tests compare the scores in the sample to a normally distributed set of scores with the same mean and standard deviation; the null hypothesis is that the sample distribution is normal. If the test is statically significant, the distribution is non-normal[1].

1   Ghasemi A, Zahedias S. Normality tests for statistical analysis: a guide for non-statisticians. *International Journal of Endocrinology and Metabolism* 2012; 10(2): 486–89.

EXCERPT 37

Adapted from: Heron N, Cupples ME. The health profile of football/soccer players in Northern Ireland – a review of the UEFA pre-participation medical screening procedure. *BMC Sports Science, Medicine and Rehabilitation* 2014; 6: 5.

This study reviewed the health profile of soccer players in Northern Ireland as described through the UEFA pre-participation medical screening procedure.

There were 89 pre-participation medical screenings conducted in 47 players, including 6 goalkeepers; 11 defenders; 22 midfielders; 8 attackers. Their mean age was 25.0 years (SD 4.86). The players had played an average of 38 games in the season previous to their medical; 24 players reported that their dominant foot was left, with no players reporting dual dominance.

Player measurement	Mean (standard deviation)
Age (years)	25.0 (4.9)
Height (cm)	179.3 (5.9)
Weight (kg)	77.6 (10.5)
BMI (kg/m^2)	24.1 (2.5)
Systolic blood pressure (mmHg)	122.5 (7.1)
Diastolic blood pressure (mmHg)	77.7 (6.9)
Games played in previous season	38 (11.3)

Commentary: The player measurements are given in the table as means with standard deviations to show the spread of values around the means.

EXCERPT 38

Adapted from: Kelly GA et al. Reduction in BMI z-score and improvement in cardiometabolic risk factors in obese children and adolescents. The Oslo Adiposity Intervention Study – a hospital/public health nurse combined treatment. *BMC Pediatrics* 2011; 11: 47.

Researchers studied the reduction in BMI z score associated with improvement in cardiometabolic risk factors in overweight and obese children and adolescents treated with a combined hospital/public health nurse model.

230 participants were included in the analyses (75%). Mean (SD) BMI z score was reduced from 2.18 (0.30) to 2.05 (0.39) (p < 0.001) in the group as a whole.

Commentary: An example of the use of z scores. The average BMI changed from 2.18 standard deviations above the mean to 2.05 standard deviations above the mean.

Non-normally distributed data (median, range, interquartile range)

As shown in Figure 30, in non-normally distributed data the data values are distributed asymmetrically across the distribution. Non-normal data can be summarised with median and (inter-quartile) range.

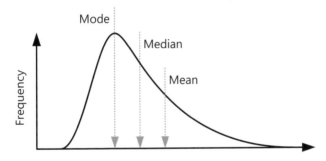

Figure 30 Non-normal distribution – positively skewed

Median: From the Latin for 'middle', the median represents the middle value of ordered data observations. With an even number of data values, the median is the average of the two values that lie on either side of the middle (Table 8).

The advantage of the median estimation is that it is robust to outliers, meaning that it is not affected by outlying points (unlike the mean). The main disadvantage of using the median is that it does not use all the data values in its determination.

SEE EXCERPT 39

Geometric mean: This is used when the distribution is positively skewed. Each value is replaced by its logarithm to base e which results in a log normal distribution. The arithmetic mean is then calculated and transformed back using the exponential transformation to give a mean. If the distribution of the log data is approximately symmetrical, the geometric mean is similar to the median and less than the mean of the original data.

Range: This is the difference between the lowest and highest values in the data set. It is useful for skewed data but it is not robust to outlying values.

DATA SET	MEDIAN	RANGE
1, 2, 3, 3, 5	3	5 − 1 = 4
1, 2, 3, 3, 5, 7, 8, 10	(3+5 / 2) = 4	10 − 1 = 9

Table 8 Example calculations of median and range

Interquartile range: This is a 'mini' range because it focuses on the spread of the middle 50% of the data. It is usually reported alongside the median value of the data set.

The data are ranked in order and divided into four equal parts (irrespective of their values). The points at 25%, 50% and 75% of the distribution are identified. These are known as the quartiles and the median is the second quartile. The interquartile range is between the first and third quartiles (Figure 31).

Unlike the range, the interquartile range is not influenced by outliers and is relatively easy to calculate. However, the interquartile range does not incorporate all the presented values.

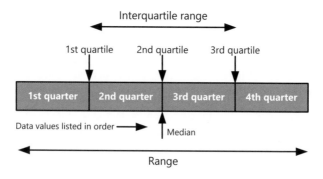

Figure 31 Comparing the range and the interquartile range

If the number of data values is not divisible by 4, first identify the median value and then calculate the first and third quartiles by the middle values between the median and the end of the ranges.

Percentiles or centiles: The data set is divided into 100 equal parts. These are sometimes used to define the normal ranges for clinical measures:

- 10% of the values lie below the 10th percentile
- 20% of the values lie below the 20th percentile
- 50% of the values lie below the 50th percentile (median)

Measures of shape

Skewness might be obvious when the data are presented on a histogram or scatter diagram.

The **coefficient of skewness** is a measure of symmetry.

The **coefficient of kurtosis** measures the peakedness of a distribution.

Positively skewed distribution: The distribution has an extended tail to the right and has a positive coefficient of skewness. The mean is larger than the median, which is larger than the mode (Figure 30).

Negatively skewed distribution: The distribution has an extended tail to the left and has a negative coefficient of skewness. The mean is smaller than the median, which is smaller than the mode.

Symmetrical distribution: This has a coefficient of skewness of zero.

Transforming data

Even for data that are not distributed normally, the data are often transformed into a distribution to allow statistical tests to be used. For example, skewed data can be transformed into a normal distribution and curved relationships can be made linear. Examples of transformations are the use of logarithms, reciprocals and square roots of the data values.

EXCERPT 39

Adapted from: Etter J-F. Electronic cigarettes: a survey of users. *BMC Public Health* 2010; 10: 231.

The aim of this study was to assess usage patterns of e-cigarettes, reasons for use, and users' opinions of these products.

The respondents were relatively young (median age 37 years), and most (77%) were men. Most (63%) were former smokers who had quit smoking relatively recently (median duration of abstinence: 100 days). Most respondents had been using the e-cigarette for slightly longer than three months, and current users took 175 puffs per day (median) from their device. Sixteen different brands of e-cigarettes were named and all these brands of e-cigarette deliver nicotine, and the median dose of nicotine per unit was 14 mg.

Commentary: Results in this study were given as median values.

Researchers experiment on a sample population, which is a representative proportion of the target population. What the researchers really want to know is the results in the target population. However, without recruiting the entire target population into their study, the only option they have is to infer the target population results from their sample results.

To generalise the results from a sample population to the target population, a few key concepts need to be understood:

- Central limit theorem
- Standard error of the mean
- 95% confidence interval

These concepts will be explained by going through an example step-by-step.

Central limit theorem

Suppose that researchers want to determine the mean height of people in the target population. A random sample of the target population is selected to take part in the study. The mean height and standard deviation is calculated for the sample population.

If the study is repeated with a new random sample, the mean height from this second sample might not be the same as that from the first sample, as the second sample is composed of different people. Indeed, repeating the study several times might produce a series of different mean heights and standard deviations. This is shown in Table 9.

	MEAN HEIGHT	STANDARD DEVIATION
Sample 1	1.65	0.12
Sample 2	1.58	0.07
Sample 3	1.63	0.10
Sample 4	1.88	0.05
Sample 5	1.59	0.09
Sample 6	1.72	0.14
Sample 7	1.63	0.08
Sample 8	1.49	0.21

Table 9 Mean heights (in metres) and standard deviations from different samples

If these sample means are themselves plotted on a graph, the distribution of the mean will follow a normal distribution (Figure 32), in line with the **central limit theorem**.

This theorem states that no matter what the probability distribution of the original variables, the sum (or mean) of a large number of random variables is distributed approximately normally. So, no matter what the distribution of heights in the target population (normal or non-normal), if we keep sampling the target population, the mean heights of the sample populations will follow a normal distribution, as long as the samples are large.

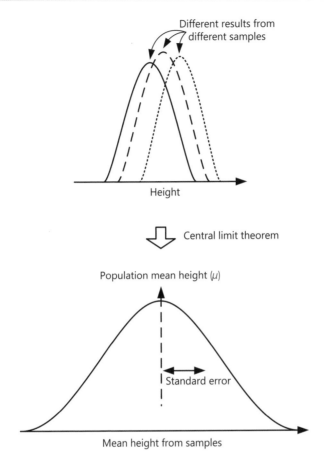

Figure 32 Population mean and standard error

Standard error of the mean (SE)

As the distribution of the mean is normal, it will have certain properties that normal distributions have.

- According to the central limit theorem, if we take enough samples, the mean of all the sample means is equal to the **population mean** (μ) (Figure 32).

- The standard deviation of the sample means has its own name, **standard error of the mean**, often shortened to **standard error** (SE) (Figure 32).

95% confidence interval

Step 1

In line with all normal distributions, 95% of the means in the samples will lie within 1.96 standard errors above or below the population mean (Figure 29).

95% of the time, the sample mean will lie in the range:	population mean ± 1.96SE

Step 2

The above equation can be rearranged by moving the population mean to the left-hand side.

95% of the time, the population mean will lie in the range:	sample mean ± 1.96SE

This gives us a range within which we expect the population mean to lie, 95% of the time. If we know the sample mean and the standard error of the mean, we can calculate this range.

Step 3

The sample mean is easy to calculate.

The standard error can be calculated from the following equation.

$$\text{standard error} = \frac{\text{standard deviation of the target population}}{\sqrt{\text{sample size}}}$$

We can make an assumption. If the sample size is large, the standard deviation of the sample population will be similar to the standard deviation of the target population. The equation for standard error is modified.

$$\text{standard error} = \frac{\text{standard deviation of the sample population}}{\sqrt{\text{sample size}}}$$

Step 4

We can now update our equation.

95% of the time, the population mean will lie in the range:	sample mean $\pm 1.96 \dfrac{SD}{\sqrt{n}}$

We are now able to work out the range in which the population mean will lie 95% of the time, by working out the sample mean, the standard deviation of the sample and the square root of the sample size.

This is the origin of the 95% confidence interval – the range in which we are 95% sure the population result lies. The confidence interval is a range of values which, when quoted in relation to a result from a sample, express the degree of uncertainty around that result.

It doesn't have to be 95%. The general equation for a confidence interval is:

$$\text{confidence interval} = z \frac{SD}{\sqrt{n}}$$

The constant z refers to the number of standard deviations that cover the chosen percentage of a normal distribution. For 95%, $z = 1.96$.

Making sense of confidence intervals

Imagine that we want to know the mean height of 500 pupils attending a school.

- If all 500 pupils are in our sample, we are 100% confident that we will calculate the correct mean height from all the height measurements we take.

- If our sample is 499 pupils, we are still very confident that the mean height we calculate from our sample will be very similar to the mean height of the target population. The mean height for all 500 pupils might be a bit higher or a bit lower, but the difference, if it exists, will be very small indeed.

- If our sample is 400 pupils, we are slightly less confident that the mean value we calculate lies close to the real mean value for all the pupils. If we had to guess where the real value lies, we would quote a small range either side of the value we have calculated.

- If our sample is only 50 pupils, we would be even less confident in our result. Even if the result is correct, we don't know it is, so we are less confident. The range in which we think the true value lies will be wider.

When researchers give a result from a sample, they may indicate their confidence in the result by stating a **confidence interval** which is a range of values. By convention, the 95% confidence interval is usually given, which is the range in which 95% of the time the population result will lie.

- If the mean height in the sample is given as 1.4 m $\pm$ 0.1 m, this means the mean height from the sample was 1.4 m. The 95% confidence interval is $\pm$ 0.1 m, that is, 95% of the time the real mean height in the target population will lie somewhere between 1.3 m and 1.5 m. We don't know the real mean height in the target population – we only ever know the range in which it may lie. This also means that 2.5% of the time, the target population mean height will lie below this range, and 2.5% of the time, the target population mean height will lie above this range.

- If the mean height in the sample is 1.4 m $\pm$ 0.2 m – the 95% confidence interval is from 1.2 m to 1.6 m.

- If the mean height in the sample is 1.4 m $\pm$ 0.3 m – the 95% confidence interval is from 1.1 m to 1.7 m.

As the researchers get less and less confident about a result from the sample, the confidence interval gets wider, as there is less certainty about the true result in the target population. The size of the confidence interval is inversely proportional to the sample size – as the sample size goes down, the confidence interval gets wider, as we are less sure about the result.

How are confidence intervals given?

Confidence intervals may be expressed in a number of different ways.

Using the plus/minus nomenclature after the sample result

The mean height is 1.4 m $\pm$ 0.1 m

Stating the start and end values in parentheses after the sample result

The mean height is 1.4 m (1.3 m, 1.5 m) or 1.4 m (1.3 m–1.5 m) **SEE EXCERPT 40**

Diagrammatically using error bars

The error bars in the two graphs shown in Figure 33 give the confidence limits.
SEE EXCERPT 41

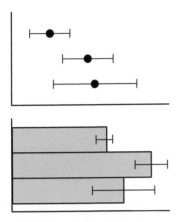

Figure 33 Confidence intervals shown as error bars

Interpreting confidence intervals

The confidence interval is a range within which we are 95% sure the true population result lies.

If the sample result is an absolute difference between two groups in a study, eg the difference in height readings, the value of **zero** difference is the value of no effect. If the confidence interval includes zero, the study result is statistically non-significant.

- The height difference between two groups is 3 cm ± 1 cm – this result is statistically significant. 95% of the time the true height difference in the target population will lie between 2 cm and 4 cm, so there will be a difference.

- The height difference between the two groups is 3 cm ± 4 cm – this result is statistically non-significant. 95% of the time the true height difference in the target population will lie between −1 cm and 7 cm. This includes the value of zero centimetres, ie no difference between the groups!

If the sample result is a ratio between two groups in a study, eg relative risk or odds ratio, the value of **one** is the value of no effect. If the confidence interval includes one, the study result is statistically non-significant.

- The relative risk is 1.6 (1.4, 1.7) – this result is statistically significant. 95% of the time the relative risk in the target population will lie between 1.4 and 1.7. The risk is higher in one of the groups.

- The relative risk is 1.6 (0.9, 2.0) – this result is statistically non-significant. 95% of the time the relative risk in the target population will lie between 0.9 and 2.0. This includes the relative risk value of one, which means no difference between the groups!

Confidence intervals involving ratios, such as relative risk or odds ratios, are usually asymmetrical and do not use the plus or minus type formula. Asymmetrical confidence intervals can be transformed into symmetrical confidence intervals if a log scale is used instead.

EXCERPT 40

Adapted from: Turner C et al. Changes in the body weight of term infants, born in the tropics, during the first seven days of life. BMC Pediatrics 2013; 13: 93.

The aim of this analysis was to describe the normal weight change in a breast fed infant in the first seven days of life in developing countries.

For all infants, the mean maximum weight loss was 4.4% (95% CI = 4.1–4.6%) and this occurred on day three. For non low birth weight infants, the mean maximum weight loss was 4.5% (95% CI = 4.2–4.8%) and for low birth weight term infants it was 4.1% (95% CI = 3.5–4.7%). Infants started to gain weight between days three and four with a mean gain of 13 g/kg/day (95% CI = 9–17 g/kg/day). Weight gain subsequently continued until day seven.

Commentary: The weight changes in the sample are given with 95% confidence intervals to show what might be expected in the target population.

EXCERPT 41

Adapted from: Abebe SM et al. Diabetes mellitus in North West Ethiopia: a community based study. *BMC Public Health* 2014; 14: 97.

This study aimed to compare the magnitude and associated risks of diabetes mellitus among urban and rural adults in northwest Ethiopia.

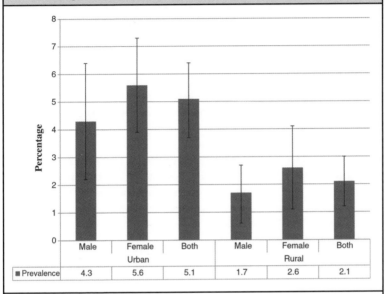

	Male	Female	Both	Male	Female	Both
		Urban			Rural	
■ Prevalence	4.3	5.6	5.1	1.7	2.6	2.1

Commentary: The graph shows the prevalence of diabetes mellitus in the sample population, by residence (urban or rural) and sex, with 95% confidence interval error bars. The true prevalence in the target population for any category will lie within the error bar 95% of the time.

Scenario 19

Dr Wilson returned from his lunch break with renewed vigour. He had just read the conclusion of a trial on the treatment of ear infections. 500 children were given a new antibiotic, zapitillin, and compared with 500 children who were given his usual choice, amoxicillin. In the zapitillin arm, 240 out of 300 children who completed the study improved (80%). In the amoxicillin arm, 300 out of 400 children who completed the study improved (75%). He sent a copy of the paper to his colleague, proposing that zapitillin be the first-choice antibiotic in the hospital formulary.

In most studies some of the subjects who participate in a trial do not make it to the end of the trial. There are many reasons why such **drop-outs** occur, including death, loss to follow-up (subjects who cannot be contacted or who have moved out of the study area), voluntary withdrawal from the trial and non-compliance with the trial conditions. Some subjects might also not be able to take the treatments offered to them in the trial.

Ideally, researchers should account for all the subjects who were eligible and started the trial, and explain the reasons behind subjects not finishing the trial. This may be depicted in a flow diagram or table. The CONSORT 2010 flow diagram shown Figure 34 has been adopted by many medical journals[1]. Flow diagrams should be studied closely to make sure the numbers add up.

---

1   Schulz et al. CONSORT 2010 Statement: updated guidelines for reporting parallel group randomised trials. *BMC Medicine* 2010; 8: 18.

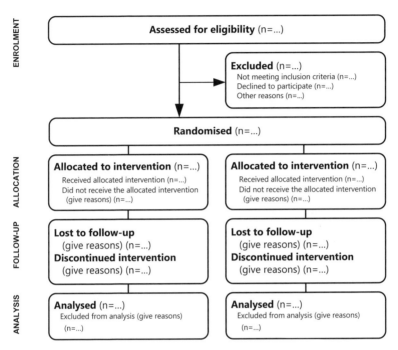

Figure 34 CONSORT 2010 flow diagram – adapted from Schulz et al. BMC Medicine 2010; 8: 18

It is important to understand the flow of subjects through the trial because incidence, prevalence and success rate calculations give different results depending on which numbers are used. **SEE EXCERPT 42**

Per-protocol (PP) analysis

In a **per-protocol** or **on-treatment analysis** only data from those subjects who complied with the trial protocol through to completion are considered in the analysis (Figure 35). The researchers ignore subjects who violated the trial protocol, for example, through non-compliance, switching groups or missing measurements[1]. **SEE EXCERPT 42**

The advantage of this **explanatory approach** is that it shows how things might be if processes are completed and gives an indication of the true effect of a treatment. The disadvantage of this method is that it can introduce bias

1   Gupta SK. Intention-to-treat concept: A review. *Perspectives in Clinical Research* 2011; 2(3): 109–12.

related to excluding subjects from analysis (attrition or exclusion bias) – the results and conclusions can be misleading and important effects of the intervention (eg intolerable side-effects) can be lost. Often the subjects who are not accounted for are the ones who failed to improve.

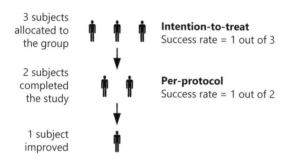

Figure 35 Per-protocol analysis versus intention-to-treat analysis

Intention-to-treat (ITT) analysis

In an **intention-to-treat analysis** all the subjects randomised are included in the analyses as members of the groups to which they are allocated, regardless of whether they completed the study or not (Figure 35)[1].

The intention-to-treat method is also known as the **pragmatic approach**. Success rates based on intention-to-treat analyses tend to mirror the results seen in real-life practice. As a result, the intention-to-treat analysis is usually considered as the analysis of choice. Whereas a per-protocol analysis tends to enhance any difference between the different groups in a study, an intention-to-treat analysis tends to produce more conservative results. **SEE EXCERPT 43**

Steps to achieve an intention-to-treat analysis should be considered in both the design and conduct of a trial. In some studies, an active run-in phase is introduced at the start of the study and this can help identify subjects who are likely to drop out. During the trial, continuing clinical support should be available to all subjects. In studies that have an anticipated high drop-out rate, the drop-out event itself should be considered as an important endpoint.

Handling missing data

If drop-outs occur in a study that is using intention-to-treat analysis, the

1   Gupta SK. Intention-to-treat concept: A review. *Perspectives in Clinical Research* 2011; 2(3): 109–12.

researchers have to decide how to include these subjects in the analysis. Data may have been collected up to the point at which these subjects left the trial, but the data that would have been collected at the end of the trial for these subjects are missing. In this situation, results can be imputated. In **imputation**, missing data are substituted to allow the data analysis to proceed. Imputation can be implemented using a variety of methods, none of which is perfect.

- In a **worst-case scenario analysis**, subjects who drop out are treated as failures and recorded as having the worst outcome possible. This is the most cautious and pessimistic approach. This is the assumption being made in Figure 35 – even if subjects were better by the time they prematurely left the study, they are treated as failures when the final results are calculated. **SEE EXCERPT 44**

- In **hot deck imputation**, values from similar subjects with complete records (the donors) can be used to fill in missing values in the drop-outs[1].

- In **last observation carried forward (LOCF)**, the last recorded results of subjects who drop out are carried forward to the end of the trial and incorporated into the final analysis of the results. **SEE EXCERPT 45**

- In a **sensitivity analysis**, assumptions are made when the missing values are put in. Sensitivity analyses can also be carried out to include different scenarios of assumptions, such as the worst-case and best-case scenarios. Worst-case scenario sensitivity analysis is performed by assigning the worst outcomes to the missing patients in the group who show the best results. These results are then compared with the initial analysis, which excludes the missing data.

It is important to establish whether the reasons drop-outs are no longer taking part are in some way attributable to the intervention.

The pitfalls of using LOCF

The use of 'last observation carried forward' can lead to underestimation or overestimation of treatment effects. Figure 36 shows the result of treating a depressed patient with an antidepressant. Over the trial, the patient's depressive symptoms improve gradually, so that at the end of the trial they were less depressed than at the start.

1   Andridge RR, Little RJA. A review of hot deck imputation for survey non-response. *Int Stat Rev.* 2010; 78(1): 40–64.

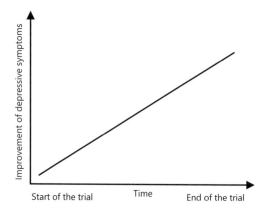

Figure 36 The result of treating a depressed patient with an antidepressant

If a different individual dropped out of the study at an early stage and the last observation was carried forward, the results could underestimate the true effect of the antidepressant, which would have been apparent had the individual completed the trial (Figure 37). The risk of making a type 2 error is increased (see page 181).

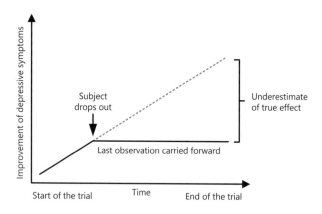

Figure 37 Underestimation of a treatment effect

Overestimation of a treatment effect can occur with 'last observation carried forward' in conditions that normally deteriorate with time. Figure 38 shows the results of the Mini Mental State Examination (MMSE) score of a dementing individual who is being treated with an anti-dementia drug. Over the trial, their dementia will progress, but at a slower rate with treatment.

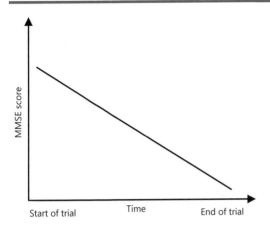

Figure 38 Decline in the Mini Mental State Examination (MMSE) score

If a different individual drops out of the trial at an early stage, the effects of the anti-dementia drug in delaying the progression of dementia might be overstated (Figure 39). The risk of making a type 1 error is increased (see page 180).

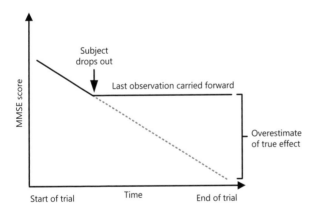

Figure 39 Overestimation of a treatment effect

EXCERPT 42

Adapted from: Rusu E et al. Effects of lifestyle changes including specific dietary intervention and physical activity in the management of patients with chronic hepatitis C – a randomized trial. *Nutrition Journal* 2013; 12: 119.

The objective of this study was to compare a normoglucidic low-calorie diet with a low-fat diet among participants with chronic hepatitis C.

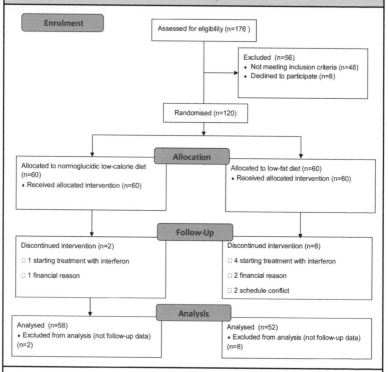

Commentary: In this CONSORT flowchart the number of subjects analysed in each arm is less than the number randomised to each arm. Subjects who dropped out of the study were not analysed – an example of a per-protocol analysis.

EXCERPT 43

Adapted from: Chen W-J et al. Employing crisis postcards with case management in Kaohsiung, Taiwan: 6-month outcomes of a randomised controlled trial for suicide attempters. *BMC Psychiatry* 2013; 13: 191.

The aim of this study was to evaluate the effectiveness of case management of suicidal patients using crisis postcards. The postcards contained coping information.

We assessed 1,218 participants for eligibility, of whom 457 failed to give consent, leaving 761 participants – 388 in the control group and 373 in the intervention group. The ITT analysis showed no effect for the crisis postcard (HR = 0.84; 95% CI = 0.56–1.29), but the per-protocol analysis showed a strong benefit for the crisis postcard (HR = 0.39; 95% CI = 0.21–0.72).

Commentary: This excerpt illustrates the importance of knowing how success rates are calculated. The authors noted, 'Although the per-protocol analysis showed a strong benefit for the crisis postcard, the primary finding of the present study was that the crisis postcard intervention did not significantly reduce subsequent suicidal behaviour in the intention-to-treat analysis. Excluding non-adherent suicide attempters might introduce bias because suicide attempters who adhered to treatments tend to have better outcome regardless of whether the treatment was effective.'

EXCERPT 44

Adapted from: Kramer JJAM et al. Effectiveness of a web-based self-help smoking cessation intervention: protocol of a randomised controlled trial. *BMC Public Health* 2009; 9: 32.

The aim of this study is to investigate the effectiveness of a web-based interactive self-help programme for smoking cessation, known as the StopSite, by comparing it to an online self-help guide. Both interventions were based on cognitive-behavioural and self-control principles, but the former provided exercises, feedback and interactive features such as one-to-one chatrooms and a user forum, which facilitated mutual support and experience sharing.

We then performed intention-to-treat (ITT) analyses including all randomised participants and classifying those not responding to follow-up questionnaires as smokers (the worst-case scenario); this is a conservative way of handling non-response.

Commentary: An intention-to-treat analysis was used in the study. Subjects who did not complete the study were given the worst possible result – that they were still smoking and therefore treatment failures.

EXCERPT 45

Adapted from: Girlanda F et al. Effectiveness of lithium in subjects with treatment-resistant depression and suicide risk: results and lessons of an underpowered randomised clinical trial. *BMC Research Notes* 2014; 7: 731.

Researchers investigated the use of lithium to reduce the risk of deliberate self-harm in adult patients with unipolar affective disorders. Patients were assessed at baseline and then every month after random allocation until the completion of the 12-month follow-up

Patients with missing values and lost during follow-up contributed to the analysis of the primary and secondary outcomes. Missing values in depressive symptom ratings were imputed using the last observation carried forward (LOCF) approach: depressive ratings were carried forward from the last available assessment to the 12-month follow-up assessment. Additionally, patients in each arm were always analysed according to the corresponding treatment group's allocation at baseline.

Commentary: An example of last observation carried forward to fill in missing values. The last depressive rating was carried forward to the 12-month follow-up assessment for subjects who were lost to follow-up.

Scenario 19 revisited

Dr Wilson's colleague read the paper too, but came to a different conclusion. He emailed Dr Wilson, 'I disagree with the conclusions the researchers have drawn. Five hundred patients were enrolled into each arm of the study. I worked out that the results did not take into account the drop-outs in both arms. Intention-to-treat analysis shows that amoxicillin gave better results, with 300 out of 500 children improving (60%). In contrast, only 240 children improved with zapitillin (48%). I won't be prescribing zapitillin unless the child has an allergy to amoxicillin, but thanks for drawing my attention to the paper.'

COMPARING GROUPS: RISKS AND ODDS

Risk: In clinical research, risk has the same meaning as probability. Risk is the probability of something happening. Risk is the number of times an event is likely to occur divided by the total number of events possible. It is expressed as P and is presented either as a number between 0 and 1 or as a percentage:

If 1 out of 6 people fall ill, the risk of falling ill is $1/6 = 0.167 = 16.7\%$

Odds: Odds is also another way of expressing chance. The odds is the ratio of the number of times an event is likely to occur divided by the number of times it is likely not to occur. This is expressed as a ratio or fraction:

If 1 out of 6 people fall ill, the odds of falling ill is $1/5 = 0.2$

Contingency tables

When comparing risks and odds across two groups, the first step is to tabulate the study results in a contingency table, also known as a 2 × 2 table (Table 10). The contingency table consists of rows and columns of cells. Cells a, b, c and d are the 2 × 2 table; the other cells help to make sense of the table.

Contingency tables can be a source of confusion because there are different ways of displaying the same information. Always maintain a consistent approach by having the exposure (to a risk factor or intervention) across the rows and the outcome event status down the columns. The 'exposure positive' row is the experimental group and is always above the 'exposure negative' row which is the control group. The 'outcome event' always refers to the worst outcome, such as death, relapse or an increase in symptoms.

| | | OUTCOME EVENT | | Totals |
		yes	no	
EXPOSURE	positive	a	b	a + b
	negative	c	d	c + d
Totals		a + c	b + d	a + b + c + d

Table 10 Generic 2 × 2 contingency table

Example 1: In a cohort study, 100 subjects are exposed to cigarette smoking and 75 subjects are not exposed to smoking. At the end of the study, 27 subjects in the smoking group developed cancer. Only four subjects in the non-smoking group developed cancer.

The steps to complete a 2×2 table (see *Table 11*) are:

- The rows are labelled 'smoking' (exposure), positive or negative.
- The columns are labelled 'cancer' (worst outcome event), yes or no.
- 100 subjects were exposed to cigarette smoking so $a + b = 100$.
- 75 subjects were not exposed to smoking, so $c + d = 75$.
- In the smoking group, 27 subjects developed the worst outcome, so $a = 27$.
- In the non-smoking group, four subjects developed the worst outcome, so $c = 4$.
- $b = 100 - 27 = 73$ subjects developed the best outcome in the smoking group.
- $d = 75 - 4 = 71$ subjects developed the best outcome in the non-smoking group.

		CANCER		Totals
		yes	no	
SMOKING	positive	27 (a)	73 (b)	100
	negative	4 (c)	71 (d)	75
Totals		31	144	175

Table 11 Completed 2×2 contingency table for Example 1

Care needs to be exercised so that the 2×2 table is completed correctly. **Some studies will report the best outcome figures, in which case the values in cells *b* and *d* are given.** If the wrong values are placed in the cells, the calculated results will be wrong – treatments will appear harmful and risk factors will appear beneficial.

Example 2: In a randomised controlled trial of an analgesic, 28/37 subjects improved on the new treatment and 12/30 subjects improved in the placebo arm.

The steps to complete a 2×2 table (see *Table 12*) are:

- The rows are labelled 'new treatment' (exposure), positive or negative.
- The columns are labelled 'pain' (worst outcome event), yes or no.
- 37 subjects were exposed to the new treatment, so $a + b = 37$.
- 30 subjects were not exposed to the new treatment, so $c + d = 30$.
- In the treatment group, 28 subjects developed the best outcome, so $b = 28$.
- In the placebo group, 12 subjects developed the best outcome, so $d = 12$.
- In the treatment group, nine subjects ($37 - 28$) developed the worst outcome, so $a = 9$.
- In the placebo group, 18 subjects ($30 - 12$) developed the worst outcome, so $c = 18$.

		PAIN		Totals
		yes	no	
NEW TREATMENT	positive	9 (a)	28 (b)	37
	negative	18 (c)	12 (d)	30
Totals		27	40	67

Table 12 Completed 2×2 contingency table for Example 2

Other aspects of risk can be derived from the 2×2 contingency table (*Table 13*).

	FORMULA
Control event rate (CER) (absolute risk of outcome in control group)	$\dfrac{c}{c + d}$
Experimental event rate (EER) (absolute risk of outcome in experimental group)	$\dfrac{a}{a + b}$
Absolute risk reduction (ARR)	$CER - EER$
Relative risk (RR)	$\dfrac{EER}{CER}$
Relative risk reduction (RRR)	$\dfrac{CER - EER}{CER}$
Number needed to treat (NNT)	$\dfrac{1}{ARR}$
Odds of outcome in experimental group	$\dfrac{a}{b}$
Odds of outcome in control group	$\dfrac{c}{d}$
Odds ratio	$\dfrac{a/b}{c/d} = \dfrac{ad}{bc}$

Table 13 Derivation of other aspects of risk and odds from the 2×2 contingency table

Absolute risk

Absolute risk is the incidence rate of the outcome. Remember that the outcome is the worst outcome.

$$\text{control event rate (CER)} = \text{risk in subjects not exposed} = \frac{c}{c + d}$$

$$\text{experimental event rate (EER)} = \text{risk in subjects exposed} = \frac{a}{a + b}$$

The absolute risk can be expressed as a percentage.

- If the CER = 0.8, then 0.8 or 80% of subjects in the control group will get the outcome.
- If the EER = 0.4, then 0.4 or 40% of subjects in the experimental group will get the outcome.

SEE EXCERPT 46 AND EXCERPT 48

Absolute risk reduction

The absolute risk reduction (ARR) is the actual drop in risk going from the control group to the experimental group:

absolute risk reduction $= CER - EER$

The absolute risk reduction is also known as the **absolute benefit increase** (ABI).

- If CER = 0.8 and EER = 0.4, then ARR = 0.4, which means the experimental group has a risk of the outcome which is 0.4 or 40 percentage points lower than the risk of the outcome in the control group.

SEE EXCERPT 46 AND EXCERPT 48

Relative risk

The relative risk (RR) or 'risk ratio' is the ratio of the risk of the outcome in the experimental group to the risk of the outcome in the control group.

relative risk $= \dfrac{EER}{CER}$

- If the relative risk is equal to 1, there is **no risk difference** between the groups.
- If the relative risk is greater than 1, there is an **increased risk** of the outcome in the experimental group.
- If the relative risk is less than 1, there is a **reduced risk** of the outcome in the experimental group.

These explanations are assuming a standard 2×2 table is being used, with the outcome being the worst outcome.

- If the relative risk = 2, the risk of the outcome in the experimental group is twice the risk in the control group. The experimental group is doing worse than the control group.

- If the relative risk = 0.5, the risk of the outcome in the experimental arm is half the risk in the control group. The experimental group is doing better than the control group.

SEE EXCERPT 47

Note that absolute risks are more useful than relative risks. Relative risk values can be impressive even when the underlying absolute risk reductions are very small. See *Figure 40* for an example.

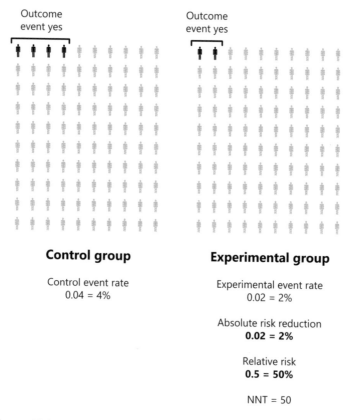

Figure 40 An impressive relative risk figure (50%) but very small absolute risk values (2% reduction)

Relative risk reduction

Relative risk reduction (RRR) is the drop in the risk of the outcome in the experimental group, expressed as a proportion of the risk in the control group.

$$\text{relative risk reduction} = \frac{CER - EER}{CER}$$

The relative risk reduction is also known as the **relative benefit increase** (RBI).

- If the CER = 0.8 and the EER = 0.4, then the RRR = 50% (risk reduces by 50% of the CER risk).
- If the CER = 0.8 and the EER = 0.6, then the RRR = 25% (risk reduces by 25% of the CER risk).

SEE EXCERPT 48

Number needed to treat

When comparing two interventions, the number needed to treat (NNT) is the number of subjects who must be treated with the intervention, compared with the control, for one additional subject to experience the beneficial outcome. It is the reciprocal of the absolute risk reduction between two interventions. The lower the value of NNT the better. The minimum value for NNT is 1; the maximum value is infinity. **SEE EXCERPT 46 AND EXCERPT 48**

$$\text{number needed to treat} = \frac{1}{ARR}$$

- If NNT = 8, for every eight patients in the experimental group, one additional person gets the beneficial outcome.

NNTs are easy to interpret but comparisons between NNTs can only be made if the baseline risks are the same. There is no cut-off level for guidance.

The NNH is the **number needed to harm**. This is the number of subjects treated for one extra subject to have the adverse outcome, compared with control intervention. Smaller NNH values are worse (ie harm is more frequent).

NNTs and NNHs should be reported as whole numbers. NNTs should be rounded up to the next whole number and NNHs should be rounded down.

The NNH:NNT ratio is indicative of the risk/benefit ratio.

Odds ratio

Odds ratio (OR) is an alternative way of comparing how likely outcomes are between two groups.

The odds ratio is the ratio of the odds of having the outcome in the experimental group relative to the odds of having the outcome in the control group.

It is used in cross-sectional studies and case–control studies. In a case–control study, the exposure is often the presence or absence of a risk factor for a disease, and the outcome is the presence or absence of the disease.

$$\text{odds ratio} = \frac{ad}{bc}$$

- An odds ratio of 1.0 (or unity) reflects exactly the same outcome rates in both groups, ie **no effect**.
- An odds ratio greater than 1 indicates that the estimated likelihood of developing the outcome is **greater** among those in the experimental arm.
- An odds ratio less than 1 indicates that the estimated likelihood of developing the outcome is **less** among those in the experimental arm.

SEE EXCERPT 49

If a 'log odds ratio' is given in the clinical paper, remember that a log odds ratio of zero reflects the same outcome rates in both groups, not the value 1.

Interpreting negative results

If the 2 × 2 table is formatted as recommended above, with the outcome event being the worst outcome possible, some results may be negative numbers.

Negative results are interpreted as follows:

A *negative* absolute risk reduction is interpreted as an **absolute risk increase**.

- Absolute risk reduction = –0.5 is an absolute risk increase = 0.5

A *negative* relative risk reduction is interpreted as a **relative risk increase**.

- Relative risk reduction = –0.3 is a relative risk increase = 0.3

A *negative* number needed to treat is interpreted as a **number needed to harm**.

- Number needed to treat = –4 is a number needed to harm = 4 ie there is one additional harmful outcome for every 4 patients.

EXCERPT 46

Adapted from: MacPherson H et al. Acupuncture for irritable bowel syndrome: primary care based pragmatic randomised controlled trial. *BMC Gastroenterology* 2012; 12: 150.

Researchers evaluated the effectiveness of acupuncture for irritable bowel syndrome in primary care when provided as an adjunct to usual care. Symptoms were quantified by the IBS Symptom Severity Score (SSS).

Treatment was assumed 'successful' ($\geq$50 points reduction on IBS SSS) in 57/116 (49%) of patients in the acupuncture group and 36/117 (31%) in those receiving usual care alone, a difference of 18% (95% CI = 6–31%). The number needed to treat was 6 (95% CI = 3–17).

Commentary: The results section gives the figures for the best outcome – a reduction in symptoms. For our calculations we'll need to work out the figures for the worst outcome.
EER (acupuncture group) = 59/116 = 0.509
CER (usual care group) = 81/117 = 0.692
ARR = 0.692 – 0.509 = 0.183 = 18.3%
NNT = 1/0.183 = 5.47 = rounded up to 6

EXCERPT 47

Adapted from: Björkenstam E et al. Associations between number of sick-leave days and future all-cause and cause-specific mortality: a population-based cohort study. *BMC Public Health* 2014; 14: 733.

This study investigated the association between number of sick-leave days and future mortality among women and men.

The relative risks (RR) of all-cause mortality displayed a gradual increase with increasing number of sick-leave days in 1995 among both women and men. In the age-adjusted models, women and men with most sick-leave days (166–365 days), had more than tripled mortality risks; women RR = 3.48; 95% CI = 3.37–3.60 and men RR = 3.29; 95% CI = 3.20–3.39 in comparison with women and men, respectively, without any sick-leave days reimbursed by the Social Insurance Agency in 1995.

Commentary: The relative risk for mortality was given separately for women and men. It was calculated by comparing the risk in those who take most sick leave with those who don't take any sick leave.

EXCERPT 48

Adapted from: Srinivasan MG et al. Zinc adjunct therapy reduces case fatality in severe childhood pneumonia: a randomized double blind placebo-controlled trial. BMC Medicine 2012; 10: 14.

Researchers investigated the effect of zinc adjunct therapy on case fatality of severe childhood pneumonia. In a double blind, randomised, placebo-controlled clinical trial, 352 children aged 6 to 59 months with severe pneumonia were randomised to zinc or a placebo, in addition to standard antibiotics for severe pneumonia.

Case fatality was 7/176 (4.0%) in the zinc group and 21/176 (11.9%) in the placebo group: Relative risk 0.33 (95% CI = 0.15–0.76). Relative risk reduction was 0.67 (95% CI = 0.24–0.85), while the number needed to treat was 13.

Commentary: Fatality was the worst outcome. The experimental event rate was 7/176 = 0.04. The control event rate was 21/176 = 0.119. The absolute risk reduction was 0.119–0.04 = 0.079. The relative risk was 0.33, meaning that children who took zinc had a third of the risk of the worst outcome compared to children who took a placebo. The relative risk reduction was 0.67 or 67%, which is the drop in the risk of the outcome in the experimental group (0.079), expressed as a proportion of the risk in the control group (0.119). The number needed to treat was 13, meaning that for every 13 children treated with zinc compared to every 13 children treated with placebo, there was one additional beneficial outcome in the zinc group.

EXCERPT 49

Adapted from: Zhou W et al. Risk of breast cancer and family history of other cancers in first-degree relatives in Chinese women: a case control study. BMC Cancer 2014; 14: 662.

This study was designed to determine the relationship between breast cancer risk and family history of other cancers in first-degree relatives.

When age, age at menarche, childbearing, and menopause status were adjusted, a significant increase in breast cancer was still observed in subjects with a family history of oesophagus cancer (OR: 2.70, 95% CI = 1.11–6.57), digestive system cancer (OR: 1.79, 95% CI = 1.14–2.79) and any other cancer (OR: 2.13, 95% CI = 1.49–3.04). Additionally, a significantly increased breast cancer risk was observed with a family history of lung cancer (OR: 2.49, 95% CI = 1.10–5.65). No significant increase in breast cancer was observed with a family history of cancer in other systems. Furthermore, no significantly increased breast cancer risk was observed in subjects with two or more family histories of other cancers (OR: 0.76, 95% CI = 0.24–2.47).

Commentary: When the odds of getting breast cancer with the risk factor are higher than the odds when the risk factor is absent, the odds ratio will be greater than one. A confidence interval for an odds ratio that doesn't include the value of no effect (one) indicates statistical significance.

COMPARING GROUPS – THE NULL HYPOTHESIS

The results from two or more groups are often being compared in research. The researcher is interested in finding out if there are any differences between the groups because this could highlight an important role for an exposure, investigation or treatment. Calculating relative risks and odds ratios helps us to compare the groups.

However, **chance** might explain why one group did better than the other. If the study was repeated, the study results might be reversed, with the other group doing better. Therefore, as part of giving the results of a study, the researchers have to decide whether the results may be due to chance. Ideally, the conclusion will be that the role of chance can be rejected, so that similar results will be seen in repeat studies.

To complicate matters, by convention this task is turned on its head, with the researcher initially assuming that any differences are due to chance (Figure 41). The researcher then calculates the value of this chance, hoping to show that it is in fact very unlikely.

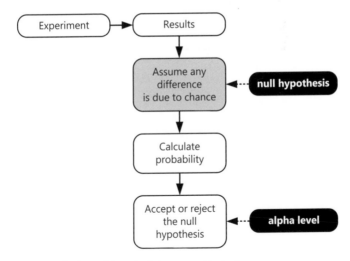

Figure 41 Initially the null hypothesis is assumed to be true

Step 1 – state the null hypothesis

The **null hypothesis** states that any difference observed in the results of two or more groups is due to chance. The null hypothesis is important because it underpins the statistical tests. However, the null hypothesis is rarely stated in clinical papers and should not be confused with the primary hypothesis.

For example, the initial research question might be, 'Does a relationship exist between smoking cannabis and schizophrenia?' The researcher might set up a case–control study to look at past cannabis smoking in a group of patients with schizophrenia and matched controls. The null hypothesis would state that no relationship exists between smoking cannabis and schizophrenia, and that any difference that does occur between the groups is due to chance.

Step 2 – set the alpha level

The researchers have to decide how they will accept or reject the null hypothesis. To do this, they specify how rare a set of results has to be that it is unlikely to be explained by chance (or the null hypothesis). They set a threshold, called the **alpha level (α)** – Figure 42.

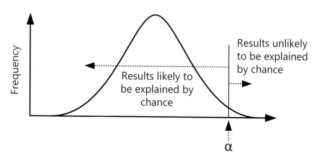

Figure 42 The alpha level is a threshold

By convention, α is usually set to **0.05**. This value of α means that if the null hypothesis is true, the observed results would have occurred by chance at most 5% of the time. Results below this threshold are considered unlikely to occur by chance.

Step 3 – calculate the P value

Probability is the likelihood of any event occurring as a proportion of the total number of possibilities. The probability of an event varies between 0.0 (will never happen) to 1.0 (certain to happen).

P values in clinical papers are probability values and are calculated using statistics. P values express the probability of getting the observed results by chance.

As the P value becomes smaller, the results are less likely to have occurred by chance and are therefore less compatible with the null hypothesis. Eventually the P value is so small that it is below α and the null hypothesis can be rejected – the results are **statistically significant** – Figure 43. The **alternative hypothesis**, which states that the result is not due to chance, is accepted.

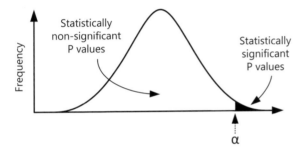

Figure 43 The alpha level and P values

With $\alpha = 0.05$, **a P value of less than 0.05 indicates statistical significance**. $P < 0.05$ means that the probability of obtaining a given result by chance is less than 1 in 20. The text in the paper might express this as, 'The results are significant at the 5% level.'

P values equal to 0.05 or above are statistically non-significant – that is, the null hypothesis is accepted. **SEE EXCERPT 50**

This is summarised in Table 14. P values can be calculated using several statistical techniques.

Remember that setting $\alpha = 0.05$ is an entirely arbitrary convention. There is no other reason that results are statistically significant when $P=0.049$ and not statistically significant when $P = 0.051$.

P < 0.05	P ≥ 0.05
Less than 1 in 20	Equal to or greater than 1 in 20
If α = 0.05, the null hypothesis is rejected	If α = 0.05, the null hypothesis is accepted
The results are statistically significant	The results are statistically non-significant
Evidence of association between variable and outcome	Association between variable and outcome not proved

Table 14 Understanding P values and significance

Step 4 – consider type 1 and type 2 errors

Type 1 and type 2 errors describe the wrongful rejection or acceptance respectively of the null hypothesis.

- Type 1 error – a false positive result; wrongful rejection.
- Type 2 error – a false negative result; wrongful acceptance.

Type 1 errors

A type 1 error occurs when the null hypothesis is true but it is rejected. A **false-positive result** has been recorded because a difference is found between groups when no such difference actually exists.

- Researchers conclude that drinking coffee increases the risk of lung cancer. This is a type 1 error. It is a false positive result. The relationship is not true.

Type 1 errors are usually attributable to bias, confounding or multiple hypothesis testing (data dredging). The possibility of a type 1 error should be considered with every statistically significant finding.

- Drinking coffee may appear to increase the risk of lung cancer but this can be explained by a confounding factor, cigarette smoking. Smoking is associated with coffee drinking and smoking is independently also associated with lung cancer. If the researchers had dealt with this confounding factor, they would have concluded that coffee drinking in itself is not associated with an increased risk of lung cancer.

The alpha level is the threshold at which researchers still accept that the result can be explained by chance. If $\alpha = 0.05$, the researchers are stating that any observations with $P < 0.05$ are a positive result. However, if the null hypothesis turns out to be actually true, results below α would be false positives – Figure 44. Therefore, if the null hypothesis is true, the risk of making a type 1 error is equal to α.

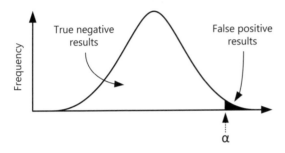

Figure 44 If the null hypothesis is true, the researchers may make a type 1 error

Type 2 errors

A type 2 error occurs when the null hypothesis is false but it is accepted. The study has returned a **false-negative** result after failing to uncover a difference between the groups that actually exists.

- Researchers conclude that smoking cigarettes does not increase the risk of lung cancer. This is a type 2 error. It is a false negative result. The relationship exists but was not uncovered in the study.

Type 2 errors usually happen because the sample size is too small and/or the measurement variance is too large. The possibility of a type 2 error should be considered with every non-significant finding.

The alpha level is the threshold at which researchers still accept that the result can be explained by chance. If $\alpha = 0.05$, the researchers are stating that any observations with $P < 0.05$ are a positive result. However, if the null hypothesis turns out to be actually false, only results below α would be correct (true positives) – Figure 45. Every other result would be incorrect (false negatives). Therefore, if the null hypothesis is false, the risk of making a type 2 error is denoted by β which is equal to $(1 - \alpha)$.

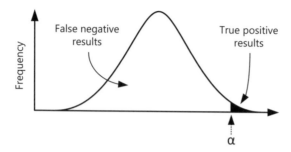

Figure 45 If the null hypothesis is false, the researchers may make a type 2 error

At the design stage of the study researchers carry out **power** calculations that give an indication of how many subjects are required in the sample to minimise the risk of making a type 2 error.

Figure 46 and Table 15 summarise the discussion so far.

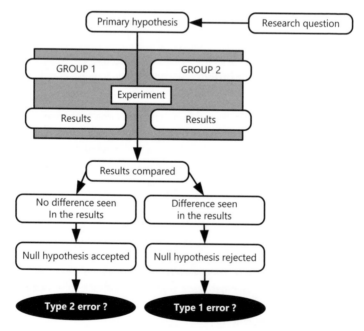

Figure 46 The null hypothesis, type 1 error and type 2 error

		NULL HYPOTHESIS	
		True	False
EXPERIMENTAL RESULT	Significant	Type 1 error	Correct
	Not significant	Correct	Type 2 error

Table 15 Type 1 and 2 errors

Sample size and power

The sample size of a study is usually determined by a power calculation.

Power is defined as the probability that a type 2 error will not be made in the study. It is a measure of the study's ability to detect the smallest possible difference between the groups that is considered clinically worthwhile, if such a difference exists. As a general rule, the larger the sample size of a study, the more power the study is said to have.

The value of power ranges from 0 to 1. **A power of 0.8 is generally accepted as being adequate in most research studies.** A study with a power of 0.8 means there is an 80% probability of finding a significant difference with a given sample size, if such a difference exists. A study with a power of 0.8 accepts a 20% chance of missing a real difference, ie a type 2 error. The risk of making a type 2 error can be reduced by using a higher value of power but then there has to be a corresponding increase in sample size – and that quickly causes recruitment problems.

Conversely, an inadequate sample size may mean the study is **underpowered** and fails to detect even large treatment effects. The key to avoiding type 2 errors is to power the study adequately. In new clinical fields, pilot studies might be carried out to estimate the difference in outcomes between experimental and control groups in order to inform a power calculation. Sometimes studies in progress are double-checked by performing an interim analysis.

Power calculations are done at the start of the study. The determinants of power are:

- The α level that is set. Power is increased with larger α levels because a type 1 error is more likely.
- The **sample size**. Power is increased with larger sample sizes.
- The **variability of the outcome measure**, as defined by its standard deviation. Power is increased as the variability decreases.

- The **minimum clinically significant difference**. Power is increased with larger clinically significant differences. This difference can be given as a difference in means or proportions. When it is expressed as a multiple of the standard deviations of the observations it is called the standardised difference.

The probability of rejecting the null hypothesis when a true difference exists is represented as $1 - \beta$. Typically, β is arbitrarily set at 0.2, meaning that a study has 80% power (0.8 of a chance) to detect a specified degree of difference at a specified degree of significance.

Power calculations can also be used to calculate the minimum effect size that is likely to be detected in a study using a given sample size and power.

A cautious researcher may recruit more subjects than is absolutely required by a power calculation, to maintain adequate numbers in the trial even if some subjects drop out. **SEE EXCERPT 51**

A power calculation can also be used to discourage researchers from recruiting too many subjects, however, bearing in mind that the excess subjects might be allocated to an inferior or ineffective intervention arm.

One-tailed versus two-tailed tests

Researchers set the alpha level to specify how rare a set of results has to be that it is unlikely to be explained by the null hypothesis.

In a **one-tailed test**, there is only one direction of interest. The α level is set to test statistical significance in one direction (Figure 47). The possibility that the results may be in the opposite direction is disregarded. **SEE EXCERPT 52**

For example, researchers may collect data from two groups. In a one-tailed test the researchers test whether the result in one group is significantly higher than the other group **or** significantly lower than the other group, but not both. If the α level is set to 0.05, a result which lies in the top 5% or bottom 5% of the distribution (depending on which direction of interest is chosen) will be statistically significant.

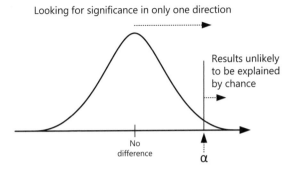

Figure 47 One-tailed test

In a **two-tailed test**, there are two directions of interest. The α level is split between the upper and lower tails in order to test statistical significance in two directions (Figure 48). The possibility of results in either direction is acknowledged.

For example, researchers may collect data from two groups. In a two-tailed test the researchers test whether the result in one group is significantly higher or lower than the other group. If the α level is set to 0.05, a result which lies in the top 2.5% or bottom 2.5% of the distribution will be statistically significant.

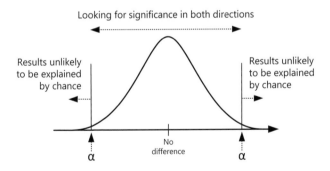

Figure 48 Two-tailed test

Compared to a two-tailed test, a one-tailed test has more power to detect a difference in one direction because it disregards the other direction. However, most analyses use two-tailed tests as the researchers are not sure in which direction the results will be.

A one-tailed test should only be used if a result in one direction is not possible or can be disregarded. **SEE EXCERPT 52**.

Bonferroni correction

Earlier in this chapter it was stated that α is usually set to 0.05. This value of α means that if the null hypothesis is true, the observed results would have occurred by chance 5% of the time, or 1 in 20.

Although results below this threshold are considered unlikely to occur by chance, they will occur 1 in 20 times by chance. This has serious implications:

- If 20 studies are done, one study will have a statistically significant test result by chance. This underlines the importance of repeating studies to confirm results.

- If one study includes 20 tests, one test will be statistically significant by chance. That is, the more tests that are done, the more likely it is that a type 1 error will occur. This underlines the importance of minimising the number of tests conducted in a study.

The **Bonferroni correction** safeguards against multiple tests of statistical significance on the same data, which might falsely give the appearance of significance. It does this by making it harder to reach statistical significance. This is done by lowering the value of α so that lower P values are required for statistical significance.

A Bonferroni correction can be implemented by dividing the value of α by the number of tests[1]. For example, if a study involves 20 tests, the α value becomes $0.05/20 = 0.0025$. This α value is harder to reach, making it harder to reach statistical significance by chance. **SEE EXCERPT 53**

If the Bonferroni correction is excessive, it may reduce the risk of making a type 1 error but it will increase the risk of making a type 2 error.

Clinical significance

Statistical significance as shown by P values is not the same as **clinical significance**. Statistical significance judges whether treatment effects are explicable as chance findings. Clinical significance assesses whether treatment effects are worthwhile in real life. Small improvements that are statistically significant might not result in any meaningful improvement clinically, for example.

Confidence intervals and significance

A significance result can be deduced from comparing the confidence intervals associated with the summary statistics from two groups. A confidence interval is

---

1   http://mathworld.wolfram.com/BonferroniCorrection.html. Accessed 10 October 2014

normally the range of values around a summary statistic in which we are 95% sure the population summary statistic lies.

- When comparing two groups, if the confidence intervals do not overlap this is equivalent to a significant result.
- If the confidence intervals overlap but one summary statistic is not within the confidence interval of the other, the result might be significant.
- If the confidence intervals overlap and the summary statistics are within the confidence interval of the other, the result is not significant.

Which is better – a confidence interval or a P value? Both can indicate statistical significance. The P value provides a measure of the strength of an association. The confidence interval indicates the magnitude of an effect and likely clinical implications because it indicates a range of possible values for the true effect in the target population.

Larger studies will in general result in narrower confidence intervals and smaller P values, and this should be taken into account when interpreting the results from statistical analyses.

EXCERPT 50

Adapted from: Gou S et al. Use of probiotics in the treatment of severe acute pancreatitis: a systematic review and meta-analysis of randomized controlled trials. *Critical Care* 2014; 18: R57.

Necrotic tissue infection can worsen the prognosis of severe acute pancreatitis, and probiotics have been shown to be beneficial in reducing the infection rate in animal experiments and primary clinical trials. This study systematically reviewed and quantitatively analysed all randomised controlled trials with regard to important outcomes in patients with predicted severe acute pancreatitis who received probiotics.

Six trials comprising an aggregate total of 536 patients were analysed. Systematic analysis showed that probiotics did not significantly affect:
– the pancreatic infection rate (RR = 1.19, 95% CI = 0.74–1.93; P = 0.47),
– total infections (RR = 1.09, 95% CI = 0.80–1.48; P = 0.57),
– operation rate (RR = 1.42, 95% CI = 0.43–3.47; P = 0.71),
– length of hospital stay (MD = 2.45, 95% CI = −2.71 to 7.60; P = 0.35) or
– mortality (RR = 0.72, 95% CI = 0.42–1.45; P = 0.25).

Commentary: In all the analyses the P values were not below the threshold for statistical significance. In all the results the confidence intervals included the value of no effect or no difference.

EXCERPT 51

Adapted from: Weight loss among female health care workers- a 1-year workplace based randomized controlled trial in the FINALE-health study. *BMC Public Health* 2012; 12: 625.

This study evaluated an intervention aiming to achieve a 12 months weight loss among overweight health care workers.

A power calculation was carried out based on weight change to ensure a copious amount of participants in the intervention and the reference group. Power was set to 0.8 with a significant level of 0.05. At least 30 participants in each group were needed to detect a difference in weight loss of at least 3 kg. With an estimated 30% drop out, 43 participants were needed in each group.

Commentary: An example of a power calculation to determine the sample size. The significance level was set to 0.05. The researchers expected a difference in weight loss between the groups of 3 kg. For a power of 0.8 they needed 30 subjects in each group. They recruited more to take account of an expected 30% drop out rate.

EXCERPT 52

Adapted from: Laiou E et al. The effects of laryngeal mask airway passage simulation training on the acquisition of undergraduate clinical skills: a randomised controlled trial. *BMC Medical Education* 2011; 11: 57.

The purpose of this study was to compare the effectiveness of two laryngeal mask airway (LMA) placement simulation courses of different durations. Medical students in the control group received brief mannequin training while the intervention group received additional more intensive mannequin training as part of which they repeated LMA insertion until they were proficient.

A one-sided test was used as it was hypothesised that the additional simulation training would not result in poorer skill than brief simulation training.

Commentary: It was assumed that the medical students who received the more intensive training would not do worse that the students who received the brief training. The study looked for a difference in one direction only – did the students who received the more intensive training do better than the control group?

EXCERPT 53

Adapted from: Analysis of the contribution of FTO, NPC1, ENPP1, NEGR1, GNPDA2 and MC4R genes to obesity in Mexican children. *BMC Medical Genetics* 2013; 14: 21.

In this study the association of six European obesity-related single nucleotide polymorphisms (SNPs) in or near FTO, NPC1, ENPP1, NEGR1, GNPDA2 and MC4R genes with risk of obesity was tested. Also assessed were the effects of these SNPs on the variation of body mass index (BMI), fasting serum insulin levels, fasting plasma glucose levels, total cholesterol and triglyceride levels.

By applying Bonferroni correction, a significant P value has been considered when below 1.4×10^{-3} (0.05/36).

Commentary: The researchers tested the effect of 6 polymorphisms on 6 different variables, making a total of 36 analyses. They adjusted the P value for statistical significance by applying a Bonferroni correction, dividing the standard value of P (0.05) by the number of analyses they wanted to do (36), to give the final value of P for statistical significance (1.4×10^{-3}).

COMPARING SAMPLES – STATISTICAL TESTS

Samples are compared using a variety of statistical tests. Not all statistical tests can be used with all data sets. The determining factors are the number of samples compared, the type of data in the samples, the distribution of the samples and whether the data are paired or unpaired.

Unpaired data refers to data from groups which have different subjects. Here the selection of the subjects for one group must not be influenced by or related to the selection of the other group. **Paired data** refers to data from the same individuals at different time points.

Table 16 summarises the statistical tests that can be used when the types of data collected from the groups are the same. These statistical tests generate values which are given with associated P values. The P values help you to decide whether to accept or reject the null hypothesis.

As many biological variables are normally distributed, the *t* test is a popular statistical test for comparing two sets of data.

	CATEGORICAL DATA	NON-NORMAL DATA	NORMAL DATA
One sample compared with a hypothetical sample	Chi-squared test Fisher's exact test (small sample)	Sign test Wilcoxon's signed rank test	One-sample t test
Comparing two groups of data	Chi-squared test (unpaired) Fisher's exact test (unpaired, small sample) McNemar's test (paired)	Mann–Whitney U test (unpaired) (equivalent to the Wilcoxon's rank sum test) Wilcoxon's matched pairs test (paired)	t test (paired or unpaired)
Comparing more than two groups of data	Chi-squared test (unpaired) McNemar's test (paired)	Kruskal–Wallis ANOVA (unpaired) Friedman's test (paired)	One-way ANOVA for unpaired groups Repeated-measures ANOVA for paired groups

Table 16 Summary of statistical tests used for comparing samples

Categorical data

Categorical statistical tests involve the use of contingency tables, also known as 2 × 2 tables (Table 17). Remember that the 'outcome event yes' column always refers to the worst outcome possible, such as death or relapse.

		OUTCOME EVENT		Totals
		yes	no	
EXPOSURE	positive	a	b	a + b
	negative	c	d	c + d
Totals		a + c	b + d	a + b + c + d

Table 17 The format of a 2 × 2 table

The statistical tests used with categorical data are the chi-squared (χ^2) test (unpaired data) and McNemar's test (paired binary data). **SEE EXCERPT 54**

For small-sized samples (fewer than five observations in any cell), Fisher's exact test can be used (Figure 49). Alternatively, the Yates' continuity correction can be used to make the chi-squared statistic have better agreement with Fisher's exact test when the sample size is small.

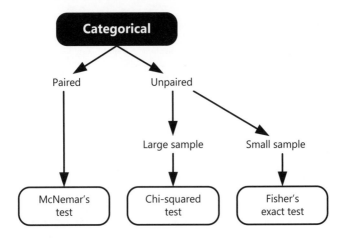

Figure 49 The statistical tests used with categorical data

Degrees of freedom: This is an estimate of the number of independent categories in a particular statistical test or experiment. Dependent categories can be calculated from the independent categories. In the case of a 2×2 contingency table, it is the number of ways in which the results in the table can vary, given the column and row totals. A 2×2 table has two columns and two rows. If the result in one of the row cells is changed, the result in the other row cell can be calculated. Similarly, if the result in one of the column cells is changed, the result in the other column cell can be calculated. Degrees of freedom is therefore:

(number of rows − 1) × (number of columns − 1)

Continuous data

Non-parametric tests, also referred to as 'distribution-free statistics', are used for analysis of non-normally distributed data (Table 18). The most commonly used tests for two independent groups are the Mann–Whitney U test (unpaired data) and Wilcoxon's matched pairs test (for paired data). The most commonly used tests for two or more groups are the Kruskal–Wallis analysis of variance (ANOVA) (for unpaired data) and Friedman's test (paired data) (Figure 50). **SEE EXCERPT 55, EXCERPT 56 AND EXCERPT 57**

The sign test is the simplest of all the non-parametric methods. It is used to compare a single sample with some hypothesised value and it is therefore useful in those situations in which the one-sample t test or paired t test might traditionally be applied.

NON-NORMALLY DISTRIBUTED DATA		
Statistical test	**Data**	**Explanation**
Sign test Wilcoxon's signed rank test	One sample data	The median of the sample is compared with a hypothetical mean
Mann–Whitney U test (equivalent to Wilcoxon's rank sum test)	Two unpaired samples	The median of one sample is compared with the median of another sample
Wilcoxon's matched-pairs test	Two paired samples	The median of one sample is compared with the median of the same sample at a different time point
Kruskal–Wallis ANOVA test	Three or more samples of unpaired data	The medians of samples from three or more groups are compared
Friedman's test	Three or more samples of paired data	The medians of samples from three or more groups are compared

Table 18 Statistical tests and non-normally distributed data

Non-normally distributed data can either be mathematically transformed into a normal-like distribution by taking powers, reciprocals or logarithms of data values or, alternatively, statistical tests can be used that don't have the assumption of normality.

Parametric tests are used for data that are normally distributed (Table 19). **SEE EXCERPT 57**

NORMALLY DISTRIBUTED DATA		
Statistical test	**Data**	**Explanation**
One-sample t test	One sample data	The mean of the sample is compared with a hypothetical mean
t test	Two unpaired samples	The mean of one sample is compared with the mean of another sample
Paired t test	Two paired samples	The mean of one sample is compared with the mean of the same sample at a different time point
Analysis of variance	Three or more samples of unpaired or paired data	The means of samples from three or more groups are compared

Table 19 Statistical tests and normally distributed data

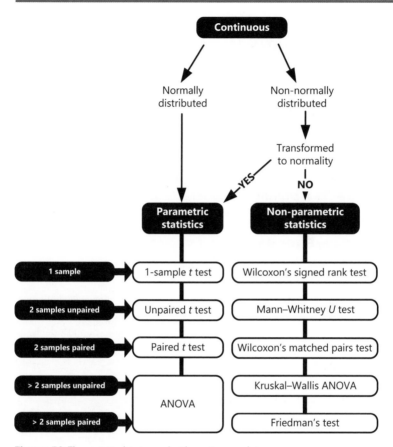

Figure 50 The statistical tests used with continuous data

Analysis of variance (ANOVA)

Instead of doing multiple *t* tests when there are more than two groups to compare in a study and risk making a type 1 error due to multiple hypothesis testing, ANOVA can be used.

ANOVA – Analysis of variance

- One dependent variable which is continuous
- One independent variable which is typically a categorical variable that represents independent groups – usually 3 or more groups
- Example: Does the written exam mark differ between Indian, Pakistani and Chinese students?

There are two main types of ANOVA:

- **One-way ANOVA:** if the independent variable is made up of just one factor. The one-way ANOVA is an extension of the independent two-sample *t* test. Example: Does the written exam mark differ between Indian, Pakistani and Chinese students?

- **Two-way ANOVA:** if the independent variable is made up of two factors. Example: Does the written exam mark differ between the ethnicity of students (Indian, Pakistani and Chinese) and their gender?

ANOVA tells you if there is a statistically significant difference but not where the difference is. The **F-statistic** is the value resulting from the analysis of variance (ANOVA) and determines the P value.

ANCOVA – Analysis of covariance

- Like ANOVA but adjusting for one or more continuous variables called covariates.

- Example: Does the written exam mark differ between Indian, Pakistani and Chinese students, controlling for age? [Note: if we wanted to know the influence of age, eg old versus young students, we could use a two-way ANOVA]

SEE EXCERPT 58

MANOVA – Multivariate analysis of variance

- Like ANOVA but with an additional related dependent variable(s).

- Example: Does the written exam mark and clinical exam mark differ between Indian, Pakistani and Chinese students?

MANCOVA – Multivariate analysis of covariance

- Like ANOVA but with an additional covariate(s) and related dependent variable(s).

- Example: Does the written exam mark and clinical exam mark differ between Indian, Pakistani and Chinese students, controlling for age?

EXCERPT 54

Adapted from: Haji Y et al. Concerns about covert HIV testing are associated with delayed presentation of suspected malaria in Ethiopian children: a cross-sectional study. *Malaria Journal* 2014; 13: 301.

This study tested the hypothesis that guardians' fear of covert human immunodeficiency virus (HIV) testing delays presentation of children with suspected malaria. In the analysis, children were divided into two groups depending on whether or not their guardians had concerns about covert HIV testing. In each group, researchers determined the number of children presenting early or late after the onset of symptoms suggestive of malaria.

The main exposure of interest was the response to the question 'do you think that HIV testing is done for all people who give blood samples for malaria testing at the heath facility?' The time between the onset of symptoms suggestive of malaria to presentation to the health centre was the primary outcome. The outcome variable was categorized into 'early' (≤2 days) and 'late' (≥3 days) as used in previous studies of this topic and also as categorisation using this cut-off approximated to the median value. Initial analysis was by chi-squared testing.

Commentary: An example of the use of the chi-squared test. There were two unpaired groups in this analysis and two possible outcome categories.

EXCERPT 55

Adapted from: Carter EM et al. Predicting length of stay from an electronic patient record system: a primary total knee replacement example. *BMC Medical Informatics and Decision Making* 2014; 14: 26.

Data were extracted from the electronic patient record system for discharges from primary total knee operations at one UK hospital and analysed for their effect on length of stay using Mann–Whitney and Kruskal–Wallis tests for discrete data and Spearman's correlation coefficient for continuous data.

Length of stay is naturally a skewed distribution in most cohorts of patients. Data were analysed on the significant effect on length of stay using the following non-parametric statistical tests: the Mann–Whitney test where only two groups exist, Kruskal–Wallis test where more than two groups exist. Factors found to have a significant effect on length of stay were age, gender, consultant, discharge destination, deprivation and ethnicity.

Commentary: An example of the use of the Mann–Whitney U test and Kruskal–Wallis test for analysing non-normal data.

EXCERPT 56

Adapted from: Hechler T et al. Chronic pain treatment in children and adolescents: less is good, more is sometimes better. *BMC Pediatrics* 2014; 14: 262.

This study aimed to compare outpatient and inpatient treatment of childhood chronic pain in a number of domains, including school absence.

School absence was assessed via parental report on the number of days missed at school within the preceding 20 school days for schoolchildren aged 6 years and above. Days of school missed were categorised into three categories: low (0–1 days missed), moderate (2–5 days missed), and high school absences (more than 5 days missed). Differences between outpatients and inpatients in the distribution of children in the school absence categories were calculated by the use of Mann–Whitney U-tests.

Commentary: An example of the use of non-normal tests to analyse categorical data that can be measured on an ordinal scale.

EXCERPT 57

Adapted from: Vanderlei FM et al. Characteristics and contributing factors related to sports injuries in young volleyball players. *BMC Research Notes* 2013; 6: 415.

The objectives of this study were to identify the characteristics of sports injuries in volleyball players and associate anthropometric and training variables with contributing factors for injuries. A total of 522 volleyball players were interviewed. Those who suffered injuries and those who did not suffer injuries were compared.

For comparison of factors associated with the occurrence of injury the Student's t-test was applied for non-paired data in cases of normal distribution (height) and the Mann–Whitney test for cases in which normal distribution was not found (age, body mass, BMI and duration of training).

Commentary: An example of the use of different statistical tests for analysing normal and non-normal data.

EXCERPT 58

Adapted from: Yaw YH et al. Weight changes and lifestyle behaviors in women after breast cancer diagnosis: a cross-sectional study. *BMC Public Health* 2011; 11: 309.

This study described changes in weight before and after breast cancer diagnosis and examined lifestyle behaviours of breast cancer survivors with stable weight, weight gain or weight loss.

One way analysis of variance (ANOVA) was used to examine weight change according to selected socio-demographic characteristics. The analysis of covariance (ANCOVA) was used to test the differences in dietary intake, and physical activity by weight change groups with household income, years of education, age at diagnosis and time since diagnosis as covariates.

Commentary: An example of the use of ANOVA to look for statistically significant differences in weight change among different socio-demographic groups and the use of ANCOVA to separately examine for statistical significant differences in dietary intake and physical activity between three weight change groups – stable weight, weight gain and weight loss – while controlling for four covariates.

CORRELATION AND REGRESSION

So far, we have described the data from a single sample, inferred population data from data samples and compared samples using the null hypothesis. Sometimes it is necessary to establish the nature of the relationship between two or more variables to see if they are associated.

Correlation

Correlation assesses the **strength** of the relationship between two quantitative variables (Figure 51). It examines whether a linear association exists between two variables, X and Y. X is usually the independent variable and Y is usually the dependent variable.

- A **positive correlation** means that Y increases linearly as X increases.

- A **negative correlation** means that Y decreases linearly as X increases.

- **Zero correlation** reflects a complete non-association between the compared variables.

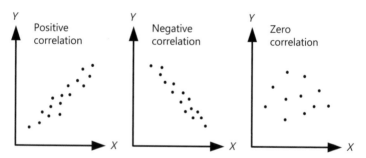

Figure 51 Scatter graphs illustrating three types of correlation

Correlation coefficient

The relationship on a scatter graph can be quantified by the correlation coefficient (r):

- If r is positive the variables are directly related. As one variable increases, so does the other.

- If r is negative the variables are inversely related. As one variable increases, the other decreases.

- *r* has no units.
- The value of *r* varies from −1 to +1:
  - o if *r* = 0 there is no correlation
  - o the closer *r* is to 0, the weaker the correlation
  - o if *r* = −1 or *r* = +1 there is perfect correlation (all the points fall on a line)
  - o the closer *r* is to −1 or +1, the stronger the correlation
  - o *r* is regarded as strong if r < −0.5 or r > 0.5
  - o *r* is not the gradient of the line – the value of *r* reflects both the direction of any relationship and how tight that relationship is.

Correlation coefficients are usually presented with *P* values. The null hypothesis states that there is no correlation. The *P* value is dependent on the strength of the correlation but also the sample size, so a small correlation coefficient can be statistically significant if the sample size is large and vice versa, making interpretation more difficult.

SEE EXCERPT 59

Importantly, correlation coefficients describe **associations**, that two or more variables vary in a related way. Correlation coefficients do not describe causal relationships.

Even when there is a strong correlation between *X* and *Y*, explanations can include any of the following:

- This correlation is a chance finding.
- *X* partly determines the value of *Y*.
- *Y* partly determines the value of *X*.
- The changes in *X* and *Y* are explained by a confounding variable.

There are different types of correlation coefficients. The correlation coefficient used to describe the relationship between two variables depends on the type of data being compared.

Pearson (product moment) correlation coefficient (r): This parametric statistic measures the linear association between two normally distributed variables measured on either an interval or ratio scale. The two variables do not need to be measured on the same scale. It is assumed the variables have a linear relationship[1].

1   Hauke J, Kossowski T. Comparison of values of Pearson's and Spearman's correlation coefficients on the same sets of data. *Quaestiones Geographicae* 2011; 30(2): 88–93.

Spearman's rank correlation (rho, ρ) and Kendall's correlation coefficient (tau, τ): These are non-parametric measures of correlation for ordinal data[1].

Regression

Whereas correlation quantifies the strength of the linear relationship between a pair of variables, regression expresses the relationship between two or more variables in the form of an equation.

The relationship between variables can be represented by the **regression line** on a scatter graph. The regression line is constructed using a **regression equation**. The regression equation has predictive value but it does not prove causality.

Simple linear regression (univariate regression)

Simple linear regression is concerned with describing the linear relationship between a dependent (outcome) variable, Y, and single explanatory (independent or predictor) variable, X.

Where there is one independent variable, the equation of the best fit for the regression line is:

$Y = a + bX$

Y = the value of the dependent variable

a = intercept of the regression line on the Y axis, ie the value of Y when X = 0

b = regression coefficient (slope or gradient of the regression line). If the regression coefficient is positive, there is a positive relationship between X and Y. If the regression coefficient is negative, there is a negative relationship.

X = the value of the independent variable

For a given value of X, a corresponding value of Y can be predicted (see Figure 52). The predicted values should be presented with their 95% confidence intervals to indicate the precision with which they have been estimated.

1   Hauke J, Kossowski T. Comparison of values of Pearson's and Spearman's correlation coefficients on the same sets of data. *Quaestiones Geographicae* 2011; 30(2): 88–93.

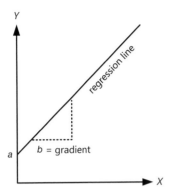

Figure 52 Simple linear regression

SEE EXCERPT 60

Method of least squares

This method determines which line out of several options fits best on a scatter plot. For each line, the vertical distance of each data point from the line is measured and squared. All squared distances are added together to produce a 'sum of squared distances' measure for that line. The eventual linear regression line is determined by finding the line that results in the least 'sum of squared distances'.

Coefficient of determination

In simple linear regression, the square of the correlation coefficient (r^2) is the **coefficient of determination**. This is a goodness-of-fit test. It is a measure of how much of the variation can be explained by the regression equation[1]. The value of r^2 is from 0 to 1. If the regression line on the scatter plot passed through every data point, all the variation would be explained by the regression equation ($r^2 = 1$). The further the data points are from the regression line, the less the regression line is able to explain all the variation and the lower is the value of r^2.

This is useful when interpreting relevance. For example, let's suppose that the correlation between exam revision time and exam mark was found to be 0.8, which would indicate the importance of revision in exam results. In this case $r^2 = 0.8 \times 0.8 = 0.64$. This means that 64% of the variation in exam results was accounted for by this simple linear model. A more complex model,

1   Coefficient   of   determination.   http://en.wikipedia.org/wiki/Coefficient_of_determination. Accessed 10 October 2014.

involving more factors such as inborn intelligence, may be better able to explain all the variation in exam results. The coefficient of determination for more complex models is denoted by R^2.

SEE EXCERPT 61

Multiple linear regression (multivariable regression)

Multiple linear regression is concerned with describing the relationship between a dependent (outcome) variable, Y, and two or more independent variables. The independent variables can be continuous or categorical.

The equation is more complex:

$$Y = a + b_1X_1 + b_2X_2 + ...$$

$a = Y$ when all the independent variables are zero

$b_1, b_2, ...$ = partial regression coefficients for the independent variables

$X_1, X_2, ...$ = value of the independent variables

The partial regression coefficients are calculated by the **least squares method**. This is usually presented along with a 95% confidence interval and a P value. If $P < 0.05$ or the confidence interval does not contain zero, then the independent variable has a significant influence on the dependent variable. As with simple linear regression, the direction of the relationship between each independent variable and the dependent variable is given by the partial regression coefficient.

Stepwise method regression model: The statistically significant independent variables are selected in order of their importance. The regression procedure looks for the independent variable that most correlates with the dependent variable at step one, then searches for the next significant variable, if any, at step two and produces regression data based on those two variables. This continues until all significant variables are entered into the equation; the final step represents the best regression model[1]. Alternatively, in the 'backward stepwise method', all the variables are included at the start and the weakest ones eliminated step by step until the final model is developed[1].

Multiple linear regression is used to assess what effect different variables might have on the study outcome. It is also used to assess the effects of possible confounding factors that may be present in the study.

SEE EXCERPT 61

1   Nardi PM. Chapter 5 Reading regressions. In: *Interpreting Data: A Guide to Understanding Research*. 1st ed. Pearson, 2005.

In a multiple linear regression equation, what is the relative importance of the independent variables in determining the final value of the dependent variable? There are two types of regression coefficients to help us to decide.

- **B** is the un-standardised regression coefficient. It is the slope of the regression line. The B values of independent variables can only be compared if the variables are measured in the same units.

- **Beta (β)** is the regression weight for standardised variables – it is an approach to allow coefficients of variables measured in different units to be compared, by standardising all the variables[1]. Beta values represent the change in the dependent variable (in standard deviations) associated with a change of one standard deviation of an independent variable. The beta values give an indication of the relative weighting of all the independent variables irrespective of their units of measurement. **SEE EXCERPT 62**

Logistic regression
Linear and multiple regression assume that the dependent variable is continuous. Logistic regression is used when we have a binary outcome of interest.

Proportional Cox regression
This is also known as the 'proportional hazards regression' and can be used to determine the influence of variables on survival or on other time-related events. The outcome measure used is not actual survival time. Instead, the concept of hazard rate is used. See also page 237.

Factor analysis
This is a statistical approach that can be used to analyse inter-relationships among a large number of variables and can be used to explain these variables in terms of their common underlying factors.

Cluster analysis
This is a multivariate analysis technique that tries to organise information about variables so that relatively homogeneous groups (clusters) can be formed.

---

1   Standardised coefficients. http://en.wikipedia.org/wiki/Standardized_coefficient. Accessed 10 October 2014.

EXCERPT 59

Adapted from: Becker C et al. CAT correlates positively with respiratory rate and is a significant predictor of the impact of COPD on daily life of patients: a cross sectional study. *Multidisciplinary Respiratory Medicine* 2014; 9: 47.

The COPD Assessment Test (CAT) is a questionnaire designed to measure the impact of COPD. The aim of this study was to evaluate the impact of the disease through the CAT in a sample of COPD patients and to correlate symptoms at rest with the CAT score in these patients.

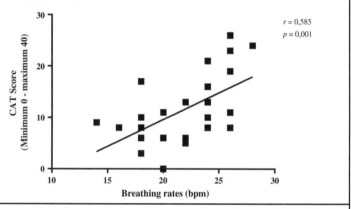

Commentary: The figure shows a positive correlation between breathing rate (breaths per minute) and CAT score. The strength of this correlation is given by the r value.

EXCERPT 60

Adapted from: Sugawara N et al. Effect of age and disease on bone mass in Japanese patients with schizophrenia. *Annals of General Psychiatry* 2012; 11: 5.

The aim of this study was to compare the bone mass of schizophrenia patients with that of healthy subjects in Japan. Bone mass was measured using quantitative ultrasound densitometry of the calcaneus. The osteosono-assessment index (OSI) was calculated as a function of the speed of sound and the transmission index.

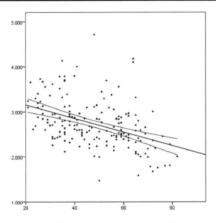

Commentary: This scatterplot depicts the relationship between osteosono-assessment index (OSI) on the vertical axis and age on the horizontal axis for male patients with schizophrenia. A line indicates the slope of best fit with a 95% confidence interval by simple linear regression analysis.

EXCERPT 61

Adapted from: Böhmer AB et al. Factors influencing lengths of stay in the intensive care unit for surviving trauma patients: a retrospective analysis of 30,157 cases. *Critical Care* 2014; 18: R143.

The aim of this study was to investigate to what extent specific factors influenced length of stay (LOS) in intensive care units in surviving trauma patients.

Univariate analysis confirmed the impact of all analysed factors. In subsequent multiple linear regression analyses, coefficients ranged from minus 1.3 to plus 8.2 days. The factors that influenced the prolongation of ICU LOS most were renal failure (+8.1 days), sepsis (+7.8 days) and respiratory failure (+4.9 days). Patients spent one additional day in the ICU for every 5 additional points on the Injury Severity Score (regression coefficient +0.2 per point). Furthermore, massive transfusion (+3.3 days), invasive ventilation (+3.1 days), and an initial Glasgow Coma Scale score ≤8 (+3.0 days) had a significant impact on ICU LOS. The coefficient of determination for the model was 44% (R^2).

Commentary: The researchers confirmed using simple linear regression that all the factors were associated with the length of stay. Using multiple linear regression they were able to put together a model involving several variables that was able to explain nearly half (44%) of the variation in length of stays.

EXCERPT 62

Adapted from: Dias S et al. Health workers' attitudes toward immigrant patients: a cross-sectional survey in primary health care services. *Human Resources for Health* 2012; 10: 14.

This study aimed to examine attitudes of different health workers' groups toward immigrant patients and to identify the associated factors.

A multiple linear regression analysis was used to estimate the relationship between the different [independent] variables and 'attitudes toward immigrant patients'. This [dependent] variable ranges from 1 to 25 (higher scores reflected more positive attitudes). Doctors (beta = 0.895; P = 0.004) and nurses (beta = 0.311; P < 0.001) were more likely to show positive attitudes when compared with office workers. Among doctors, age was significantly associated with attitudes: the older ones had a lower probability of reporting positive attitudes than the younger ones (beta = −0.678; P = 0.030). Workers who have daily contact with three or fewer immigrant patients (beta = 0.258; P = 0.001) and with four to seven (beta = 0.209; P = 0.008) were more likely to report positive attitudes, compared with those workers who had contact with eight or more immigrant patients per day.

Commentary: The researchers were able to elicit the relative importance of the different variables by standardising all the variables and quoting beta values.

Trials can take several months from start to finish. Interim analyses allow researchers to see the results at specific time points before the end of the study. Interim analyses can help to identify flaws in the study design and can help in identifying significant beneficial or harmful effects that may be occurring. This can sometimes result in the study being stopped early for ethical reasons if it is clear that one group is receiving treatment that is more harmful or less beneficial than another.

There is a potential problem with interim analyses. If multiple analyses are performed, positive findings might arise solely by chance and mislead the researchers into making a type 1 error. Several statistical methods are available to adjust for multiple analyses. Their use should be specified in the trial protocol.

In March 2009 Pfizer stopped a randomised placebo-controlled trial of its drug Sutent (sunitinib) in patients with pancreatic islet cell tumours. The trial began in 2007 and was expected to be completed in 2011. The primary measure of effectiveness was progression-free survival, or time until death or disease progression. An independent data-monitoring committee recommended stopping the trial early after it concluded the drug improved progression-free survival versus placebo. All patients were given the option to continue taking Sutent or be switched from placebo to Sutent.

In April 2009 Pfizer stopped a phase 3 trial comparing its drug Sutent (sunitinib) with Xeloda (capecitabine) in the treatment of advanced breast cancer. The primary endpoint was progression-free survival. An independent monitoring committee found that Sutent was unlikely to prove better as a stand-alone treatment than Xeloda among patients who had not previously benefited from standard treatments.

NON-INFERIORITY AND EQUIVALENCE TRIALS

A researcher may pit a new drug against a placebo preparation to illustrate the new drug's efficacy in the management of a condition. However, a placebo-controlled trial does not give clinicians the information they want if there is already a treatment available for the condition. In that situation a trial comparing a new drug to the standard drug is more useful.

A researcher can of course set up a trial to assess whether a new drug is better than the standard drug. In such **superiority trials** significance testing is used to determine if there is a difference between the treatments. Superiority studies require large numbers of subjects to ensure adequate power and to minimise type 2 errors because less difference is expected when a new treatment is compared with a standard treatment instead of with a placebo.

Equivalence

In an **equivalence study** the researcher attempts to show equivalence between drugs. It is difficult to show exact equivalence so the trial is designed to demonstrate that any difference in outcome between the two drugs lies within a specified range called the 'equivalence margin' or 'delta'. Delta should represent the smallest clinically acceptable difference. Equivalence can be assumed if the confidence interval around the observed difference in effect between the two drugs lies entirely within delta[1]. If the equivalence margin is too wide, the risk of getting a false–positive result increases (the two drugs are wrongly accepted as equivalent).

Non-inferiority

In a **non-inferiority study** the researcher assesses whether a new drug is no worse within a specified margin than the standard drug. If the confidence interval for the difference between the two drugs is not more negative than a pre-specified amount, called the non-inferiority margin or delta, then non-inferiority can be assumed[1]. A non-inferiority study is a one-sided version of an equivalence study. Inferiority trails should be avoided in situations where any

1   Piaggio G, Elbourne DR, Altman DG, Pocock SJ, Evans SJ. Reporting of noninferiority and equivalence randomized trials: An extension of the CONSORT statement. *JAMA* 2006; 295: 1152–60.

inferiority is unacceptable, for example where the treatment is used to avoid a seriously undesirable outcome such as death.

What is the purpose of non-inferiority trials? The answer is that pharmaceutical companies might not need to show that their new drug is better than the standard drug in order to gain market share. For example, if a drug can be shown to be non-inferior and has advantages such as being cheaper or causing fewer adverse effects, the new drug is likely to be prescribed by clinicians. Non-inferiority trials usually require smaller sample sizes and are cheaper and quicker to run than superiority or equivalence trials. Once non-inferiority has been established, further statistical tests can be performed on the data to test for superiority.

Selecting interventions based on class effect

Grouping drugs together depends on the drugs having similar characteristics, which may include chemical structure, pharmacokinetics and pharmacodynamics. A **class effect** exists if the drugs grouped together have similar therapeutic effects and similar adverse effects.

Choosing a drug which belongs to a group and which shares a class effect is relatively straightforward, as usually the cheapest option is selected.

CONFOUNDING REVISITED

We revisited bias at the end of the **methods** section of this book because once a mistake has happened, there is little the researcher can do apart from admit the mistake and discuss its impact in the discussion section of the paper.

Confounding has been revisited at the end of the **results** section of this book because to deal with confounding, there are a number of things a researcher can do both in the methods section and the results section of the paper.

Methods to control confounding

At the time of designing the study

- **Restriction:** Certain confounding factors are restricted from entering the sample population using inclusion and exclusion criteria.
- **Matching:** People with confounding factors are allocated equally in the different arms of a study.
- **Randomisation:** Confounding factors, known or unknown, can be evenly distributed among the study groups, depending on the method of randomisation.

At the time of analysis of the study

- **Standardisation:** The risk in the exposed group is adjusted to that which would have been observed had there been the same confounder distribution as in the unexposed group. For example, if age is a confounding factor, the risk in the exposed group could be adjusted to the age-standardised risk. Standardisation is flexible and reversible. Data collection can be completed before potential confounders are dealt with. However, standardisation becomes difficult when dealing with more than one confounder.
- **Statistical adjustment using multivariate analysis:** This statistical method is used to take confounding factors into account. It analyses the data by taking the outcome as the dependent variable and includes the causal factor and any confounding factors into the equation. The equation allows you to check how much the confounding factors contribute to the overall effect. When the dependent variables are continuous in nature, multiple linear regression is used. If the variables are binary, logistic regression is

used. The advantage of using multivariate analysis is that more than one potential confounder can be considered and the technique is flexible and reversible.

SECTION G

CHECKLISTS

SECTION 9

CHECKLISTS

INTRODUCTION TO CHECKLISTS

All clinical papers can be understood and critically appraised using the structure that we have described so far. The clinical question and study type are considered before the methods and results are appraised.

As well as classification of research work by the type of study design used, it can be classified by the subject area of the clinical question. For example, some studies look at aetiological factors; others look at the usefulness of diagnostic tests. Within different clinical areas, there might be specific questions to ask, particularly with regard to the methods and results. Applicability concerns tend to be the same.

Checklists provide a way to work through the key considerations when critically appraising different study types, by listing the key points in the methods, reporting of results and applicability. Many institutions have published checklists, but the most highly acclaimed checklists were published in the Users' guides to the medical literature series, published between 1993 and 2000 in the *Journal of the American Medical Association* (*JAMA*) by the *Evidence-Based Medicine Working Group* (see the 'Further reading' chapter on page 298). The checklists in this section are based on the work of this group.

The chapters in this section give a concise overview of the checklists that we use in our clinical practice. To avoid duplication, we will only elaborate on new terms and concepts.

AETIOLOGICAL STUDIES

Aetiological studies compare the risk of developing an outcome in one or more groups exposed to one or more risk factors (Figure 53, Table 20). Study types commonly used include case–control and cohort studies.

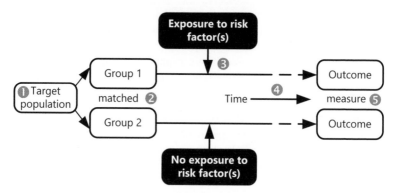

Figure 53 Aetiological studies (the numbered steps in the methodology are explained in Table 20)

METHODOLOGY
Was there a clearly defined group of patients? (1) Except for the exposure studied, were the groups similar to each other? (2) Did the exposure precede the onset of the outcome? (3) Was the follow-up of the subjects complete and of sufficient duration? (4) Were exposures and clinical outcomes measured in the same way in both groups? (5)
RESULTS
Relative risk in a randomised trial or cohort study Odds ratio in a case–control study Precision of the estimate of risk – confidence intervals Is there a dose–response gradient? Does the association make biological sense?
APPLICABILITY
Are your patients similar to the target population? Are the risk factor(s) similar to those experienced in your population? What are your patients' risks of the adverse outcome (number needed to harm)? Should exposure to the risk factor(s) be stopped or minimised?

Table 20 Aetiological studies checklist (the numbers relate to the study pathway outlined in the Figure 53)

The STROBE checklist

The 'STROBE' acronym stands for **ST**rengthening the **R**eporting of **OB**servational studies in **E**pidemiology. This is the aim of an international group of epidemiologists, methodologists, statisticians, researchers and journal editors involved in the conduct and dissemination of observational studies. Checklists for appraising cohort, case–control and cross-sectional studies can be downloaded from the STROBE website (www.strobe-statement.org).

DIAGNOSTIC OR SCREENING STUDIES

A diagnostic study compares a new test for diagnosing a condition with the gold-standard method (Figure 54, Table 21).

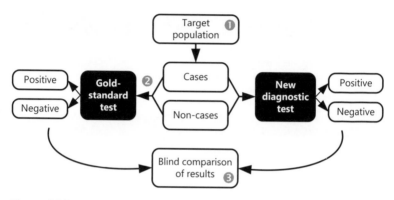

Figure 54 Diagnostic studies (the numbered steps in the methodology are explained in Table 21)

A good test will correctly identify patients with the condition (**true positives**) while minimising the number of patients without the condition who also test positive (**false positives**). Similarly, it will correctly identify patients who do not have the condition (**true negatives**) and minimise the number of patients given negative results when they do have the condition (**false negatives**).

Screening tests look for the early signs of a disease in asymptomatic people so that the disease can be treated before it gets to an advanced stage. The acceptability of false-positive and false-negative results depends in part on the seriousness of the condition and its treatment. A false-positive result causes unnecessary anxiety for the patient and can lead to expensive, unpleasant or dangerous treatments that are not indicated. A false-negative result on the other hand can lull a patient into a false sense of security and other symptoms and signs of disease might be ignored.

METHODOLOGY
Did the patient sample include an appropriate spectrum of patients to whom the test will be applied? (1) Was the gold standard applied regardless of the diagnostic test result? (2) Was there was an independent and blind comparison with a gold standard of diagnosis? (3)

RESULTS
Sensitivity Specificity Positive predictive value Negative predictive value Likelihood ratios Pre-test probability and odds Post-test probability and odds Receiver operating curve

APPLICABILITY
Are your patients similar to the target population? Is it possible to integrate this test into your clinical settings and procedures? Who will carry out the test in your clinical setting and who will interpret the results? Will the results of the test affect your management of the patient? Is the test affordable?

Table 21 Diagnostic or screening studies checklist (the numbers relate to the study pathway outlined in Figure 54)

Characteristics of the test

The results of the comparison of a diagnostic test with a gold-standard test need to be tabulated in a 2×2 table, as shown in Table 22. Note that each subject needs to take **two** diagnostic tests – the gold-standard test and the new test. The values of a, b, c and d will either be given or can be deduced from other data given in the results section.

		DISEASE STATUS BY GOLD STANDARD		Totals
		positive	negative	
DISEASE STATUS BY DIAGNOSTIC TEST	positive	a	b	$a + b$
	negative	c	d	$c + d$
Totals		$a + c$	$b + d$	$a + b + c + d$

Table 22 A 2×2 table for the results of diagnostic tests

There are a number of words and phrases used to describe the characteristics of a diagnostic test (Table 23). Each of these values should be calculated. A learning aid to help remember the formulae is shown in Figure 55.

TEST CHARACTERISTICS	DESCRIPTION	FORMULA
Sensitivity (true-positive rate)	The proportion of subjects with the disorder (by gold standard) who have a positive result (by new test)	$\dfrac{a}{a+c}$
Specificity (true-negative rate)	The proportion of subjects who do not have the disorder and who have a negative test	$\dfrac{d}{b+d}$
Positive predictive value (PPV)	The proportion of subjects with a positive test result who do have the disorder	$\dfrac{a}{a+b}$
Negative predictive value (NPV)	The proportion of subjects with a negative test result who do not have the disorder	$\dfrac{d}{c+d}$
Likelihood ratio for a positive test result (LR+)	How much more likely is a positive test to be found in a person with, as opposed to without, the condition?	$\dfrac{sensitivity}{1-specifity}$
Likelihood ratio for a negative test result (LR–)	How much more likely is a negative test to be found in a person with, as opposed to without, the condition?	$\dfrac{1-sensitivity}{specifity}$
Accuracy of a test	The proportion of subjects given the correct result	$\dfrac{(a+d)}{(a+b+c+d)}$

Table 23 Diagnostic test characteristics

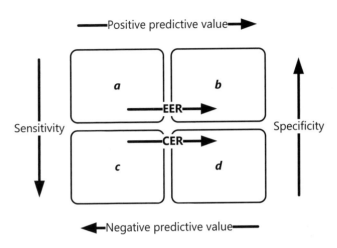

Figure 55 Learning aid for the characteristics of a diagnostic test. For example, the arrow for sensitivity starts at box a and goes over boxes a and c; sensitivity therefore equals a / (a + c). EER = experimental event rate; CER = control event rate.

SEE EXCERPT 63

There are also a number of risks and odds that can be calculated for the patient (Table 24).

PATIENT RISKS & ODDS	DESCRIPTION	FORMULA
Pre-test probability (equivalent to prevalence)	The probability that a subject will have the disorder.	$\dfrac{a + c}{a + b + c + d}$
Pre-test odds	The odds that a subject will have the disorder.	$\dfrac{\text{pre-test probability}}{1 - \text{pre-test probability}}$
Post-test odds	The odds that a subject, scoring positive on the diagnostic test, actually has the disorder	$\text{pre-test odds} \times LR+$
Post-test probability	The probability that a subject, scoring positive on the diagnostic test, actually has the disorder	$\dfrac{\text{post-test odds}}{\text{post-test odds} + 1}$

Table 24 Patient risks and odds

Understanding results

Sensitivity, specificity and predictive values can be confusing. The following statements clarify the difference between sensitivity and positive predictive value:

- **Sensitivity:** If a patient has a disorder, what is the chance of getting a positive result on the new test?

- **Positive predictive value:** If a patient has a positive result on the new test, what is the chance that they do have the disorder?

The following statements clarify the difference between specificity and negative predictive value:

- **Specificity:** If a patient does not have the disorder, what is the chance of getting a negative result on the new test?

- **Negative predictive value:** If a patient has a negative result on the new test, what is the chance that they do not have the disorder?

The sensitivity and specificity of a test can be interpreted using the following statements and aides-mémoires:

- **SpPin** – when a highly **sp**ecific test is used, a **p**ositive test result tends to rule **in** the disorder.

- **SnNout** – when a highly **sn**sitive test is used, a **n**egative test result tends to rule **out** the disorder.

The sensitivity and specificity are not affected by changes in the prevalence of the disorder.

Predictive values depend on the prevalence of the disorder. As the prevalence of a disorder in the population goes up:

- Positive predictive value will increase.
- Negative predictive value will decrease.
- Post-test probabilities also change.

It is important to determine where a diagnostic study was done in order to decide whether predictive values are applicable to your local population, as the results are only applicable if the prevalence of the disorder is the same.

Likelihood ratios are more useful than predictive values. As likelihood ratios are calculated from sensitivity and specificity, they remain constant even when the prevalence of the disorder changes, unlike predictive values.

Likelihood ratios show how many times more likely patients with a disorder are to have a particular test result than patients without the disorder.

- The likelihood ratio for a positive test result should be high as possible above 1. Positive results are desirable in patients with the disorder.

- The likelihood ratio for a negative test result should be as low as possible below 1. Negative test results are undesirable in patients with the disorder.

The likelihood ratio nomogram (or 'Fagan nomogram') enables the post-test probability to be graphically calculated if the pre-test probability and likelihood ratio are known (Figure 56). If a line is drawn connecting the pre-test probability of disease and the likelihood ratio, it intersects at the post-test probability of disease when extended to the right.

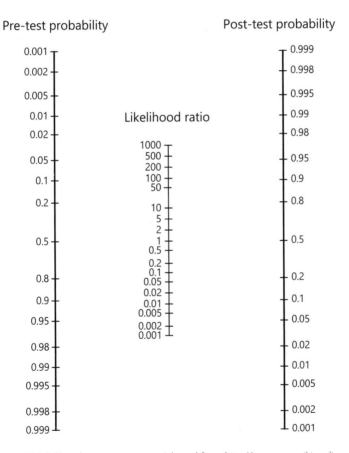

Figure 56 Likelihood ratio nomogram. Adapted from http://commons.wikimedia.org/wiki/File:Fagan_nomogram.svg

The performance of a diagnostic test often varies from one clinical location to another and the interpretation of results might also differ. This needs to be considered when deciding the applicability of any research findings.

Multiple testing

Serial testing (eg diagnosing HIV – if the first test is positive, another test is done to confirm) increases specificity (the true-negative rate).

Parallel testing (eg diagnosing myocardial infarction – history, ECG, enzymes) increases sensitivity (the true-positive rate).

Receiver operating characteristic (ROC) curve

There is a threshold with any diagnostic test above which a positive result is returned and below which a negative result is returned. During the development of a diagnostic test, this threshold can be varied to assess the trade-off between sensitivity and specificity. With any change in the cut-off point the sensitivity can increase and the specificity can decrease, or vice versa.

A good diagnostic test would, ideally, be one that has low false-positive and false-negative rates. A bad diagnostic test is one in which the only cut-offs that make the false-positive rate low lead to a high false-negative rate and vice versa. To find the optimum cut-off point, a **receiver operating characteristic curve** is used. This is a graphical representation of the relationship between the false-negative and false-positive rates for each cut-off. The plot shows the false-positive rate (1 – specificity) on the X axis and the true-positive rate (sensitivity or 1 – false-negative rate) on the Y axis (Figure 57).

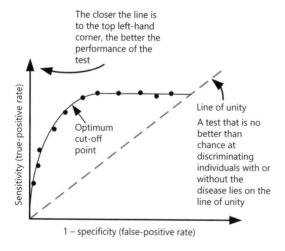

Figure 57 Receiver operating curve

The **area under the curve** represents the probability that the test will correctly identify true-positive and true-negative results. An area of 1 represents a perfect test, whereas an area of 0.5 represents a worthless test.

The closer the curve follows the left-hand border and then the top border of the receiver operating curve space, the more accurate the test – the true-positive rate is high and the false-positive rate is low. This is the point where the area under the curve is the greatest. The best cut-off point is the point at which the curve is closest to the top left-hand corner.

If two different tests or continuous variables are plotted on the same receiver operating characteristic curve, the test or variable with the curve that lies above the curve of the other test or variable is the best choice. It will have the greatest area under the curve. **SEE EXCERPT 64**

STARD statement

The objective of the STARD initiative (STAndards for the Reporting of Diagnostic accuracy studies) is to improve the accuracy and completeness of reporting of studies of diagnostic accuracy. The STARD statement consists of a checklist of 25 items which can be viewed on their website (http://www.stard-statement.org/).

EXCERPT 63

Adapted from: Bello IS et al. Reliability of Rapid Diagnostic Tests in the diagnosis of malaria amongst children in two communities in South West Nigeria. *Malaria Journal* 2014; 13(Suppl 1): P10.

Researchers evaluated the ability of a rapid diagnostic kit (RDK) to diagnose malaria compared to the gold standard malaria microscopy method. A total of 132 children age were screened.

In the microscopy category, 35 (26.5%) children tested positive while 97 (73.5%) tested negative for malaria parasite. Out of the 35 children tested positive, RDT picked 33 as positive and 2 as negative, (sensitivity = 94.3%). While out of the 97 that tested negative for microscopy, RDT picked 94 as negative and 3 as positive (specificity = 96.9%). The positive predictive value and negative predictive values are 91.7% and 97.9% respectively.

Commentary: The rapid diagnostic kit performed well compared to the gold-standard method for diagnosing malaria infection. The researchers suggest its use can help clinicians decide whether treatment is indicated.

EXCERPT 64

Adapted from: Sammalkorpi HE et al. A new adult appendicitis score improves diagnostic accuracy of acute appendicitis – a prospective study. *BMC Gastroenterology* 2014; 14: 114.

In this study a new scoring system for more accurate diagnostics of acute appendicitis was constructed. The new Adult Appendicitis Score was compared to two other scoring methods, the Alvarado score and the Appendicitis Inflammatory Response (AIR) score. The scores were compared to the gold-standard diagnosis of acute appendicitis based on histological examination showing transmural infiltration of neutrophils in the appendix.

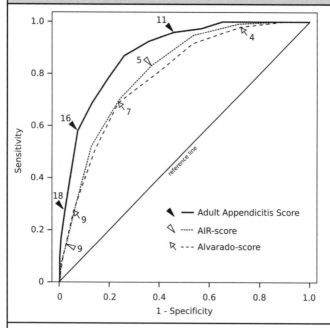

Commentary: The area under the curve in this ROC curve was significantly larger with the new Adult Appendicitis Score (0.882) compared with AUC of Appendicitis inflammatory response score (0.810) and Alvarado score (0.790).

Treatment studies compare the effects of a new intervention with those of another intervention (Figure 58, Table 25). A good intervention will improve the outcome compared with previously available interventions. The improvement can be stated in absolute terms, in relative terms or by the number needed to treat (NNT).

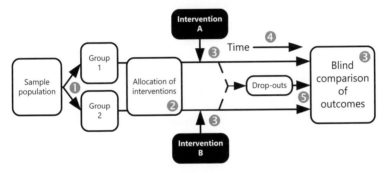

Figure 58 Treatment studies (the numbered steps in the methodology are explained in Table 25)

METHODOLOGY
Was there a clearly focused clinical question and primary hypothesis?
Was the randomisation process clearly explained? (1)
Were the groups similar at the start of the study?
Was concealed allocation used in the allocation of interventions? (2)
Were the groups treated equally apart from the experimental intervention?
Was blinding used effectively? (3)
Was follow-up complete and of sufficient duration? (4)
Was this an intention-to-treat study? (5)

RESULTS
Control event rate
Experimental event rate
Absolute risk reduction / benefit increase
Relative risk reduction / benefit increase
Numbers needed to treat
Precision of the estimate of treatment effect – confidence intervals

APPLICABILITY
Are your patients similar to the target population?
Were all the relevant outcome factors considered?
Will the intervention help your patients?
Are the benefits of the intervention worth the risks and costs?
Have patients' values and preferences been considered?

Table 25 Treatment studies checklist (the numbers relate to the study pathway outlined in Figure 58)

The CONSORT statement

First published in the *Journal of the American Medical Association* in August 1996, the Consolidated Standards of Reporting Trials (CONSORT) statement introduced a set of recommendations to improve the quality of randomised controlled trial reports[1]. The statement was updated in 2010. This checklist is summarised in Table 26. The same structure can also be used to critically appraise trials. Further information is available on the CONSORT website at www.consort-statement.org.

1   Moher D, Schulz KF, Altman DG. The CONSORT statement: revised recommendations for improving the quality of reports of parallel-group randomised trials. *Lancet* 2001; 357: 1191–94.

SECTION OF PAPER	DESCRIPTION
Title and abstract	
	Identification as a randomised trial in the title. Structured summary of trial design, methods, results and conclusions (for specific guidance see CONSORT for abstracts)
Introduction	
Background and objectives	Scientific background and explanation of rationale. Specific objectives or hypotheses
Methods	
Trial design	Description of trial design (such as parallel, factorial), including allocation ratio Important changes to methods after trial commencement (such as eligibility criteria), with reasons
Participants	Eligibility criteria for participants Settings and locations where the data were collected
Interventions	The interventions for each group with sufficient details to allow replication, including how and when they were actually administered
Outcomes	Completely defined, prespecified primary and secondary outcome measures, including how and when they were assessed Any changes to trial outcomes after the trial commenced, with reasons
Sample size	How sample size was determined When applicable, explanation of any interim analyses and stopping guidelines
Randomisation – sequence generation	Method used to generate the random allocation sequence Type of randomisation; details of any restriction (such as blocking and block size)
Randomisation – allocation concealment	Mechanism used to implement the random allocation sequence (such as sequentially numbered containers), describing any steps taken to conceal the sequence until interventions were assigned
Randomisation – implementation	Who generated the random allocation sequence, who enrolled participants and who assigned participants to interventions

Blinding	If done, who was blinded after assignment to interventions (eg participants, care providers, those assessing outcomes) and how If relevant, description of the similarity of interventions
Statistical methods	Statistical methods used to compare groups for primary and secondary outcomes Methods for additional analyses, such as subgroup analyses and adjusted analyses

Results

Participant flow	For each group, the numbers of participants who were randomly assigned, received intended treatment and were analysed for the primary outcome For each group, losses and exclusions after randomisation, together with reasons
Recruitment	Dates defining the periods of recruitment and follow-up Why the trial ended or was stopped
Baseline data	A table showing baseline demographic and clinical characteristics for each group
Numbers analysed	For each group, number of participants (denominator) included in each analysis and whether the analysis was by original assigned groups
Outcomes and estimation	For each primary and secondary outcome, results for each group and the estimated effect size and its precision (such as 95% confidence interval) For binary outcomes, presentation of both absolute and relative effect sizes is recommended
Ancillary analyses	Results of any other analyses performed, including subgroup analyses and adjusted analyses, distinguishing prespecified from exploratory
Harms	All important harms or unintended effects in each group

Discussion

Limitations	Trial limitations, addressing sources of potential bias, imprecision and, if relevant, multiplicity of analyses
Generalisability	Generalisability (external validity, applicability) of the trial findings
Interpretation	Interpretation consistent with results, balancing benefits and harms and considering other relevant evidence

Other information	
Registration	Registration number and name of trial registry
Protocol	Where the full trial protocol can be accessed, if available
Funding	Sources of funding and other support (such as supply of drugs), role of funders

Table 26 The CONSORT 2010 checklist[1] – adapted from Schulz et al. 2010. *BMC Medicine*, 8, 18

The Standards for Quality Improvement Reporting Excellence (SQUIRE) Group has also published guidelines to improve standards[2] (guidelines available at www.squire-statement.org).

1   Schulz et al. CONSORT 2010 Statement: updated guidelines for reporting parallel group randomised trials. *BMC Medicine* 2010; 8: 18.
2   Davidoff F, Batalden P, Stevens D, Ogrine G, Mooney SE. Publication guidelines for quality improvement studies in health care: evolution of the SQUIRE project. *BMJ* 2009; 338: a3152.

PROGNOSTIC STUDIES

A prognostic study examines the characteristics of the patient (prognostic factors) that might predict any of the possible outcomes and the likelihood that different outcome events will occur (Figure 59, Table 27). Outcomes can be positive or negative events. The likelihood of different outcomes occurring can be expressed absolutely, relatively or in the form of a survival curve.

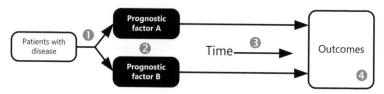

Figure 59 Prognostic studies (the numbered steps in the methodology are explained in Table 27)

METHODOLOGY
Was a sample of patients recruited at a common point in the course of the disease? (1) Was there adjustment for important prognostic factors? (2) Was follow-up complete and of sufficient duration? (3) Was there blind assessment of objective outcome criteria? (4)
RESULTS
Absolute risk – eg 5-year survival rate Relative risk – eg risk from a prognostic factor Survival curves – cumulative events over time Precision of the prognostic estimates – confidence limits
APPLICABILITY
Are your patients similar to the patients in this study? Does this study give you a better understanding of the progress of disease and the possible outcomes? Does this study help you to decide whether to reassure or counsel your patients?

Table 27 Prognostic studies checklist (the numbers relate to the study pathway outlined in Figure 59)

Survival analysis

Survival analysis studies the time between entry into a study and a subsequent occurrence of an event. Originally, such analyses were performed to give information on time to death in fatal conditions, but they can be applied to many other outcomes as well as mortality.

Survival analysis is usually applied to data from longitudinal cohort studies. There are, however, problems when analysing data relating to the time between one event and another:

- All times to the event occurring will differ, but it is unlikely that these times will be normally distributed.
- The subjects might not all have entered the study at the same time, so there are **unequal observation periods**.
- Some patients might not reach the endpoint by the end of the study. For example, if the event is recovery within 12 months, some patients might not have recovered in the 12-month study period.
- Patients can leave a study early, not experience the event or be lost to follow-up. The data for these individuals are referred to as **censored**.

Both censored observations and unequal observation periods make it difficult to determine the mean survival times because we do not have all the survival times. As a result, the curve is used to calculate the **median survival time**.

Median survival time

Median survival time is the time from the start of the study that coincides with a 50% probability of survival – that is, the time taken for 50% of the subjects not to have had the event. This value is associated with a P value and 95% confidence intervals.

Kaplan–Meier survival analysis

The Kaplan–Meier survival analysis looks at event rates over the study period, rather than just at a specific time point. It is used to determine survival probabilities and proportions of individuals surviving, enabling the estimation of a cumulative survival probability. The data are presented in life tables and survival curves (Figure 60).

The data are first ranked in ascending order over time in life tables. The survival curve is plotted by calculating the proportion of patients who remain alive in the study each time an event occurs, taking into account censored observations. The survival curve will not change at the time of censoring, but only when the next event occurs. Censored patients are assumed to have the same survival prospects as those who continue in the study.

Time is plotted on the x axis, and the proportion of people without the outcome (survivors) at each time point are plotted on the y axis. A cumulative curve is achieved, with steps at each time an event occurs. Small vertical ticks on the curve indicate the times at which patients are censored.

A survival curve can be used to calculate several parameters:

- The **median survival time**, which is the time taken until 50% of the population survive

- The **survival time**, which is the time taken for a certain proportion of the population to survive

- The **survival probability** at a given time point, which is the probability that an individual will not have developed an endpoint event.

A survival curve can also be used to compare the difference in the proportions surviving in two groups and their confidence intervals, such as when comparing a control population with an experimental population. **SEE EXCERPT 65**

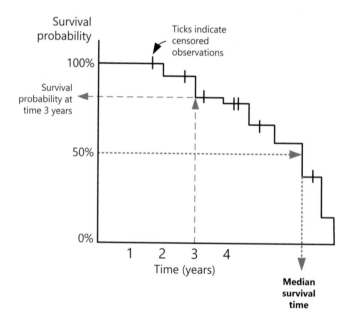

Figure 60 Survival curve

Log-rank test

To compare the survival experiences of two or more populations, the proportion of people surviving in each population at any given time point can be compared. This snapshot does not, however, reflect the total survival experience of the two groups.

The **log-rank test** is a better method as it takes the entire follow-up period into account. It is a significance test and helps to decide whether or not to accept the null hypothesis that there is no difference in the probability of survival in the different groups. It does not indicate the size of the difference between the groups, unlike the hazard ratio.

The log-rank test is so called because the data are first ranked and then compared with observations and expected outcome rates in each of the groups (similar to a chi-squared test). The log-rank test does not take other variables into consideration.

Cox proportional hazards regression

The **hazard rate** is the probability of an endpoint event in a time interval divided by the duration of the time interval. The hazard rate can be interpreted as the instantaneous probability of an endpoint event in a study if the time interval is short. The hazard rate might not be constant during the study.

The **hazard ratio** is the hazard rate in the experimental arm divided by the hazard rate of the control arm. The hazard ratio is complemented by a P value and confidence intervals. It is assumed that the hazard ratio remains constant throughout the study. **SEE EXCERPT 66**

If the hazard ratio is 1, the two arms have an equal hazard rate.

If the hazard ratio is > 1, the experimental arm has an increased hazard.

If the hazard ratio is < 1, the experimental arm has a reduced hazard.

Although the interpretation of hazard ratio is similar to that of relative risk and the odds ratio, the terms are not synonymous. The hazard ratio compares the experimental and control groups throughout the study duration, unlike the relative risk and odds ratio, which only compare the proportion of subjects that achieved the outcome in each group at the end of the study.

It is not possible to calculate the hazard ratio from a 2 × 2 contingency table.

Cox proportional hazards regression is used to produce the hazard ratio. It is the multivariate extension of the log-rank test. It is used to assess the impact of treatment on survival or other time-related events and adjusts for the effects of other variables.

EXCERPT 65

Adapted from: Sonmez M et al. Effect of pathologic fractures on survival in multiple myeloma patients: a case control study. *Journal of Experimental & Clinical Cancer Research* 2008; 27: 11.

In this study, researchers determined the impact of pathological fractures on survival in patients with multiple myeloma.

Survival was studied from the date of diagnosis to the last contact with the patient. Survival curves were calculated using the Kaplan–Meier method and statistical comparisons were performed by the log-rank test. While overall survival was 17.6 months in the patients with pathological fractures, it was 57.3 months in the patients with no pathological fracture (according to Kaplan–Meier test, log rank p = 0.03).

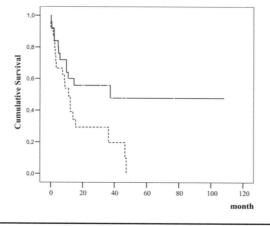

Commentary: An example of a survival curve. The researchers concluded that pathological fractures may cause reduced survival and increased mortality in the multiple myeloma patients.

EXCERPT 66

Adapted from: Anderson J et al. The impact of renal insufficiency and anaemia on survival in patients with cardiovascular disease: a cohort study. *BMC Cardiovascular Disorders* 2009; 9: 51.

The aim of this study was to establish the prevalence of chronic kidney disease and anaemia in patients with cardiovascular disease in the community and to examine whether the presence of anaemia was associated with increased morbidity and mortality.

The estimated risk of death from any cause, when compared to patients with cardiovascular disease only, was almost double (HR = 1.98, 95% CI = 0.99=3.98) for patients with both cardiovascular disease and chronic kidney disease and was over 4 times greater (HR = 4.33, 95% CI = 1.76–10.68) for patients with cardiovascular disease, chronic kidney disease and anaemia.

Commentary: Hazard ratios (HR) were calculated to compare different groups of patients. The researchers concluded that the presence of chronic kidney disease carries an increased mortality risk which increases in an additive way with the addition of anaemia.

ECONOMIC STUDIES

Resources within the NHS are finite. Not every activity can be funded. Economic analyses evaluate the choices in resource allocation by comparing the costs and consequences of different actions. They tend to take a wider perspective on healthcare provision than other types of studies, because they do not just focus on whether one intervention is statistically better than another. They aim to discover which interventions can be used to produce the maximum possible benefits.

Economic analyses can be appraised in much the same way as other types of studies (Table 28). All direct, indirect and intangible costs and benefits should be included in a good economic analysis. Much of the debate regarding economic analyses tends to focus on the assumptions made in order to calculate monetary values for the use of resources and the consequent benefits. Such assumptions are based on large amounts of information collected from different sources, including demographic data, epidemiological data, socioeconomic data and the economic burden of disease.

METHODOLOGY
Is there a full economic comparison of healthcare strategies? Does it identify all other costs and effects? Were the costs and outcomes properly measured and valued? Were appropriate allowances made for uncertainties in the analysis? Are the costs and outcomes related to the baseline risk in the treatment population?
RESULTS
Incremental costs and outcomes of each strategy Cost-minimisation analysis Cost-effectiveness analysis Cost–utility analysis Cost–benefit analysis
APPLICABILITY
Can I use this study in caring for my patients? Could my patients expect similar outcomes? Do the costs apply in my own setting? Are the conclusions unlikely to change with modest changes in costs and outcomes?

Table 28 Economic studies checklist

A subdiscipline of health economics is pharmacoeconomics. This refers to the scientific method that compares the value of one drug with the value of another. A pharmacoeconomic study evaluates the cost (expressed in monetary terms) and effects (expressed in terms of monetary value, efficacy or enhanced quality of life) of a drug.

Examples of input costs:

- Direct medical costs – hospitalisations, equipment and facilities, medical and nursing time, drugs and dressings
- Direct non-medical costs – out-of-pocket expenses, time costs, volunteer time
- Indirect costs – productivity changes
- Intangible costs – quality of life, pain, suffering.

Examples of output benefits:

- Associated economic effects – direct medical savings, direct non-medical savings, indirect savings, intangible savings
- Natural units (health effects) – endpoints, surrogate endpoints, survival
- Utility units (preference-weighted effects) – health status, quality of life.

There are several types of economic evaluation and they differ in which consequences they measure.

Cost-of-illness study

This is not a true economic evaluation in fact, because it does not compare the costs and outcomes of alternative courses of action. It actually measures all the costs that are associated with a particular condition and these can include some of the following:

- Direct costs – where real money is actually changing hands, eg health service use
- Indirect costs –costs that are not directly accountable to a particular function, eg the costs of lost productivity from time taken off work due to the condition
- Intangible costs – the costs associated with the disvalue to a patient of pain and suffering.

Cost-minimisation analysis

This analysis is used when interventions are being compared which produce the same beneficial outcome and the benefit is of the same order of magnitude (Figure 61).

- Example: The treatment of headache using paracetamol or aspirin.

The analysis simply aims to decide the least costly way of achieving the same outcome. Any difference in outcome is not taken into consideration.

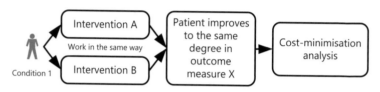

Figure 61 Cost-minimisation analysis

Cost-effectiveness analysis (CEA)

This type of analysis is used in situations where the outcome is the same for the alternative interventions but achieved by different mechanisms and to different degrees (Figure 62). The amount of improvement therefore has to be factored in to the economic analysis as well as the cost of the interventions. Only one outcome is considered.

- Example: The treatment of back pain using physiotherapy or surgery.

The cost-effectiveness of an intervention is the ratio of the cost of the intervention to the improvement in the outcome measure, which is expressed in non-monetary units (eg the number of pain-free days). The cost-effectiveness of an intervention is only meaningful when compared with other interventions.

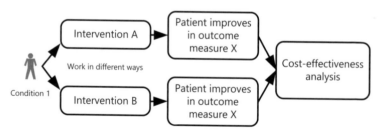

Figure 62 Cost-effectiveness analysis

Cost–consequences analysis

Cost–consequences analysis is a form of cost-effectiveness analysis for situations where there is more than one outcome measure. Instead of combining several outcomes to create a single index of health utility, in a cost–consequence analysis all outcomes are presented with relevant cost-effectiveness ratios, and the reader can judge the relative importance of the outcomes.

Cost–utility analysis

A cost–utility analysis is used to make choices between interventions for different conditions in which the units of outcome differ (Figure 63). Cost–utility analysis is better than cost-effectiveness analysis in situations where interventions give outcomes which are not perfect health.

- Example: The treatment of breast cancer using a new drug versus hip replacement surgery.

As the outcomes cannot be directly compared, a common unit or **utility measure** (which is indicative of both the quantity and quality of life afterwards) is used.

The best known utility measure is the **quality-adjusted life year** or QALY.

$$QALY = \frac{\text{number of extra years}}{\text{of life obtained}} \times \frac{\text{the value of the quality of life}}{\text{during those extra years}}$$

In terms of the quality of life over 1 year, death is equal to 0 QALYs and 1 year of perfect health is 1 QALY. The competing interventions are compared in terms of cost per utility (cost per QALY).

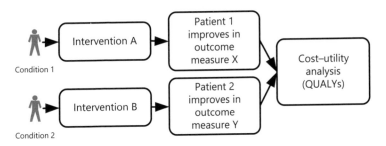

Figure 63 Cost–utility analysis

Example of a cost–utility analysis

A patient needs life-saving treatment.

Intervention A costs £1000 and gives a patient 10 additional years of life with a quality of life of 0.2. This is equal to $10 \times 0.2 = 2$ QALYs. The cost of each QALY is £500.

Intervention B costs £2160 and gives a patient three additional years of life with a quality of life of 0.9. This is equal to $3 \times 0.9 = 2.7$ QALYs. The cost of each QALY is £800.

Over 10 years, Intervention B gives 0.7 additional QALYs over Intervention A.

There are two ways that this result can influence practice:

1. If the clinician wants to offer the intervention that offers the highest number of QALYs, Intervention B is the treatment of choice. The patient might disagree and want to live longer, even if their life is harder.

2. If the clinician wants to offer the intervention that offers best value for money for the health service, Intervention A is the treatment of choice. The patient might disagree and want a better quality of life, even if their life is shorter.

For another example: **SEE EXCERPT 67**

Cost–benefit analysis

This analysis is used to compare the costs and benefits of different treatments for different patient groups by putting a **monetary value** on the outcomes resulting from each alternative intervention (Figure 64). The results for each intervention are expressed as the ratio of economic benefits to costs or as net economic benefit (ie benefits minus costs). A cost–benefit analysis for a single intervention can be considered on its own so a comparison intervention is not always necessary.

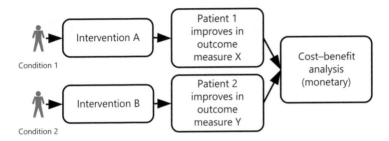

Figure 64 Cost–benefit analysis

Cost–benefit analysis considers the **opportunity cost** of a treatment choice rather than just the direct cost. Using a resource prevents it being used in some other way. For example, if an intervention is chosen, as well as the direct cost of the intervention itself one has to consider the foregone benefits that may have been gained from choosing an alternative intervention. Only if the costs and benefits associated with the chosen intervention outweigh those of the alternative intervention should the decision to spend go ahead.

Sensitivity analysis

Economic evaluations are models based on assumptions and estimates, and aim to capture and summarise what happens in reality. Sensitivity analysis assists in assessing how robust the conclusions are, considering that there will be a degree of uncertainty about some elements of any economic analysis. It tests the consistency of the results by repeating the comparison between inputs and consequences, while varying the assumptions used. The figures are adjusted to account for the full range of possible influences.

A **one-way (univariate) sensitivity analysis** changes the value of one parameter at a time. **SEE EXCERPT 68**

A **multi-way (multivariate) sensitivity analysis** alters two or more parameters simultaneously to show the effect of combined changes.

A **probabilistic sensitivity analysis** looks at the effect on the results of an evaluation when the underlying parameters are allowed to vary simultaneously across a range according to predefined distributions. The results this kind of analysis produces represent a more realistic estimate of uncertainty. Techniques such as a Monte Carlo simulation have been developed.

EXCERPT 67

Adapted from: Angus C et al. Cost-effectiveness of a programme of screening and brief interventions for alcohol in primary care in Italy. *BMC Family Practice* 2014; 15: 26.

Researchers assessed the cost-effectiveness of the Screening and Brief Intervention (SBI) programmes in primary healthcare to reduce alcohol consumption in Italy.

The cost of delivering SBIs over the 10 year programme is estimated to be €411 million. This is offset by a total reduction in hospital costs over 30 years of €370 million. The total gain in Quality-Adjusted Life Years (QALYs) is estimated to be 75 200 giving an Incremental Cost-Effectiveness Ratio (ICER) of €550/QALY, suggesting that such a programme is close to being cost-neutral. As a large proportion of the health benefits are experienced by men (69% of total QALYs), delivering SBIs to men only is estimated to be cost-saving, although the estimated ICER for a female-only SBI programme of €3 100/QALY is still well within the recommended Italian threshold of €25 000–€40 000/QALY.

Commentary: The researchers calculated that each QALY would cost €550.

EXCERPT 68

Adapted from: van Boven JFM et al. Improving inhaler adherence in patients with Chronic Obstructive Pulmonary Disease: a cost-effectiveness analysis. *Respiratory Research* 2014; 15: 66.

This study evaluated the cost-effectiveness of the PHARMACOP-intervention which improved medication adherence and inhalation technique for patients with COPD compared with usual care.

The average overall costs per patient for the PHARMACOP-intervention and usual care were €2 221 and €2 448, respectively within the 1-year time horizon. Results showed robust cost-savings in various sensitivity analyses. In univariate sensitivity analyses, all relevant parameters were varied within their 95% CI of the basecase values. The model was most sensitive to the number of hospital-treated exacerbations in the PHARMACOP-trial and the relative risk reduction due to the intervention. The medication costs and adherence improvement were of somewhat less influence.

Commentary: The researchers found that the PHARMACOP intervention was less expensive compared to usual care. They then did a sensitivity analysis of the model they used to compute costs to see which factors had the most influence.

QUALITATIVE RESEARCH

In contrast to the objective counting and measuring approach of quantitative research, qualitative research concerns itself with the subjective measurement of the processes that underlie behavioural patterns. It can investigate meanings, attitudes, beliefs, preferences and behaviours. It aims to provide complex textual descriptions instead of statistical analyses. Unlike the artificial experiments of quantitative research, the focus of qualitative research is on natural settings. Context is important, making the results less generalisable.

Qualitative research relies on inductive reasoning processes. Few assumptions are made in advance of the study. Data are used to generate theories. This is the opposite of the deductive inquiry processes seen in quantitative research, where data are used to confirm or refute a hypothesis.

Qualitative research helps doctors to understand people and the social and cultural contexts within which they live and there has been an increasing recognition over recent years of the important role such research can play in the formation and development of medical services. Qualitative methods help to bridge the gap between scientific evidence and clinical practice and help doctors to understand the barriers to using evidence-based medicine and its limitations in informing decisions about treatment.

A checklist approach can be applied to the evaluation of qualitative research (Table 29). As with other types of research, a qualitative study should start with a clearly formulated question that addresses a specific clinical problem and that is amenable to investigation by qualitative methods. Examination of the research question takes place in a natural setting where the patient might normally be.

METHODOLOGY
Did the paper describe an important clinical problem?
Was a qualitative approach appropriate?
Was the setting clearly described?
How were the participants chosen?
Was the data collection comprehensive and detailed?
Were the data collected in a way that addresses the research issue?
Is there a relationship between researchers and participants that needs consideration?

RESULTS
Was the data analysis sufficiently rigorous?
Were the data analysed appropriately?
Were any quantitative methods used appropriately?
Are the results credible and repeatable?
Is there a clear statement of the findings?

APPLICABILITY
Are your patients similar to the patients in this study?
Do the results help you to understand your medical practice and outcomes better?
Does the study help you to understand your relationship with your patients and carers better?

Table 29 Qualitative research checklist

Approaches

Grounded theory: Qualitative researchers do not usually start with a theory which they aim to test. Instead, a theory is developed from the data as they are collected. The theory is said to be 'grounded' in the data. The theory is updated as new data are collected and compared with existing data. The outcome is a theory which explains the phenomenon that is under investigation.

Phenomenological: Aims to answer the question, 'What is the meaning of one's lived experience?' The researcher seeks subjects who are willing to describe their thoughts, feelings and interpretations that are related to the phenomenon under investigation.

Ethnographic: Aims to learn from (rather than to study) members of a community in order to describe and interpret a cultural or social group or system.

Historical: Aims to explain present events and anticipate future events by collecting and evaluating data about past events.

Sampling methods

Qualitative studies do not use random methods to select a sample from the target population.

Convenience/accidental: The selection of subjects is simply based on ease of access. Anyone who might be able to offer an insight into the phenomenon under study is selected if they are available. **SEE EXCERPT 69**

Opportunistic: The research takes advantage of unforeseen opportunities as they arise to recruit more subjects. **SEE EXCERPT 70**

Purposive: The researcher consciously selects subjects who have knowledge or experience of the area being investigated. **SEE EXCERPT 70**

Quota: A type of purposive sampling. Quotas are set for subjects with certain characteristics. This allows the researchers to focus on those people most likely to be able to help.

Snowball: Researchers identify subjects, who are then used to refer researchers on to other subjects in their social network. This provides a means of gaining access to people who would not be readily available to take part in a study, such as those living on the periphery of society. This is also known as 'chain-referral sampling'. **SEE EXCERPT 70**

Sample size

Data saturation: Researchers continue to collect data until they are no longer hearing or seeing new information. **SEE EXCERPT 71**

Data gathering

Participant observation: The researcher not only observes a group but adopts a role within the group from which to participate in some manner, usually over an extended period of time. This method allows for data to be collected on naturally occurring behaviours in their usual contexts. There can be a conflict between a researcher's dual role as a researcher and a participant. An added danger is that the researcher might end up over-identifying with the group, impairing analytical objectivity.

Focus groups: The researcher interviews groups of people with something in common. The people are free to talk to each other in the group. The data arise out of the interaction between group members, rather than from interaction between the researcher and the group. Focus groups can provide data on the cultural norms of the group and are helpful for exploratory research into issues of concern to the group. However, focus groups are not naturalistic, the discussions can be dominated by some participants and there are issues around confidentiality. **SEE EXCERPT 72**

In-depth interviews:

- **Structured interviews** aim to focus on certain areas in order to find answers to predetermined questions. The interviewer is in control so this technique is less naturalistic.

- **Semi-structured interviews** follow a topic guide but allow for open-ended answers and follow-up of points raised.

- **Unstructured interviews** aim to discuss a limited number of topics in great depth, with no structure or preconceived plan. The interviewee is in control.

Documents: The researcher or subject keeps a personal diary account of events, interactions, discussions and/or emotions. Official documents and questionnaires might be used.

Role-play: Subjects can be asked to give their personal feedback after playing a role or observing role-play.

Minimising bias

Complete objectivity is neither achievable nor necessarily desirable in qualitative research.

Reflexivity: The researcher acknowledges the central role they play in the research process. There is an understanding of the bidirectional effect the researcher might have had on the research findings.

Bracketing: The identification and temporary setting aside of the researcher's assumptions.

Validating data

A number of techniques are available to researchers to minimise the biases and problems that arise with qualitative studies.

Member checks: The subject confirms whether the researcher has accurately recorded data. This can be done during the interview process itself or at the end of the study. This is also known as 'informant feedback' or 'respondent validation'.

Triangulation: Data are cross-verified using more than two different sources. **SEE EXCERPT 72**

Analysing data

Constant comparison analysis: This strategy involves taking individual data as they are collected and comparing them to all the other data collected, in order to make tentative conclusions, hypotheses and themes. Initial ideas and concepts are tested and new data sources are found in order to develop a grounded theory.

Content analysis: Documents, text or speech are examined to see what themes emerge. Many words of text are compressed into fewer content categories based on explicit coding rules. **SEE EXCERPT 73**

EXCERPT 69

Adapted from: Sadr S et al. The treatment experience of patients with low back pain during pregnancy and their chiropractors: a qualitative study. *Chiropractic & Manual Therapies* 2012; 20: 32.

The objective of this study was to explore the experience of chiropractic treatment for pregnant women with low back pain, and their chiropractors.

Chiropractors were asked to recruit any of their patients who they determined would meet the inclusion criteria. As such, any pregnant women who met the inclusion criteria were initially asked by their treating chiropractor if they were interested in participating in this study, and were then referred to the investigators to confirm their interest, eligibility for inclusion and availability for an interview.

Commentary: An example of convenience sampling. Any person who met the inclusion criteria was invited to take part in the study.

EXCERPT 70

Adapted from: Whelan B et al. Healthcare providers' views on the acceptability of financial incentives for breastfeeding: a qualitative study. *BMC Pregnancy and Childbirth* 2014; 14: 355.

This study was part of a larger project looking at the development and feasibility testing of a financial incentive scheme for breastfeeding. Researchers gathered healthcare providers' views around whether using financial incentives in areas with low breastfeeding rates would be acceptable in principle.

Participants were purposively sampled to include a wide range of experience and roles associated with supporting mothers with infant feeding. In particular, three strategies were used to purposefully select information-rich cases: politically important case sampling which allowed for key stakeholders who could be potential research collaborators to voice their opinions on the intervention; snowball sampling whereby interviewees identified key informants whose opinions were important to capture; and opportunistic sampling which allowed for the researchers to take opportunities during data collection to select potentially important cases.

Commentary: The sampling methods used included purposive sampling, snowball sampling and opportunistic sampling.

EXCERPT 71

Adapted from: Sedibe HM et al. Qualitative study exploring healthy eating practices and physical activity among adolescent girls in rural South Africa. *BMC Pediatrics* 2014; 14: 211.

This paper explored perceptions, attitudes, barriers and facilitators related to healthy eating and physical activity among adolescent girls in rural South Africa.

Debriefing sessions were held daily by researchers after the fieldwork to discuss issues and themes emerging from the interviews and to ensure consistency of question meaning. Preliminary analysis occurred concurrently with the continued administration of interviews to identify emergent sub-themes to be pursued in subsequent interviews. Data saturation was reached by the 11th interview. The 11 recorded interviews were transcribed and translated into English by the field worker.

Commentary: The researchers analysed incoming data and modified their interviews to take account of emerging themes. Data saturation was reached with the 11th subject, at which point the data collection was complete.

EXCERPT 72

Adapted from: Sunaert P et al. Engaging GPs in insulin therapy initiation: a qualitative study evaluating a support program in the Belgian context. *BMC Family Practice* 2014; 15: 144.

This study explored the factors influencing the engagement of general practitioners in insulin therapy initiation.

We used semi-structured interviews to answer the first research question: two focus group interviews with GPs and 20 one-to-one interviews with GPs who were not regular users of the overall support programme in the region. The data from the GPs were triangulated with data obtained from one-to-one interviews with patients, the diabetes nurse educator and the specialist involved in the program development, and data extracted from meeting reports evaluating the insulin initiation support programme.

Commentary: The information gathered from focus groups and one-to-one interviews was confirmed by comparing it to information from other sources.

EXCERPT 73

Adapted from: Perceptions of HIV/STI prevention among young adults in Sweden who travel abroad: a qualitative study with focus group and individual interviews. *BMC Public Health* 2014; 14: 897.

This study aimed to describe the experiences of and attitudes towards prevention efforts against HIV/STIs among young adults who travel abroad, as well as investigate what kind of prevention efforts young adults want before travelling abroad.

The interviews were transcribed verbatim by the first author and analysed using thematic content analysis. The transcribed material was read through to get a picture of the whole and understand the importance of the material, after which the parts that affected the study's purpose and the overall research questions were identified. In the process of creating preliminary categories, the following aspects were taken into consideration: the number of times the subject came up, the number of people who discussed the topic, the intensity of the conversation around the topic as well as the group's interaction around the topic. Together, the authors discussed the content and boundaries of the preliminary categories. The categories were processed so that they would be exclusive and have an internal consistency; furthermore, the number of categories was reduced in an ongoing creative process until only seven categories remained, where all raw data for the relevant issues could be placed. During categorisation, the authors switched from looking at the text as a whole to studying parts in order to understand it in context.

Commentary: The researchers describe the process of content analysis. The content of the transcribed interviews was reduced to seven categories.

GUIDELINES

Clinical guidelines aim to improve clinical effectiveness and efficiency. They assist clinicians and patients by using a combination of research evidence, clinical experience and expert opinion to recommend assessment and management strategies for patients in specific clinical situations. As most recommendations are based on high-quality research such as systematic reviews and meta-analyses, guidelines can help clinicians keep up to date with the medical literature and improve communication with patients.

Many local, national and international organisations produce clinical guidelines. However, guidelines vary in quality. They need to be critically appraised just like individual research studies. There can be issues with the process of guideline development as well as the choice and interpretation of evidence used to support recommendations.

Guideline development

1. Confirm a need for the proposed clinical guideline.
2. Identify individuals and stakeholders who will help develop the guideline.
3. Identify the evidence for the guideline.
4. Evaluate current practice against the evidence.
5. Write the guideline.
6. Agree how change will be introduced into practice.
7. Engage in consultation and peer review and amend guideline if necessary.
8. Gain ratification.
9. Implement and disseminate the guideline.
10. Audit the effectiveness of the guideline.

Appraising guidelines

AGREE

The Appraisal of Guidelines Research & Evaluation (AGREE) Instrument provides a framework for assessing the quality of clinical practice guidelines (available at http://www.agreetrust.org). The AGREE 11 Instrument assesses both the quality of the reporting and the quality of some aspects of the recommendations. It provides an assessment of the predicted validity of a guideline, ie the likelihood that it will achieve its intended outcome. It does not assess the impact of a guideline on patients' outcomes.

AGREE 11 (September 2013) consists of 23 key items organised in six domains:

- **Scope and purpose** is concerned with the overall aim of the guideline, the specific clinical questions and the target patient population.

- **Stakeholder involvement** focuses on the extent to which the guideline represents the views of its intended users.

- **Rigour of development** relates to the process used to gather and synthesise the evidence and the methods used to formulate and update the recommendations.

- **Clarity and presentation** deals with the language and format of the guideline.

- **Applicability** pertains to the likely organisational, behavioural and cost implications of applying the guideline.

- **Editorial independence** is concerned with the independence of the recommendations and acknowledgement of possible conflicts of interest from the guideline development group.

Each item is rated on the extent to which a criterion has been fulfilled and scored on a four-point scale where 4 = Strongly Agree, 3 = Agree, 2 = Disagree and 1 = Strongly Disagree.

Guidelines in practice

- Clinical guidelines are not designed to replace the knowledge, skills and clinical judgment of clinicians. Guidelines need to be interpreted sensibly and applied with discretion.

- Courts are unlikely to adopt standards of care advocated in most clinical guidelines as legal 'gold standards'. The mere fact that a guideline exists does not of itself establish that compliance with it is reasonable in the circumstances or that non-compliance is negligent[1].

- If a guideline has been accepted by a large part of the medical profession, a clinician will need a strong reason for not following the guidance as it is likely to constitute a reasonable body of opinion for the purposes of litigation. The standards enshrined in the Bolam test may apply – minimum acceptable standards of clinical care derive from responsible customary practice[1].

1   Hurwitz B. Legal and political considerations of clinical practice guidelines. *BMJ* 1999; 318: 661–64.

SYSTEMATIC REVIEWS AND META-ANALYSES

So far, we have been critically appraising individual studies. However, a literature search often reveals many studies with similar aims and hypotheses. Examining one study in isolation can mean that we miss out on findings discovered by other researchers. Ideally, all the studies around one subject area should be collated.

Reviews of articles provide a useful summary of the literature in a particular field. The main flaw with many of these reviews is that they are based on a selection of papers collected in a non-systematic way, so that important research might have been missed.

Systematic review

A systematic review attempts to access and review systematically all of the pertinent articles in the field. A systematic review should effectively explain the research question, the search strategy and the designs of the studies that were selected. The results of these studies are then pooled. The evidence drawn from systematic reviews can therefore be very powerful and valuable. The overall conclusions are more accurate and reliable than those of individual studies. Systematic reviews are the gold-standard source of research evidence in the hierarchy of research evidence.

Research question

As with all research, a systematic review should begin with a focused clinical question. The study types, outcomes of interest, inclusion criteria and exclusion criteria should be clearly stated.

Search strategy

A systematic review is only as good as the search strategy employed to find evidence. To avoid accusations of bias, the search should transcend geographical, language, cultural, academic and political barriers.

- A good systematic review will give a comprehensive account of the search strategy. This usually starts with a search of electronic databases, such as MEDLINE and EMBASE, and trial registers. Search terms include types of studies, exposures and outcomes. To aid transparency, the search terms and Boolean operators ('and', 'or', 'not') can be listed, together with the number of search results returned. This will enable other researchers to assess the thoroughness of the search strategy and allow the search to be repeated.

- Bibliographies of the identified articles can be scanned. Although this hand-searching technique is labour-intensive, links to more articles might be uncovered. Hand-searching can be extended to other sources of information, including grey literature. One advantage of manually searching the content lists of recent journals is that articles not yet included in medical databases might be found.

- Citation searching involves searching for articles that cite studies that have already been identified, with the expectation that such articles will be closely related and therefore relevant to the systematic review.

- The researchers may contact recognised experts and organisations in the field to find out about any other ongoing, missed or unpublished evidence.

SEE EXCERPT 74

Quality assessment

The abstracts of all the identified articles are reviewed and the studies that are deemed suitable are selected for a full review. Each article is then examined to ensure that it meets eligibility requirements and quality thresholds. Essentially, every piece of research is critically appraised with a view to eliminating biased studies that could overestimate or underestimate the treatment effect size. Reasons should be given for excluding studies.

This process is normally carried out by more than one researcher. The level of agreement between the researchers might be given. Any disagreements about whether a study should be included in the review are dealt with using agreed procedures in order to reach a consensus.

SEE EXCERPT 75

Interpretation of the data

Comparing data from different studies involves identifying common units of measurement. Outcomes such as relative risks and odds ratios are usually straightforward to compare. Exposures can be more problematic. Different studies may describe different doses of risk factors or treatments, in which case the researchers should explain how such doses were standardised across the studies.

Meta-analysis

A meta-analysis is the quantitative assessment of a systematic review. It involves combining the results of independent studies to produce an overall estimate of effect. Meta-analyses are performed when more than one study has estimated the effect of an intervention and when there are no differences in participants, interventions and settings that are likely to affect the outcome significantly. It is also important that the outcome in the different trials has been measured in similar ways.

A good meta-analysis is based on a systematic review of studies rather than a non-systematic review, which can introduce bias into the analysis. Adding a meta-analysis to a systematic review brings advantages:

- Improved detection of statistically significant differences between groups, even if effect sizes are small. Combining small studies increases the sample size and consequently the power of the analysis. The risk of making a type 2 error is reduced.

- Improved precision of the result. By increasing the sample size of the analysis, the overall estimate of effect is associated with a narrower confidence interval.

- Improved clarity about the direction and magnitude of any effect. Single studies can have confusing and conflicting results due to the scattering of results. A meta-analysis can provide conclusive evidence for or against an intervention, even when individual studies are inconclusive.

The key steps to remember for a meta-analysis are:

- Synthesis using statistical techniques to combine results of included studies

- Calculation of a pooled estimate of effect of an intervention together with its P value and confidence interval

- A check for variations between the studies (heterogeneity)

- A check for publication bias

- Review and interpretation of the findings.

Forest plots

The results of a meta-analysis are presented as a forest plot (or blobbogram) of pooled results. Figure 65 summarises the components of a forest plot.

The forest plot is a diagram with a list of studies on the vertical axis, often arranged in order of effect or chronologically, and the common outcome measure on the horizontal axis. The outcome measure can be odds or risk ratio, mean differences, event rates, etc. There is a vertical 'line of no effect', which intersects the horizontal axis at the point at which there is no difference between the interventions.

The result of each study is shown by a box that represents the point estimate of the outcome measure.

- The area of the box is proportional to the weight each study is given in the meta-analysis. The researchers will explain how the weighting was calculated. Usually studies with larger samples sizes and with more precise estimates (ie tighter confidence intervals) are given more weight.

Across each box there is a horizontal line. The width of the horizontal line represents the 95% confidence interval.

- If the outcome measure on the horizontal axis is a ratio, such as the relative risk, the 95% confidence interval is asymmetrical around each study outcome. If relative risks are plotted on a logarithm scale the confidence interval will be symmetrical around each study outcome.

- If the horizontal line touches or crosses the line of no effect, either the study outcome was not statistically significant or the sample size was too small to allow us to be confident about where the true result lies (or both).

- If the horizontal line does not cross the line of no effect, the results are statistically significant.

The overall outcome of the meta-analysis is a diamond shape:

- The centre of the diamond is located at the point estimate of the pooled result.

- The horizontal width of the diamond shape is the 95% confidence interval for the overall result.

- There might be an ascending dotted line from upper corner of the diamond.

- In some forest plots the diamond shape is unfilled and the confidence interval is shown as a horizontal line through the diamond. If the confidence interval is narrow, this line might be contained within the diamond.

SEE EXCERPT 76

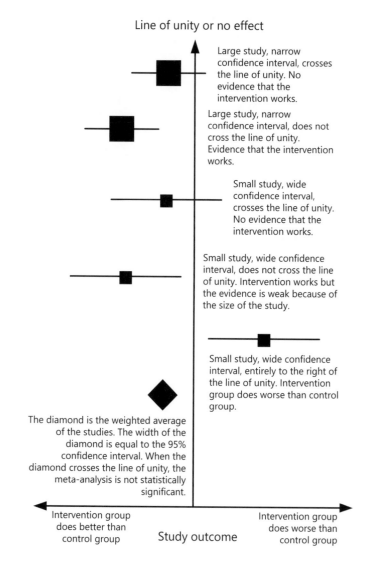

Figure 65 Understanding a forest plot

Guidelines and review libraries

The PRISMA Statement aims to help authors improve the reporting of systematic reviews and meta-analyses. PRISMA stands for Preferred Reporting Items for Systematic Reviews and Meta-Analyses. It consists of a 27-item checklist and a four-phase flow diagram. It is an evolving document that is subject to change periodically as new evidence emerges. In fact, the PRISMA Statement is an update and expansion of the now-outdated QUOROM Statement. The current definitive version of the PRISMA Statement can be found on the PRISMA website (www.prisma-statement.org).

The MOOSE group (the Meta-analysis Of Observational Studies in Epidemiology) has published a checklist containing specifications for reporting of meta-analyses of observational studies in epidemiology[1]. Use of the checklist should improve the usefulness of meta-analyses for authors, reviewers, editors, readers and decision makers (www.consort-statement.org).

PROSPERO is a prospective register of systematic reviews of health and social care interventions produced and maintained by the University of York Centre for Reviews and Dissemination (www.crd.york.ac.uk/prospero).

The Cochrane Collaboration, established in 1993, is an international network working to help healthcare providers, policy makers, patients and their advocates and carers make well-informed decisions about healthcare, based on the best available research evidence. The Cochrane Collaboration prepares, updates and promotes the accessibility of **Cochrane Reviews**, which are systematic reviews of primary research in human healthcare and health policy. They are published online in The Cochrane Library (www.thecochranelibrary. com).

1   Stroup DF, Berlin JA, Morton SC, et al. Meta-analysis of observational studies in epidemiology: a proposal for reporting. Meta-analysis Of Observational Studies in Epidemiology (MOOSE) group. *JAMA* 2000; 283: 2008–12.

EXCERPT 74

Adapted from: Khokhar B et al. Effectiveness of mobile electronic devices in weight loss among overweight and obese populations: a systematic review and meta-analysis. *BMC Obesity* 2014; 1: 22.

Researchers reviewed the medical literature for research on the use of mobile electronic devices to facilitate and maintain weight loss.

Two reviewers performed independent searches of the following online electronic databases (Medline, PsycINFO, Embase and CENTRAL). The search of online databases was not restricted by language or date. The search was broken down into four main categories. To identify the relevant population, the first Boolean search was done using the term 'OR' to explode [search by subject heading] and map [search by keyword] the following MeSH headings 'overweight' or 'obese'. To identify relevant interventions the second Boolean search used the term 'OR' to explode and map 'mobile phone' or 'internet' or 'computers handheld' or 'wireless technology' or 'text messaging' or 'electronic mail' or 'smartphone' or '[iPad or iPhone or iPod touch]' or 'mHealth'. The third category of MeSH headings was also related to the intervention and included: 'exercise' or 'motor activity' or 'physical fitness' or 'diet'. Finally, the fourth group of key terms was used to identify study design. A Boolean search using the term 'or' to explode and map the keywords 'controlled clinical trials' or 'randomized controlled trials' or 'meta-analysis' or placebo*' or 'random*' or 'groups'. These four search categories were then combined using the Boolean operator 'AND'. In addition, two individuals searched the reference lists of prior review papers and all identified research articles were hand searched. Clinical trial registries were also consulted to identify all ongoing trials (www.clinicaltrials.gov, www.controlled-trials.com/mrct, www.isrctn.com). Tables of contents of key journals [Telemedicine Journal and E-Health, Health Informatics Journal and Journal of Medical Internet Research] were also hand searched. Finally, experts identified during the review process were contacted for clarifications on their published trials.

Commentary: An example of a search strategy, including searching multiple databases, multi-level Boolean searches using many keywords, hand-searching and contacting experts in the field.

EXCERPT 75

Adapted from: Manyanga T el al. Pain management with acupuncture in osteoarthritis: a systematic review and meta-analysis. *BMC Complementary and Alternative Medicine* 2014; 14: 312.

The objective of this systematic review was to identify, and synthesise data from prospective randomised controlled trials comparing acupuncture to sham acupuncture, usual care, or no treatment, in adults diagnosed with osteoarthritis.

We used a two-step process for trial screening and selection. Two reviewers independently screened the titles and abstracts to determine if a citation met the general inclusion criteria. We included randomised controlled trials (RCTs) of acupuncture administration to adults diagnosed with osteoarthritis. We excluded non-RCTs, trials involving animals and trials in which electro-needle stimulation was performed. The full text of citations classified as include or unclear were reviewed independently with reference to the predetermined inclusion and exclusion criteria. Non-English full text citations were first translated and then reviewed independently. Disagreements between the two reviewers were resolved through consensus and by third-party adjudication, as needed.

Commentary: Two researchers assessed the quality of each study against the inclusion and exclusion criteria. Any disagreements were settled by the intervention of a third researcher.

EXCERPT 76

Adapted from: Li L et al. Meta-analysis of the risk of cataract in type 2 diabetes. *BMC Ophthalmology* 2014; 14: 94.

This meta-analysis aimed to investigate the association between type 2 diabetes and the risk of cataract.

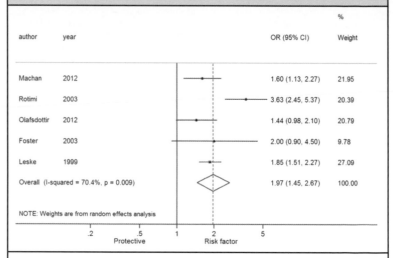

Commentary: A forest plot of the association between type 2 diabetes and any cataract. The diamond does not touch the (solid) line of no effect (at odds ratio = 1).

SYSTEMATIC REVIEWS – HOMOGENEITY AND HETEROGENEITY

Because the aim of the meta-analysis is to summate the results of similar studies, there are tests to ensure that the studies merit combination. Any variation seen to occur between study results can be due to chance or systematic differences or both.

Homogeneity is when studies have similar and consistent results and any observed differences are due to random variation.

When there is more variation than would be expected by chance alone, even after allowing for random variation, this is referred to as **heterogeneity**.

Clinical heterogeneity occurs when the individuals, interventions or outcomes chosen in studies differ from one another significantly, making the results of these studies difficult to collate.

Statistical heterogeneity occurs when the results of the studies differ from one another in magnitude or direction significantly more than would be expected by chance.

Substantial heterogeneity between studies can bias the summary effect making it unreliable, so it is important to detect.

Summary effect size

There are two approaches to calculate the effect size to summarise the results for a meta-analysis:

- **Fixed-effects model:** This assumes that there is no heterogeneity between the studies, ie that the trials are all comparable and the effect is the same in all the studies (homogeneity). **SEE EXCERPT 77**

- **Random-effects model:** This allows for between-study variations, ie the effect is not the same in all the studies (heterogeneity).

If heterogeneity has been ruled out, a fixed-effects model is used. If heterogeneity does exist, a random-effects model is used. The random-effects model will give wider confidence intervals than fixed-effect models in the presence of significant heterogeneity.

The two types of fixed-effects models for relative risk and odds ratio used to produce a summary statistic are:

- **The Mantel–Haenszel method:** The most widely used statistical method for producing the final result of a forest plot. It combines the results of trials to produce a single-value overall summary of the net effect. The result is given as a chi-squared statistic associated with a P value.

- **The Peto method for odds ratio:** This is for individual and combined odds ratios. This method produces biased results in some circumstances, especially when calculated odds ratios are far from 1.

Methods to test for heterogeneity

- **Forest plot:** This provides visual evidence of heterogeneity if present. Heterogeneity is indicated if the confidence interval of a study does not overlap with any of the confidence intervals of the other studies. If the confidence intervals of all the studies partly overlap the studies are homogeneous.

- **Cochran's Q (Chi², X²):** Calculated as the weighted sum of the squared differences between each study's estimate and the pooled estimate across all the studies. P values are obtained by comparing the statistic with a chi-squared distribution with n − 1 degrees of freedom, where n is equal to the number of studies. Cochran's Q has low power to test heterogeneity if the number of studies is small[1]. Usually a P value < 0.1 is used as a cut-off to declare heterogeneity[2].

- **I² statistic:** Describes the percentage of total variation across studies that is due to heterogeneity rather than chance[1]. It ranges in value from 0% (no heterogeneity) to 100%. Heterogeneity is considered to be present if I² ≥ 50%. **SEE EXCERPT 78**

- **Galbraith plot:** A graph with 1/SE on the X axis and the Z score on the Y axis. The summary effect line goes through the middle of the plot. Parallel to this line, two lines (usually at a distance of two standard deviations) create an interval in which most dots would be expected to fall if the studies were estimating a single fixed

1   Higgins JPT et al. Measuring inconsistency in meta-analyses. *BMJ* 2003; 327: 557.
2   Deeks JJ, Higgins JPT, Altman DG (editors). Chapter 9: Analysing data and undertaking meta-analyses. In: Higgins JPT, Green S (editors). *Cochrane Handbook for Systematic Reviews of Interventions*. Version 5.0.1 [updated September 2008]. The Cochrane Collaboration, 2008. Available from www.cochrane-handbook.org.

parameter. Heterogeneity is indicated by studies lying outside these parallel lines[1].

- **L'Abbé plot:** This plots the rate of successful outcome in the control group on the horizontal axis, and the rate of successful outcome in the experimental group on the vertical axis. A diagonal line is drawn between the two axes indicating identical rates in each group. Above the line represents effective treatment; below the line represents ineffective treatment. The more compact the distribution of the points on the graph, the more likely it is that homogeneity is present and the less likely it is that there is heterogeneity present[1].

Meta-regression analysis

Meta-regression is a method that can be used to try to adjust for heterogeneity in a meta-analysis. It can determine if there is evidence of different effects in different subgroups of trials.

Meta-regression analysis aims to relate the size of a treatment effect to factors within a study, rather than just generating one summary effect across all the trials. For example, the use of statins to lower cholesterol levels may be investigated by a series of trials. A meta-analysis of these trials might produce a summary effect size across all the trials. A meta-regression analysis will provide information on the role of statin dosage or duration of treatment, helping to explain any heterogeneity of treatment effect between the studies present in the meta-analysis.

SEE EXCERPT 78

1   Bax L et al. More than numbers: The power of graphs in meta-analysis. *Am. J. Epidemiol* 2009; 169(2): 249–55.

EXCERPT 77

Adapted from: Wang C et al. Heparin therapy reduces 28-day mortality in adult severe sepsis patients: a systematic review and meta-analysis. *Critical Care* 2014; 18: 563.

Researchers assessed the effects of heparin on short-term mortality in adult patients with sepsis and severe sepsis.

Between study heterogeneity was assessed using an I^2 statistic. There was no evidence of between study heterogeneity ($I^2 = 0.0\%$), and a sensitivity analysis was not performed. The fixed effects model was applied and pooled odd ratios were estimated using the Mantel–Haenszel method.

Commentary: In this meta-analysis, heterogeneity was not found so the fixed effects model was used.

EXCERPT 78

Adapted from: Berhan A et al. Vortioxetine in the treatment of adult patients with major depressive disorder: a meta-analysis of randomized double-blind controlled trials. *BMC Psychiatry* 2014; 14: 276.

The objective of this meta-analysis was to evaluate the efficacy and safety of vortioxetine in adults with major depressive disorder.

The heterogeneity among the included studies was assessed with I^2 statistics; when the value of I^2 was greater than or equal to 50% it was considered as statistically significant. To assess the possible sources of heterogeneity, subgroup analysis based on the durations of therapy and meta-regression using vortioxetine dose as a covariate were performed. Heterogeneity testing revealed the presences of significant heterogeneity among the included studies ($I^2 = 68\%$). The meta-regression using doses of vortioxetine as covariate showed a statistically significant reduction in MADRS total score with patients who used higher doses of vortioxetine (slope $= -0.031$; 95% CI $= -0.053$ to -0.009; $P = 0.005$).

Commentary: In this study heterogeneity was found to be present. Meta-regression analysis revealed one cause of the heterogeneity was the doses of vortioxetine used in the different studies.

Reporting bias is the term applied to a group of related biases that can lead to over-representation of significant or positive studies in systematic reviews. Types of reporting bias include time-lag bias, language bias, citation bias, funding bias, outcome variable selection bias, developed country bias, publication bias and multiple publication bias.

Publication bias

Large studies tend to get published, whether they have a positive finding or a negative finding. Small studies with positive findings are more likely to be submitted and published than small studies with negative findings. As a result, smaller studies with negative findings tend to get missed in systematic reviews and meta-analyses[1].

The exclusion of small studies means that the overall results of a systematic review or meta-analysis may be misleading. The over-representation of positive studies may mean that the results are biased toward a positive result.

There are several methods available to identify publication bias, including **funnel plots**, the **Galbraith plot** and tests such as the **Egger's test**, **Begg's rank correlation test** and **Rosenthal's fail-safe N**.

Funnel plots

Funnel plots are scatter plots of treatment effects estimated from individual studies on the horizontal axis and a measure of study size on the vertical axis[1]. The shape of the funnel depends on what is plotted on the vertical axis (Figure 66).

Standard error is a recommended choice for the vertical axis: the expected shape in the absence of bias corresponds to a symmetrical funnel, straight lines to indicate 95% confidence intervals can be included and the plot emphasises smaller studies which are more prone to bias[2].

1   Sterne JAC et al. Investigating and dealing with publication and other biases in meta-analysis. BMJ 2001; 323: 101.
2   Sterne JAC et al. Funnel plots for detecting bias in meta-analysis: guidelines on choice of axis. Journal of Clinical Epidemiology 2001; 54(10): 1046–55.

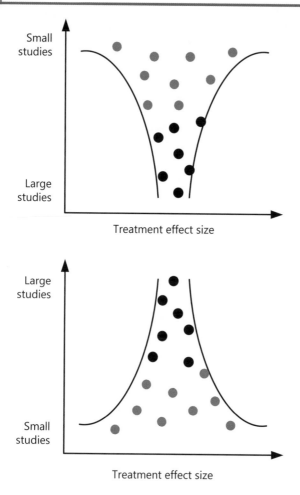

Figure 66 The shape of the funnel plot depends on what is plotted on the vertical axis

Each point on the graph represents one of the studies. In the absence of publication bias, the plot resembles a symmetrical funnel.

Large studies have large sample sizes. The results from large studies have narrow confidence intervals and tend to be close to the true result in the target population. Large studies lie close together on the horizontal axis and sit in the narrow part of the funnel.

Small studies have small sample sizes. The results from small studies tend to vary considerably and have large confidence intervals. On the horizontal axis, small studies scatter widely and sit in the wide part of the funnel.

Asymmetry of funnel plots

If there is publication bias, there will be asymmetry at the wide part of the funnel plot end due to the absence of small negative results (Figure 67)[1]. Asymmetry might also be due to other reasons, including the tendency for the smaller studies to show larger treatment effects and heterogeneity between trials[2].

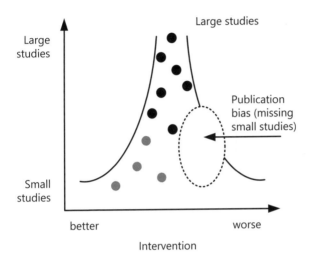

Figure 67 A funnel plot can reveal publication bias

SEE EXCERPT 79

The **'trim and fill' method** can be used with funnel plots to correct for publication bias[2]. Studies which are the cause of asymmetry in the funnel plot are removed (the trim) so that the true centre of the funnel can be ascertained. The removed studies are then replaced together with imputed mirror-image counterparts (the fill), with the mirror axis placed at the pooled estimate[3]. There may be a resulting change in the overall effect shown in the updated meta-analysis.

The plot itself is similar to a regular funnel plot with additional dots (usually not filled) representing the imputed studies, and an additional vertical line that indicates the summary effect when these studies are included in the meta-analysis[3].

1   Egger M et al. Bias in meta-analysis detected by a simple, graphical test. *BMJ* 1997; 315: 629.
2   Sterne JAC et al. Investigating and dealing with publication and other biases in meta-analysis. *BMJ* 2001; 323: 101.
3   Sutton AJ et al. Empirical assessment of effect of publication bias on meta-analyses. *BMJ* 2000; 320: 1574–77.

EXCERPT 79

Adapted from: Mytton OT et al. Systematic review and meta-analysis of the effect of increased vegetable and fruit consumption on body weight and energy intake. *BMC Public Health* 2014; 14: 886.

This study is a systematic review of trials that sought to increase vegetable and fruit consumption to understand the effect on body weight and energy intake.

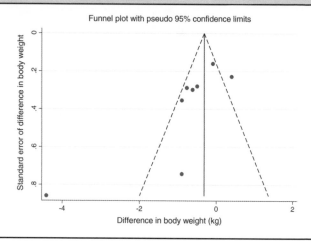

Commentary: The funnel plot is a test for publication bias. Publication bias may be indicated by an absence of small negative trials, in this case trials missing from the bottom right-hand corner.

SECTION H

APPLICABILITY

There is a well-established hierarchy of research methodologies. The hierarchy is based on the premise that the study designs differ in their ability to predict what will happen to patients in real life. The studies at the top of the hierarchy carry more weight than studies lower down, because their evidence is of a higher grade.

Systematic review / meta-analysis
Randomised controlled trial (RCT)
Non-randomised controlled trial
Cohort studies
Case–control studies
Cross-sectional surveys
Case series
Case report
Expert opinion
Personal communication

Studies that carry greater weight are not necessarily the best in every situation and are unlikely to be appropriate for all situations. For example, a case report can be of great importance, even though in terms of the hierarchy of studies a case report normally carries low weight. Also note that the hierarchy is for guidance only; not all studies using the same design are of equal quality.

Levels of evidence

Many organisations write systematic reviews and guidelines after reviewing the medical literature. Grading systems tend to have their foundations in the hierarchy of evidence but might be fine-tuned by giving higher scores to specific examples of good methodological practice. Ideally, grading systems should indicate the strength of the supporting evidence and the strength of the recommendation.

GRADE

Since 2000 the Grading of Recommendations Assessment, Development and Evaluation (GRADE) Working Group has developed an approach to grading quality of evidence and strength of recommendations (see http://www.gradeworkinggroup.org/). The overall quality of evidence is categorised as 'high', 'moderate', 'low' or 'very low'. Recommendations are only at two levels, strong or weak.

Only if clinicians are very certain that benefits do, or do not, outweigh risks and burdens on the basis of the available evidence will they make a strong recommendation. Conversely, a weak recommendation indicates that benefits and risks and burdens are finely balanced, or there is appreciable uncertainty about the magnitude of benefits and risks. A weak recommendation might also indicate that patients are liable to make different choices.

SIGN

The Scottish Intercollegiate Guidelines Network (SIGN) develops evidence-based clinical guidelines. In 2008 SIGN published *A Guideline Developer's Handbook (SIGN 50)*, which describes their approach to levels of evidence and grades of recommendation (see Table 30; the full document is accessible at http://www.sign.ac.uk/).

LEVELS OF EVIDENCE	
1++	High-quality meta-analyses, systematic reviews of RCTs, or RCTs with a very low risk of bias
1+	Well-conducted meta-analyses, systematic reviews or RCTs with a low risk of bias
1−	Meta-analyses, systematic reviews or RCTs with a high risk of bias
2++	High-quality systematic reviews of case control or cohort or studies High-quality case–control or cohort studies with a very low risk of confounding or bias and a high probability that the relationship is causal
2+	Well-conducted case–control or cohort studies with a low risk of confounding or bias and a moderate probability that the relationship is causal
2−	Case–control or cohort studies with a high risk of confounding or bias and a significant risk that the relationship is not causal
3	Non-analytic studies, eg case reports, case series
4	Expert opinion

GRADES OF RECOMMENDATION	
A	At least one meta-analysis, systematic review or RCT rated as 1++, and directly applicable to the target population; or A body of evidence consisting principally of studies rated as 1+, directly applicable to the target population, and demonstrating overall consistency of results
B	A body of evidence including studies rated as 2++, directly applicable to the target population, and demonstrating overall consistency of results; or Extrapolated evidence from studies rated as 1++ or 1+
C	A body of evidence including studies rated as 2+, directly applicable to the target population and demonstrating overall consistency of results; or Extrapolated evidence from studies rated as 2++
D	Evidence level 3 or 4; or Extrapolated evidence from studies rated as 2+
√	Recommended best practice based on the clinical experience of the guideline development group

Table 30 SIGN levels of evidence and grades of recommendation. Reproduced with permission from Scottish Intercollegiate Guidelines Network.

Centre for Evidence-Based Medicine

The Oxford Centre for Evidence-Based Medicine grades the level of evidence from 1 to 5 (see the full document at http://www.cebm.net/ocebm-levels-of-evidence).

CRITICAL THINKING

The final stage of critical appraisal is to determine the applicability of the research findings. By this stage you will have decided that the methodology of the study is robust and the results are significant in some way. Some research findings might be of academic interest only while others could potentially help your patients. Providing your patients are demographically and clinically similar to the sample population, it might be worth applying the results to your clinical practice, in the expectation that the results on your patients will be similar to the results found in the study population. One could argue that the most useful research is that which can be generalised most easily to a wider population.

Adopting an evidence-based approach to medical practice is a positive move but it is important to acknowledge that evidence-based medicine is not without its critics. The shift to statistical number crunching, the pressure to publish and the financial gains that are possible have led to abuses by doctors, researchers and marketing teams. The recommendations in a clinical paper should never be accepted at face value without considering whether a study could be accidentally or deliberately misleading.

Good critical appraisal skills will detect flaws in studies. The points listed below illustrate that the monitoring of any changes to your clinical practice is a vital step in modifying your service to an evidence-based model. If changes do not lead to improved patient care, the research should be revisited to understand why the expected benefits did not materialise.

The abstract is a summary

- The abstract is a summary of the paper, briefly describing the study's methodology, important results and key recommendations. The abstract should be considered as the sales pitch, highlighting all that is good about the paper and omitting anything bad. Abstracts are easy to read but can also mislead.

The clinical question might not be the right question

- The clinical question could have been clearly defined but might not reflect the complexity of real clinical practice. Applied in isolation, the research results might not improve practice because other important factors have not been addressed.

- Research teams composed solely of academic doctors might have priorities and viewpoints that do not reflect those of doctors at the coalface of clinical practice. Translating statistically significant results into clinical practice is not easy.

The target population is not the same as your patient population

- The target population will rarely match your patients, diminishing the generalisability of the results. The target population will be unique because of its geographical location, its culture, its morbidity and mortality levels, and differences in healthcare standards and provision.

The sample population is a sample

- The sample population is not your clinical population. It is a proportion of the target population. Whatever happens in the sample population might not happen in the target population, let alone your patients.

- People will have been excluded from the sample population but you will not be able to apply the same exclusions as easily in practice. The study results might not extrapolate to all your patients, leading to unexpected outcomes.

- People entering trials are motivated to improve their health and to follow trial protocols. They are not representative of your patients, many of whom will not meet this ideal.

- Results from small sample sizes are poor evidence for supporting big changes in clinical practice.

Randomisation might not be random

- Randomisation is vulnerable to manipulation. A poorly described allocation process, lack of robust concealment and unequal groups at baseline are warning signs that the difference between groups might have been exaggerated.

Don't be blinded by blinding

- Blinding can be compromised and almost always in favour of the researcher, improving the results because of observation bias. Open-label trials are poor evidence for change.

- Placebo preparations vary in quality. Poor matches are easily uncovered. The expectations of doctors and patients are lowered, disadvantaging those in the control arm.

- Researchers might minimise the importance of the placebo effect. Building relationships with patients and offering them hope are powerful interventions in clinical practice but are rarely discussed in research papers.

Losing subjects is carelessness

- Results may be boosted by poor handling of subjects who withdraw or who are lost to follow-up. Every subject should be accounted for, from recruitment to outcome. Not accounting for all subjects or dismissing subjects for spurious reasons is nearly always in the researcher's favour. You will not be able to get rid of patients so easily in order to achieve comparable success rates.

Unfavourable comparisons

- Researchers sometimes compare favoured interventions with 'nobbled' comparators. Doses in the control arm might be too small for therapeutic benefit, doses might be too high and cause adverse reactions, or dosing regimens might be too onerous for subjects to follow.

- Researchers like comparing new treatments with placebo preparations but head-to-head trials with established treatments are more useful to you.

- Patients with chronic health problems are treated for months or years, yet the researchers might only provide evidence for the first few days or weeks of intervention.

- Side-effects are as important to patients as benefits but often omitted or minimised as outcome measures in research studies.

- Composite endpoints might not be valid and are difficult to translate into clinical practice and monitoring.

Statistics

- There are lies, damned lies and statistics! Data are manipulated, presented and interpreted in whichever way the researchers choose. Like a magic show, what you see is what they want you to see.

- Subgroup analyses allow researchers to focus on artificial subsets of the sample population, an exercise you will find difficult to justify to your patients.

- The focus on P values is unhealthy. Statistical significance is based on an arbitrary cut-off value. The magnitude of any effect should always be reported – it shows the potential impact on your patients.

- Be wary of small effect sizes, even if statistically significant. They are unlikely to benefit your patients and might not be confirmed by repeat studies.

- Small effect sizes shouldn't lead to discussions about cause and effect without a thorough examination of other factors that could play a role. Causation is usually multifactorial and not as simple as portrayed by some researchers.

- Relative risk results are less useful to you than absolute risk numbers and more likely to mislead. The impact of research is easier to exaggerate with relative risks.

- A reduction in undesirable outcomes is often presented as applying to the whole sample population whereas it only applies to those at risk. A 20% reduction in risk only applies to those who are at risk of the outcome; everyone else is unaffected. This may mean interventions are more expensive than they first appear.

The larger perspective

- Many medical breakthroughs and discoveries did not come from research trials. To practise only evidence-based medicine is to miss or ignore opportunities for improving the care of your patients.

- In some situations we cannot wait for gold-standard trials to be conducted. We should not withhold experimental treatments if patients are facing death. Any evidence is better than no evidence.

- Statistical results apply to groups, not to individuals. Medical care should also be patient-centred, not just population-centred. Evidence-based medicine can impair the doctor–patient relationship.

- Clinical trials and marketing often overlap and can be difficult to separate. Did the clinical trial lead to the marketing campaign or did the intended marketing approach impact on the clinical trial design?

- Positive trials are much more likely to get published than negative trials. Is your impression of research skewed by publication bias? You don't know what you don't know.

CRITICAL APPRAISAL IN PRACTICE

Databases and search engines

There are many different databases that cover health and medical subject areas and index research and/or high-quality information resources.

MEDLINE is produced by the National Library of Medicine in the United States (http://www.nlm.nih.gov). It is a major source for biomedical information and includes citations to articles from more than 4000 journals. It contains over 12 million citations dating back to the mid-1960s from international biomedical literature on all aspects of medicine and healthcare. It contains records of journal articles, bibliographic details of systematic reviews, randomised controlled trials and guidelines. There are many organisations that offer access to MEDLINE, with different ways of searching. The key MEDLINE service is offered by the US National Library of Medicine itself, in their PubMed service (www.pubmed.gov).

Current Index to Nursing and Allied Health Literature (CINAHL) is a nursing and allied health database and covers topics such as health education, physiotherapy, occupational therapy, emergency services and social services in health care (http://www.ebscohost.com/nursing/products/cinahl-databases/cinahl-complete). Coverage is from 1982 to the present and it is updated bimonthly.

Embase is the European equivalent of MEDLINE, the *Excerpta Medica* database, and is published by Elsevier Science (http://www.embase.com). It focuses mainly on drugs and biomedical literature and also covers health policy, drug and alcohol dependence, psychiatry, forensic science and pollution control. It covers more than 8400 journals and with the Embase Classic extension it includes data from 1947 onwards. The search engine at www.embase.com includes EMBASE and unique MEDLINE records.

MEDLINE, CINAHL and Embase are well-established, comprehensive databases and possess sophisticated search facilities. The size of these databases requires that the searcher first defines the search terms and then refines them to reduce the number of results. Although this can be done by limiting the search by publication date, language or 'review articles only' (for example), a more valid way of limiting results is to focus on those articles that are more likely to be of high quality. This is done by using 'filters'.

NHS Economic Evaluations Database (NHS EED) is a database that focuses on economic evaluations of healthcare interventions. Economic evaluations are appraised for their quality, strengths and weaknesses. NHS EED is available from the website of the Centre for Reviews and Dissemination (http://www.crd.york.ac.uk/crdweb). The database will not be updated from January 2015.

The **NIHR Dissemination Service** (http://www.disseminationcentre.nihr.ac.uk/) is a new resource from the National Institute for Health Research, producing summaries of research which have been identified as important to clinicians, patients and managers. Commentaries and insights are added to make the findings more relevant to key people.

The **Turning Research Into Practice (TRIP)** database is a meta-search engine that searches across 61 sites of high-quality information (http://www.tripdatabase.com). Evidence-based publications are searched monthly by experts and indexed fully before being presented in an easy-to-use format with access to full-text articles, medical images and patient leaflets.

APA PsycNET allows users to search **PsycInfo**, an abstract database of psychological literature from the 1800s to the present (http://psycnet.apa.org/). It covers more than 2000 titles, of which 98% are peer-reviewed.

Ovid HealthSTAR contains citations to the published literature on health services, technology, administration and research. It focuses on both the clinical and non-clinical aspects of healthcare delivery. (http://library.mcmaster.ca/articles/healthstarovid-healthstar).

The **British Nursing Index (BNI)** indexes citations from British and English-language nursing-related journals (http://www.proquest.com/products-services/bni.html).

System for Information on Grey Literature in Europe (SIGLE) is a bibliographic database covering non-conventional literature (http://www.opengrey.eu).

Google Scholar is a service from the Google search engine (http://scholar.google.com). It provides the ability to search for academic literature located across the world wide web, including peer-reviewed papers, theses, books, abstracts and articles, from academic publishers, professional societies, preprint repositories, universities and other scholarly organisations. Google has worked with leading publishers to gain access to material that wouldn't ordinarily be accessible to search engines because it is locked behind subscription barriers. This allows users of Google Scholar to locate material of interest that would not normally be available to them. Google Scholar even attempts to rank results in order of importance.

Evidence-based medicine resources

Several journals, bulletins and newsletters cover evidence-based medicine and clinical effectiveness. Some evidence-based journals, such as the **ACP Journal Club** (www.acpjc.org), a monthly feature in Annals of Internal Medicine, and **Evidence-Based Medicine** (http://ebm.bmj.com) scrutinise articles and summarise the studies in structured abstracts, with a commentary added by a clinical expert. These journals cover reviews and choose articles that meet strict selection criteria.

Clinical Evidence (http://www.clinicalevidence.com/) is a regularly updated guide to best available evidence for effective healthcare. It is a database of hundreds of clinical questions and answers and is designed to help doctors make evidence-based medicine part of their everyday practice. Topics are selected to cover important clinical conditions seen in primary care or ambulatory settings. There is rigorous peer review of all material by experts, to ensure that the information is of the highest quality. It is updated and expanded regularly.

The **Cochrane Library** (http://www.cochrane.org) is an electronic publication designed to supply high-quality evidence to inform people providing and receiving care, and those responsible for research, teaching, funding and administration at all levels. It is a database of the Cochrane Collaboration, an international network of individuals committed to 'preparing, maintaining and promoting the accessibility of systematic reviews of the effects of healthcare'.

Development and dissemination of guidelines

The **National Institute for Health and Clinical Excellence (NICE)** was set up as a Special Health Authority for England and Wales on 1 April 1999. It is part of the NHS and it is responsible for providing national guidance on the promotion of good health and the prevention and treatment of ill health (http://www.nice.org.uk). **Evidence Search** (https://www.evidence.nhs.uk/) provides clinicians with access to the best current know-how and knowledge to support healthcare-related decisions.

The **NHS Centre for Reviews and Dissemination (CRD)** (http://www.york.ac.uk/inst/crd/) is based at the University of York and provides research-based information about the effects of health and social care interventions via databases and systematic reviews.

The **Scottish Intercollegiate Guidelines Network (SIGN)** was formed in 1993 and its objective is to improve the effectiveness and efficiency of clinical care for patients in Scotland by developing, publishing and disseminating guidelines that identify and promote good clinical practice (http://www.sign.ac.uk).

The **National Guideline Clearinghouse (NGC)** is a US-based public resource for evidence-based clinical practice (http://www.guideline.gov).

Other sources of information

Conference proceedings: Papers given at conferences can provide important information on new research that is either in progress or recently completed. Some trials are only ever reported in conference proceedings. Databases such as the **Conference Papers Index** (http://www.proquest.com/products-services/cpi-set-c.html) hold records and/or abstracts of some proceedings.

Grey literature: This is material that is not published in the standard book or journal formats. It includes reports, booklets, technical reports, circulars, newsletters and discussion papers.

Citation searching: This involves using reference lists of articles already retrieved or citation indices to trace other useful studies. The **Science Citation Index** (http://ip-science.thomsonreuters.com/mjl/) allows searching for references using cited authors' surnames.

Hand searching: Journals can be physically examined for their contents. This is time-consuming, but might be a viable proposition when the published data on a topic concentrates around a few key journals.

Journal clubs are a routine fixture in academic programmes at teaching hospitals. A successful presentation requires preparation, good presentation skills and clinical relevance for the audience.

Preparation

Different journal clubs take different approaches to the running of the meetings. Some journal clubs are very prescriptive – the clinical paper is already chosen and the doctor has to simply appraise it. Other clubs rely on the doctor to choose a paper of his or her choice. Some clubs ask the doctor to search for and appraise a paper related to a clinical question of interest, such as a question raised by a recent case presentation. However the clinical paper is chosen, preparation has to start well in advance of the presentation.

Ideally, you should distribute the clinical paper to the journal club members at least a week in advance. Most articles are available to download as Adobe Acrobat files from the journal websites; this format maintains their original formatting and provides an excellent original for photocopying. However, be aware of copyright restrictions on distribution. An alternative approach is to publicise the link to the article on the World Wide Web. When you distribute information about your chosen paper, include information on the timing of the journal club and intimate that you will expect everyone to have read the paper before the presentation, which will focus on the critical appraisal of it.

Presentation skills

Nowadays it is not excusable to use anything less than an LCD projector with Microsoft PowerPoint or an equivalent software package for your presentation.

Using PowerPoint

PowerPoint makes it easy to produce great-looking presentations, but its flexibility and ease of use also allow doctors to produce presentations that look anything but professional. Use its template features to give your presentation a consistent and professional appearance. Journal clubs are formal affairs, so stick to a dark background colour for your slides, such as blue or black, with lightly coloured text to keep the presentation sober-looking and to aid readability. Avoid patterned backgrounds and fussy templates, which will distract the audience from your presentation. Use a traditional serif typeface, such as

Times New Roman, and avoid typefaces that give an informal impression or try to mimic handwriting.

Slide content

Keep each slide brief and to the point. Every slide should have a title and up to five bullet points, which you will expand on during the presentation. Consider using tables or diagrams to summarise information. Avoid abbreviations and acronyms in your presentation, unless your audience is familiar with them. Make sure you double-check your spelling and grammar. Pay particular attention to the appropriate use of capital letters and punctuation marks. Avoid fancy slide transitions, animations and sound effects.

Delivering the slide show

Dress smartly for your presentation. Leave your mobile phone or pager with a colleague. Arrive early at the journal club, set up your presentation and make sure all the slides appear as designed – don't expect that the technology will always work.

During the presentation, stand to one side of the screen. Talk clearly to the audience, and not too quickly. Make eye contact with different members of the audience for a few seconds at a time. Wireless remote controls, such as the Logitech Cordless Presenter with its built-in timer and laser pointer, enable you to advance through your slides without having to use the keyboard or stand next to the computer. Using such a device can be a liberating experience.

Slides

The organisation of the slides depends on the subject matter. Below is an example of a slide presentation. Resist the temptation to simply read out an abbreviated form of the research paper – your audience has already read it!

SLIDE 1	**SLIDE 2**
The title of the paper The author(s) of the paper Journal name and date of publication Your name and other details	The clinical question The primary hypothesis Comment on the background to this project Comment on originality

SLIDE 3	**SLIDE 4**
The study design – is it appropriate?	The target population Sampling method The sample size and power calculation

SLIDE 5	**SLIDE 6**
Inclusion and exclusion criteria	The randomisation process Concealed allocation

SLIDE 7	**SLIDE 8**
Baseline characteristics Comment on likelihood of selection bias	Interventions in the groups Use of placebos The blinding process

SLIDE 9	**SLIDE 10**
The outcome measures Validity and reliability of measurements Endpoints	Which group did best? Risks, RR Odds, OR NNT

SLIDE 11	**SLIDE 12**
Are the results statistically significant? Null hypothesis, P values Statistical tests	Were the aims of the study fulfilled? Are the relevant findings justified? Are the conclusions of the paper justified?

SLIDE 13	**SLIDE 14**
Are the results clinically significant? Can the results be generalised to your population?	What do you think of the paper? Summarise the good and bad points What future work can be done? Any questions?

TAKING PART IN AN AUDIT MEETING

The word 'audit' is guaranteed to divide doctors into two camps. On one side are those doctors who leap at the opportunity to improve the services they offer patients. On the other side are those doctors who detest the idea that they should be taken away from clinical work to engage in what they perceive to be a managerial duty. Whatever their attitude to audit is, however, most doctors find themselves doing audits because career progression often depends on being able to show evidence of completed audit projects. Importantly, successful audit outcomes depend on a multidisciplinary team approach to ensure practical and timely interventions to improve services. Doctors not engaging in audit do so at their peril and to the detriment of the service as a whole.

Audit meetings usually take place regularly on a monthly basis. To maintain audience interest and continuity, each audit meeting should have on its agenda a mixture of audit presentations, audit protocols for approval and an opportunity for members of the audience to propose audit titles. A rolling agenda should be kept to ensure that teams present their audit projects at the proposal and protocol stages as well as at the end of the first and second cycles of data collection. Only then will audit projects be completed and make a meaningful difference to service provision. Unfortunately it is all too common to see audit projects abandoned after the first data collection as a result of apathy, doctors moving to different hospitals or a poor understanding of the audit cycle. Each project should have an audit lead who will see the project through to its conclusion.

It is important to distinguish between audits, surveys and research projects. Far too often, surveys of service provision are presented as audits where there is no intention of comparing the findings to a gold standard or repeating the data collection after putting an intervention in place. Other doctors present research projects as audits as a way of sidestepping ethical committees because audit projects do not normally require ethical approval. The chair of the audit meeting needs to keep the meeting focused on audit projects and nothing else.

Below is an example of a slide presentation of an audit protocol. Discussions after such presentations tend to focus on the details of the gold standard of service provision with which the local service will be compared. It is imperative that research is done prior to selecting the gold standard to ensure that it is the gold standard! This can mean seeking out national as well as local guidelines on best practice. In the absence of a recognised gold standard, the team might need to make one up or follow the advice of a key opinion leader.

SLIDE 1	SLIDE 2
The title of the audit project The names of the audit lead and participants Date of presentation	A description of the aspect of the service that might need to be improved

SLIDE 3	SLIDE 4
The gold standard for that part of the service	Details of the first cycle of data collection Who will collect the data and when? What data will be collected?

SLIDE 5	SLIDE 6
The audit tool in more detail	Date of presentation of first data collection and comparison with the gold standard Any questions?

The audit tool is an instrument that facilitates the data collection and this can be done on a retrospective or prospective basis. It is usually a blank form to be filled in with data. The audit tool should be designed to collect only meaningful data and not be over inclusive. The simpler the audit project, the more likely it is to be completed!

After the first collection of data, the comparison of the local service with the gold standard should be presented at the audit meeting. It is at this point that possible interventions to bring the standard of the local service closer to the gold standard should be discussed with the audience. As far as possible the selected interventions should be pragmatic, likely to succeed and incorporate fail-safe methods.

The completion of the audit cycle requires a final presentation on the second collection of data after the implementation of the agreed interventions. There is, however, no limit to the number of times any aspect of the service can be re-audited.

Done well, audit projects can lead to healthcare environments and procedures that are better suited to the needs of both doctors and patients. It is unlikely that any doctor would complain about that!

WORKING WITH PHARMACEUTICAL REPRESENTATIVES

Doctors differ in their attitudes towards the pharmaceutical industry.

Without a doubt, pharmaceutical companies have revolutionised the practice of medicine. They have invested tremendous amounts in research activity to bring products to the marketplace that benefit our patients. Without their financial clout, many products would simply never have been in a position to be licensed.

The reputation of some pharmaceutical companies has been tarnished in recent years, however, because of the conflict between their research and marketing departments. The companies exist, after all, to sell products and generate profits. However, as doctors, we should be able to focus our attention on the research work, so that we can decide whether or not our clinical practice can be improved.

The company representative role has evolved over the years in recognition of the changes in the NHS and the acceptance of an evidence-based approach to treatments. In addition to representatives who focus purely on sales in primary and/or secondary care, there are representatives who work on NHS issues with Primary Care Trusts and, in some companies, staff who work with outcomes research. Different representatives' objectives will not be the same! An understanding of the roles and responsibilities of pharmaceutical representatives will enable you to maximise the benefits of meeting with them regularly.

The sales representative dissected

Before meeting with you, a pharmaceutical sales representative will know a lot about you. Information about your prescribing habits will have been gleaned from data on dispensed prescriptions. The representative wants to meet you because you are in a position to increase the sales of their company's products. This might be accomplished by issuing more prescriptions, by advocating the use of their products to other prescribers, or because you are involved in research that could be favourable to their products.

After the usual greetings and niceties, the focus of the discussion will move to your prescribing habits. The representative wants to gain an insight into how you make decisions about prescribing issues. This involves asking questions about the types of patients you see, the products you prescribe, the reasons for your choice of first-line medications and your experiences with and prejudices against alternative approaches.

The representative will assess your needs in terms of identifying groups of patients in which your outcomes could be improved. They will talk about their company's products and show you evidence of the benefits of prescribing these products for your patients. Sales aids, PowerPoint presentations, promotional literature and clinical papers will magically appear from black briefcases. The effect can be overwhelming, as you are blinded by volumes of impressive data. The representative finishes off the presentation and questioning and asks for some commitment in terms of trying the company's product.

The doctor's viewpoint

Being a passive observer in a meeting with a sales representative is not good use of your time. The representative is usually very knowledgeable about his specialist field and is a potential source of a lot of useful information. You will have your own needs in terms of information you require in order to be a better doctor, and by identifying these needs to the representative, you can both be in a win–win situation.

There are general questions you can ask to update your knowledge base:

- What is the latest research the company is doing?
- Are there any impending licence changes or new launches?
- Are there any forthcoming NHS initiatives that I should be aware of?
- Which guidelines are in vogue, and who are the key opinion leaders?

If the representative is selling a product to you, you need to focus the discussion on information that will help you to decide whether or not to prescribe the product. Questions you might ask about the data presented can include the following:

- Are these efficacy data or effectiveness data?
- Is the sample population similar to our own?
- What were the inclusion and exclusion criteria?
- What was the comparative treatment? Was it a placebo or was it a head-to-head trial?
- Do the doses used in the study reflect everyday clinical practice?
- What was the absolute risk reduction with the new treatment?
- What was the number needed to treat?
- Are the results statistically significant and clinically significant?
- In which situations should the new treatment not be prescribed?

- Are there any safety data we need to be aware of?
- Why should we not prescribe a competitor product?
- Is this a cost-effective intervention?
- Are there any post-marketing studies in progress?
- Has the drug been through the Drugs and Therapeutics Committee, or has a pharmaceutical advisor been presented with the data?

If you are presented with any graphs, put your analytical skills to the test by looking for marketing tricks in the presentation of data. Examples include magnification of the y axis to exaggerate differences in comparative results, and poor labelling of the x axis in an attempt to hide the short duration of a trial.

Sources of information

Promotional material

The representative can give you approved promotional materials that list product features and benefits. Sales aids help convey important information such as data on efficacy, safety, tolerability, compliance, comparative data with competitors, health–economic data, the summary of product characteristics and the price.

Clinical papers

Clinical papers provide you with the original data on which promotional material is based. If you prefer to look at the clinical papers, ask the representative to go through the relevant papers or, alternatively, ask for copies to be sent to you. Once you have the paper, you will want to appraise it critically yourself and then arrange to meet with the representative to discuss any issues or questions that you have. An experienced representative will be able to critique the paper as they use it to sell to you, and point out key details.

Key opinion leaders

You might want to know the opinion of specialists in a field before you prescribe a certain drug. Ask your representative about key opinion leaders and whether they can arrange for you to meet with these people or hear them speak at an appropriate scientific meeting. Alternatively, ask to set up a round-table meeting with you and your colleagues so that you can have an open discussion with the expert about the product and how it would benefit your patients. If you would like to be an advocate for the product, then tell the representative to arrange meetings for you to discuss this with your colleagues.

Data on file

If there is information presented that you are interested in but which has not yet been published, it is usually referenced as 'data on file'. If you would like to see these data, you can request the information and the representative will contact their medical department, who will send this on to you.

Off-licence data

If you have queries that are off-licence, you should let the representative know. They will contact their medical department, and either someone from that department will come and see you or they will send you the requested information. The representative is not allowed to discuss off-licence information.

FURTHER READING

The *JAMA* series

1. Guyatt GH, Sackett DL, Cook DJ, for the Evidence-Based Medicine Working Group. Users' guides to the medical literature. II. How to use an article about therapy or prevention. A. Are the results of the study valid? *Journal of the American Medical Association* 1993; 270: 2598–601.

2. Guyatt GH, Sackett DL, Cook DJ, for the Evidence-Based Medicine Working Group. Users' guides to the medical literature. II. How to use an article about therapy or prevention. B. What were the results and will they help me in caring for my patients? *Journal of the American Medical Association* 1994; 271: 59–63.

3. Jaeschke R, Guyatt G, Sackett DL, for the Evidence-Based Medicine Working Group. Users' guides to the medical literature. III. How to use an article about a diagnostic test. A. Are the results of the study valid? *Journal of the American Medical Association* 1994; 271: 389–91.

4. Jaeschke R, Gordon H, Guyatt G, Sackett DL, for the Evidence-Based Medicine Working Group. Users' guides to the medical literature. III. How to use an article about a diagnostic test. B. What are the results and will they help me in caring for my patients? *Journal of the American Medical Association* 1994; 271: 703–7.

5. Levine M, Walter S, Lee H, et al., for the Evidence-Based Medicine Working Group. Users' guides to the medical literature. IV. How to use an article about harm. *Journal of the American Medical Association* 1994; 271: 1615–19.

6. Laupacis A, Wells G, Richardson S, Tugwell P, for the Evidence-Based Medicine Working Group. Users' guides to the medical literature. V. How to use an article about prognosis. *Journal of the American Medical Association* 1994; 272: 234–37.

7. Oxman AD, Cook DJ, Guyatt GH, for the Evidence-Based Medicine Working Group. Users' guides to the medical literature. VI. How to use an overview. *Journal of the American Medical Association* 1994; 272: 1367–71.

8. Drummond MF, Richardson WS, O'Brien BJ, Levine M, Heyland D, for the Evidence-Based Medicine Working Group. Users' guides to the medical literature. XIII. How to use an article on economic analysis of clinical practice. A. Are the results of the study valid? *Journal of the American Medical Association* 1997; 277: 1552–57.

9. O'Brien BJ, Heyland D, Richardson WS, Levine M, Drummond MF, for the Evidence-Based Medicine Working Group. Users' guides to the medical literature. XIII. How to use an article on economic analysis of clinical practice. B. What are the results and will they help me in caring for my patients? *Journal of the American Medical Association* 1997; 277: 1802–6. Published erratum appears in *JAMA* 1997; 278: 1064.

10. Barratt A, Irwig L, Glasziou P, et al., for the Evidence-Based Medicine Working Group. Users' guide to medical literature. XVII. How to use guidelines and recommendations about screening. *Journal of the American Medical Association* 1999; 281: 2029–34.

11. Giacomini MK, Cook DJ, for the Evidence-Based Medicine Working Group. Users' guides to the medical literature. XXIII. Qualitative research in health care. A. Are the results of the study valid? *Journal of the American Medical Association* 2000; 284: 357–62.

12. Giacomini MK, Cook DJ, for the Evidence-Based Medicine Working Group. Users' guides to the medical literature. XXIII. Qualitative research in health care. B. What are the results and how do they help me care for my patients? *Journal of the American Medical Association* 2000; 284: 478–82.

The 'How to read a paper' series

A readable and practical series, originally published in the *BMJ*.

1. Greenhalgh T. How to read a paper: the Medline database. *BMJ* 1997; 315: 180–83.

2. Greenhalgh T. How to read a paper: getting your bearings (deciding what the paper is about). *BMJ* 1997; 315: 243–46.

3. Greenhalgh T. How to read a paper: assessing the methodological quality of published papers. *BMJ* 1997; 315: 305–8.

4. Greenhalgh T. How to read a paper: statistics for the non-statistician. I: Different types of data need different statistical tests. *BMJ* 1997; 315: 364–66.

5. Greenhalgh T. How to read a paper: statistics for the non-statistician. II: 'Significant' relations and their pitfalls. *BMJ* 1997; 315: 422–25.

6. Greenhalgh T. How to read a paper: papers that report drug trials. *BMJ* 1997; 315: 480–83.

7. Greenhalgh T. How to read a paper: papers that report diagnostic or screening tests. *BMJ* 1997; 315: 540–43.

8. Greenhalgh T. How to read a paper: papers that tell you what things cost (economic analyses). *BMJ* 1997; 315: 596–99.

9. Greenhalgh T. How to read a paper: papers that summarise other papers (systematic reviews and meta-analyses). *BMJ* 1997; 315: 672–75.

10. Greenhalgh T. How to read a paper: papers that go beyond numbers (qualitative research). *BMJ* 1997; 315: 740–43.

A FINAL THOUGHT

It is never an easy task to initiate, plan and complete a research project. It requires dedication, hard work and a willingness to work long hours, which are often unpaid and unrecognised. Few researchers aim deliberately to publish poor-quality research. More often than not, limitations in trial design and conduct are due to a lack of resources, ethical considerations or simply that pragmatic solutions have to be found to enable the research project to take place.

The attainment of critical appraisal skills allows doctors to evaluate the quality of research papers. Such skills should be used not only to find flaws in clinical papers, but also to comment positively on the good points. Taking a balanced approach will ensure that all research, good and bad, generates ideas for future projects. It is this endless cycle of thinking, questioning and doing that has brought us so far. The journey is far from complete.

In 1676, Isaac Newton wrote to a fellow scientist, acknowledging the work of others in his own research: *'If I have seen further, it is by standing on the shoulders of giants.'*

INDEX